Gender, Identity, and the Production of Meaning

Gender, Identity, and the Production of Meaning

Tamsin E. Lorraine

Westview Press
BOULDER • SAN FRANCISCO • OXFORD

Feminist Theory and Politics

Copyright © 1990 by Westview Press, Inc.

Published in 1990 in the United States of America by Westview Press, Inc., 5500 Central Avenue, Boulder, Colorado 80301, and in the United Kingdom by Westview Press, 36 Lonsdale Road, Summertown, Oxford OX2 7EW

Library of Congress Cataloging-in-Publication Data
Lorraine, Tamsin E.
    Gender, identity, and the production of meaning / by Tamsin E. Lorraine.
    p. cm. — (Feminist theory and politics)
    Includes bibliographical references.
    ISBN 0-8133-7877-X — ISBN 0-8133-7878-8 (pbk.)
    1. Sex role. 2. Identity (Psychology). 3. Lacan, Jacques, 1901–
4. Sexism in language. 5. Discourse analysis. 6. Feminist
criticism. I. Title. II. Series.
HQ1075.L67 1990
305.3—dc20   89-77271
                                                                      CIP

Printed and bound in the United States of America

      The paper used in this publication meets the requirements
(∞) of the American National Standard for Permanence of Paper
      for Printed Library Materials Z39.48-1984.

10   9   8   7   6   5   4   3   2   1

Contents

Preface

I had two questions in mind when I wrote this work. One concerned the various ways in which women have been silenced by men and the other was why women have allowed themselves to be silenced. There are many answers that feminists could and have given to both questions. I plan to consider these questions as they relate to the human need to create and maintain self-identity in a social context. My contention is that self-identity is a much more complex affair than we might want to think—not only are we born without any sense of self we can call our own, but we are continually having to recreate our self-identities in the face of a chaotic influx of sensation that threatens to sweep us away. A person may think her sense of self is intact—an unproblematic given—but think how it would feel to wake up to find that everyone you knew had left town and strange aliens had arrived to take their places. You would be the same person, even have the same memories—but how long would you be able to retain the identity you had before waking up that morning? And by what kind of process would you manage to retain any sort of continuity between your old identity and any new identity you might form?

Questions like these in the context of the work of such diverse feminists as Nancy Chodorow and Luce Irigaray on differences in gender identity raise the possibility that there might be something about the process by which we construct and maintain a sense of self that would explain a "masculine" need to silence women in certain ways and a "feminine" need in keeping with being silenced. This intuition is further borne out by feminist literature that examines the role of woman as "other." It is often said that men tend to have an easier time seeing themselves as subjects and seeing women as relative to them—that is, as their "other" rather than as subjects in their own right, whereas women tend to have an easier time seeing themselves as that "other." If this is so, could we account for these tendencies by pointing to differences in the ways that men and women construct and maintain their self-identities?

In this work I articulate an open-ended theory of self that delineates "masculine" and "feminine" self-strategies on the basis of the Hegelian tradition of theorizing self/other relations, psychoanalysis, and contemporary feminist theory. Far from supposing that I have captured anything essential to either masculine or feminine identity, I propose this theory as a tool for further exploring gender distinctions. I argue that selves can be maintained through the meaning produced in a subject's words and acts, and I use the two self-strategies I have characterized as interpretive tools to explore three philosophical texts. The texts I selected are all written by male philosophers. I suggest that the constraints placed on these philosophers by their own conceptions of themselves as men produce conflicts in their texts stemming from conflicts in their use of self-strategies. If these philosophers had been able to go beyond the conceptual barriers presented by their particular versions of a masculine identity, they might have been able, by varying the self-strategies they used, to resolve certain puzzles confronting them.

The possibility that the gender-differentiated self-strategies I propose could be combined in different ways underlies my intention in proposing them. I do not present these "masculine" and "feminine" strategies as indicative of all or even most men or women. In fact, it would be quite in keeping with the theory proposed here if the two self-strategies were characterized in completely different ways contingent upon places, times, and groups of human beings that are different from those explored here. I hope that some women and men may read, and recognize themselves in, the self-strategies described here and perhaps be moved to break through some conceptual barriers of their own. But these self-strategies are meant to be tools in the exploration of how varying conceptions of gender categories inform the way we think and act, rather than to provide definitive descriptions of differ-ences beween men and women. These self-strategies thus have relevance for people who can understand themselves better through them—and for the philosophers that I ex-plore here.

I hope that exploration of gender distinctions in self-constituting activity and of the relationship between the two will reveal some of the reasons for the anxiety created by women's attempts to change the status quo. Although it may be self-evident that men do not want to relinquish power, it is possible that an individual's deep-seated fear of being stripped of his/her ability to maintain a self is also an anxiety-producing factor. Articulating one story about these strategies will enable us to become more aware both of such strategies (however they may be described) and of their importance to our survival as social subjects. This awareness, in turn, will allow us to construct social theo-ries for change that are more likely to succeed because they take the human need to maintain self into account.

I would like to express my gratitude to all the people who have inspired and encouraged, both directly and indi-rectly, this work. Specifically, I would like to thank the Alternative Track of the Philosophy Department at the University of Massachusetts, Amherst, the Amherst Feminist Theory Study Group, the Society for Women in Philosophy, and the Amherst Circle for giving me the courage and the support to pursue the themes I explore here. I would also like to thank Robert Paul Wolff and Cynthia Freeland for reading earlier drafts of this work and giving me helpful criticism and advice. The feedback I obtained from audiences that heard various parts of this book was also invaluable: My thanks go to Mark Taylor and the audience of the *Science and Society and the Other Kierkegaards* Conference at the University of Mas-sachusetts in 1988, to the audience members at the Society for Women in Philosophy Conference at the College of the Holy Cross in 1988, the members of the Sofphia meeting at SUNY, Albany, in 1989, and the Friends of Minerva meeting at Rollins College in 1990. I would particularly like to thank Alison Brown and Cynthia Kaufmann for their stimulating support, and Chris Bresnahan and my sister, Shawn, for their unflagging belief in me.

My biggest debt of gratitude goes to Ann Ferguson. Without her patience, sensitivity, and encouragement this project would never have reached completion. My thanks to her and all the other women who have had the courage to create alternative visions. It is to them that I dedicate this book.

Tamsin E. Lorraine

1

Setting the Context

Introduction

The question of who we are—what kind of creature is a human being—has been with us for a long time. But the more we probe the question, the more complicated it seems. Developing scientific procedures to study objects "out there" is difficult enough, but when the object of study is ourselves, we seem to run into the paradoxical problem of trying to split ourselves in two in order to become our own objects of study.

Nowhere is this paradox more apparent than in the attempts of philosophers to theorize about the self. We feel ourselves to be the subjects of our own thoughts and actions. My thought is not your thought; you are not responsible for my actions. Not only am I the subject of my experiences as I have them, but I can also remember my past experiences as mine and respond to current situations as "me." This "me" somehow represents the sum total of who I am and who I have been—the self to which I refer all my experiences over the greater part of my life span. We all feel we have a self, and we suspect that it is a crucial aspect of being human. And yet when we try to say just what it is, it slips away. We close our eyes and stop our ears in the attempt to find it (Descartes),[1] decide it simply does not exist apart from our perceptions (Hume),[2] or turn to discussions of personal identity instead (contemporary analytic philosophers).[3] And yet a theory of self—a theory about the subjective experience we all have that "my experiences are mine"—is crucial to our understanding of human beings as subjects of knowledge, as agents of action, thought, or desire, and as participants in social and political systems. Human beings are not simply objects whose behavior can be tabulated and analyzed; they are intentional agents whose consciousness of themselves and the world they live in form an inextricable feature of everything they say, think, or do.

The traditional humanist view of human beings as unified, rational, self-interested agents has become increasingly suspect. Postmodernist and poststructuralist views of the self threaten any coherent account we might give for such notions as freedom, responsibility, and authenticity. The open-ended theory of self developed here accepts this challenge and provides an alternative conception of the self that can fulfill some of the requirements of a feminist concern for social change. Although we can no longer assume the self as a unified substratum of our experience—a given that grounds our perceptions and actions in the world—this does not mean that we have to sacrifice our notions of human agency and responsibility. Human subjects are not merely effects of the social symbolic codes and institutions within which they act, as some trends in poststructuralist thought would suggest. Rather, humans navigate these codes and institutions on the basis of embodied experience. The poststructuralist trend asserts that our bodies and our embodied experience have significance for us only insofar as that experience is mediated through the codes at our disposal, but I argue that body-based pleasure motivates us to navigate codes in personally idiosyncratic ways.

Thus, although current poststructuralist arguments portray the self in large part as the product of concepts and categories that precede it, I argue that human subjects do exercise ingenuity, creativity, and even responsibility in putting these concepts and categories into service in their goal of achieving meaningful connectedness with their world. I ground my theory in psychoanalysis because it is, so far, the most coherent account available of the origins of the self in infants and young children. Psychoanalysis does not, however, tell the whole story. It can do no more than offer suggestions about motivations in exercising our options in meaning-making that may be rooted in our earlier histories. We need to focus on, in addition to accounts of the origins of the self, the strategies for maintaining and transforming the self that become available to us later in life.

Psychoanalysis in conjunction with the other theories about the self explored in this volume can illuminate notions of agency, authenticity, and responsibility without returning us to the humanist tradition's notion of self as the unexamined given. On my view, a "self" is a construct that is crucial to social existence. Without a self that others can accept, we could not engage in the activities that maintain us as a society. This work is an attempt to provide a theory about how that self is possible. Indeed, a sensitivity and response to one's own peculiar makeup (rooted in one's own peculiar set of circumstances) make questions about agency and authenticity meaningful. Social codes and institutions exert their effects on human subjects, and human subjects in turn exert on them their own effects, in keeping with pleasures and experiences that lie on the boundary of human existence. When subjects make use of this stratum of experience, they are navigating codes and institutions in a way that is subjectively satisfying and that makes these subjects more than mere effects. Although one cannot predict the form such satisfaction might take, it would manifest itself, from a subjective perspective, in a bodily experience of pleasurable connectedness with the world. If this experience was related to the fuller context of all the meanings created by a human subject in the creation of a continuous sense of self, this pleasure would be further secured.

Bodily based pleasure that is reaffirmed and reiterated in the overall context of an individual's life could be the basis of a notion of authenticity that results from the dialectical interaction of an embodied subject with the codes at her disposal. The agent motivated by the desire for such pleasure would exert a counterforce to the codes available for the maintainence of subjectivity necessary for social survival. For subjectivity to continue, codes would have to be utilized, but the codes selected from those available would speak to the bodily based pleasures of an individual with a unique set of embodied experiences.

In this work I am particularly interested in how constraints placed on human subjects by their conception of gender categories might impede them in their attempts to come to new satisfying solutions to the problem of human identity. The theoretical framework developed here is not meant to provide final answers to this question but rather to open new ground for exploration by providing a tool for pursuing the operation of gender categories in philosophical texts. I will construct a theory of self that posits the following:

1. A theory of self should be a theory about self-constituting activity rather than about a fixed entity
2. This self-constituting activity is (at least currently) informed by gender
3. Self-constituting activity is inextricably linked with meaning-producing activity
4. Meaning-producing activity is also gender informed
5. We can trace the process of self-constituting, meaning-producing activity in the examination of philosophical texts
6. Such an examination can yield further insights into how gender informs self-constituting and meaning-producing activity
7. This new understanding of the self can give us insights into how particular perspectives inform and shape social reality and how we can move toward social change

Descartes and Hegel: Two Approaches to the Self

If it is assumed that we have direct access to reality, questions do not arise about our limitations in gaining knowledge of, and the degree to which that "knowledge" is a distortion of, reality. Once we start asking how comprehensive and accurate our knowledge is of the world we live in, the problem of how we come by that knowledge becomes important. It is then that the questions of who and what we are become inextricably linked with those about the nature of reality. For our broader understanding of the world, self-understanding is crucial. At that point, prescriptions for the "correct" way to approach questions about reality may be given. Metaphysical investigations that do not directly address the issue of how the questioning subject affects the investigation hold implicit assumptions about what the nature of that subject is or should be.

In the philosophical tradition there have been two tendencies with respect to epistemological concerns and concerns about the social order. One tendency has been to separate the two sets of concerns: Questions about truth and falsity and when and whether we attain true knowledge are completely separate from questions about how the social order is and should be constituted. This tendency, which is in the Cartesian tradition, takes epistemology as the pursuit of objective knowledge by an individual subject in contemplative seclusion from the world. Another tendency takes epistemological questions and questions about the social order as inextricably linked: There is no such thing as a knowing subject unaffected by his or her position in a particular social order. Thus, any question about how a subject comes to know must also account for the subject's position in society and what interests motivate that subject's knowing. With the latter view, which is in the Hegelian tradition, "objectivity" in the sense of the disinterested knowledge of value-free facts is rendered problematic, if not completely undermined.

Some trends in analytic philosophy assume that the ideal questioning subject is the contemplative, unextended thinking substance of Cartesian philosophy.[4] Such an assumption about the nature of the questioning subject influences what is considered relevant to metaphysical discussions. On this view the rational endeavor that will lead to true knowledge is the product of a disembodied self in contemplative seclusion from the world of everyday affairs. In order to arrive at the most comprehensive and accurate account possible of reality as it "really" is, one must detach oneself from mundane concerns and take an appropriately "objective" attitude toward the topic at hand.

On the Cartesian epistemological model, the more we can detach the object of study from its surroundings and determine the properties essential to it, the better we will know it. The more we can remove the object of study from its concrete context, the more objective our study will be. "Objectivity" here refers to the universal validity of our findings—no matter where or when or by whom the same study is carried out, the findings will be the same.

There is a current trend, particularly in continental philosophy, to question the subject/object split,[5] to assert that there is no such thing as a perspective from which we can gain disinterested, objective knowledge of objects that are "out there." Whatever viewpoint we take is selected with an end in sight. To assume that there is such a thing as the disinterested stance that can avoid subjective colorings and lay bare reality "as it is" is self-deceptive. In fact, taking the subject and object in a fully contextualized setting can be more revealing than taking the object in isolation. It is only within the context of investigation that we can know the objectives that are coloring a given interpretation.

On the Hegelian epistemological model, the questioning subject cannot be understood out of the particular context in which it is found and any questions about how that subject affects metaphysical investigations are a constant and pressing concern. This view insists that the questioning subject cannot be dropped out of consideration once, say, we reach an appropriately disembodied stance toward the topic at hand. Because any knowledge of reality is obtained in a particular context by a particular subject, the particular nature of that subject and how that subject affects the knowledge obtained must always be taken into account. Thus, instead of a distinct split between questioning subject and the world "out there" being questioned, we have a subject that is unable to take an external perspective on the world she would question because she is a part of that world. This approach makes problematic the relationship between subject and object and renders knowledge of the subject in all its changing forms crucial to our knowledge of the world. Therefore, self-understanding comes to have a transformative effect on our understanding of the nature of reality. In place of the assumption that there is a particular stance from which we can finally grasp the truth about the world, there are the assumptions that as we change, the "truths" we grasp will change and that an understanding of our changing selves will give us insight into the reality we come to know.

Questions about the nature of the self have taken different tacks depending on which tradition the questions come from. On the Cartesian view, an investigation of the self takes the self as an object like any other object; in order to understand truly what it is, one must examine it from an appropriately disinterested perspective. One does not expect the self-understanding that comes from this investigation to influence how one goes about investigating the nature of reality. On the Hegelian view, there is no disinterested perspective from which one can examine the self as an object in isolation from other objects. Self-understanding must come through an examination of the process of dialectical interaction between self and world.

The dialectical tradition of philosophy has focused on the subject and object of knowledge and desire as two moments of a whole that interact. In this dialectical interaction the object is not merely known or desired but enters into a relationship with the subject, a relationship in which both subject and object are transformed. Such a view of the subject of knowledge and desire posits the self as a material construction with a historicity that precludes easy definition rather than as a transcendental entity. On this reading, the self cannot be left out of any account of the world because the subject and object are moments in a whole of interpretation. If the self has a transformative effect, if the self creates reality as much as the self is created by reality, then an understanding of the self's motivations and interests will help us understand the constraints on our claims to knowledge as well as on our desires. Given that subject and object are moments of a whole rather than isolated from each other, the subject's self-understanding is going to affect its understanding of what is true and what is desirable. How one sees one's self and one's stake in that self as the foundation of one's subjectivity is going to play an important constraining role in how one understands one's world. Thus, the relationship between self and world becomes problematic. Personal identity plays a crucial role in determining the interpretation of reality.

In the next section I will take a closer look at approaches to the self derived from Hegel, Nietzsche, and Heidegger. The views discussed here have been taken up into poststructuralist thought and will be the context for the Lacanian approach to the self explored in Chapter 2.

Approaches to the Self in the Hegelian Tradition: Hegel, Nietzsche, and Heidegger

Hegel

It was Hegel who first approached a theory of self through a description of the changing forms of consciousness. Rather than assuming that consciousness always had one role appropriate to it, he stressed the importance of studying consciousness in relation to its object and traced the changing nature of this relationship. In addition to introducing the dialectical role of the social context into the question of consciousness, he introduced the idea that consciousness, in each turn of its transformation, needed to deal with the problem of self-certainty—not only do human beings want knowledge about their world; they want to position themselves with respect to that world.[6]

In the first two chapters of the *Phenomenology of Spirit*, Hegel takes his reader through increasingly sophisticated levels of consciousness. At the first level (sense-certainty), reality is assumed to be directly accessible to the senses. At the level of perception, the knowing subject is forced to revise this assumption because it renders the knowing subject's conception of truth impossible. In keeping with a phenomenological approach, Hegel allows the truth to determine itself completely within consciousness rather than positing truth as a standard existing somewhere outside of consciousness. He examines the actual experience of the consciousness that knows from the philosophical stance of the "we" who are investigating knowledge. He then shows how in the actual process of knowing, consciousness is forced to revise its concept of truth if it is to know at all.

At each level of consciousness a dialectic emerges in which knowledge of an object is referred to the object known for verification; but it is discovered that the object itself must be revised. In the experience of the human subject this dialectic does not explicitly emerge—it is in Hegel's philosophical perusal of what occurs in experience that a pattern of in-itself, for-itself, and in-and-for-itself becomes explicit. That is, Hegel's reconstruction of an evolving consciousness reveals a pattern in which consciousness reconstructs first its object, then itself and its relationship to the object, and then its object again in the attempt to come closer to its own experience of knowledge and truth.

In investigating sense-certainty—the first level of consciousness—as it is experienced, Hegel delineates its features: the I, the object, and the certainty that it is the object that is the essential reality. At this level, the object apprehended *is* truth. But when I point out an object "meaning" to point it out in all its particularity, I discover that rather than pointing out a concrete particular I have pointed out a universal—the "This" I point to could refer to anything. Once sense-certainty has discovered that the This taken in-itself to be essential reality turned out to be for consciousness an empty abstraction, sense-certainty is forced to alter its criterion for truth.

By examining the actual experience of sense-certainty Hegel has shown sense-certainty's conception of knowledge to be inadequate. Because of the original inadequacy of this conception, consciousness is forced past sense-certainty to the level of perception in the attempt to find a conception of knowledge that will be borne out by consciousness's experience. At the stage of sense-certainty, consciousness takes for granted that it has direct access to truth; once the object is apprehended it is known as it is. When sense-certainty is pushed to grasp the object pointed out in its entirety, sense-certainty discovers that the truth is out of reach. The subject/object distinction that was no problem for knowledge as long as the object constituted truth turns out to be problematic. But consciousness, rather than assuming the object to be truth intact and the problem to lie in gaining access to that object, shifts its perception of the subject/object relation itself.

At the level of perception the I, in order to relate a plurality of universals in the "one" that makes that plurality this particular object, takes the object as self-same—that which remains the same from perception to perception—and relates the diverse moments of its apprehension accordingly. For perception the criterion of truth is the self-same. At this stage, consciousness is freed from the self-identical relation of sense-certainty, whose truth is the bare act of intuiting, and is able to ferret out the truth of multiple acts of perception. Consciousness is forced back upon itself in that it takes the diversity of properties to be due to the perceiving I, and any untruth of its perception as being within consciousness rather than within the object. Truth lies in the entire process of I and object rather than in either the one or the other.

Instead of a direct access to truth from subject to object, a more complicated criterion for truth emerges, a criterion that requires more and more participation on the part of the subject in order to provide any sort of verification for knowledge. At the end of consciousness's experience of perception the object is no longer a tenable criterion for truth—it has broken up into two opposing elements (multiple acts of perception and the "one" of the object), which can be brought together only through the perceiving subject.

By tracing the shifting subject/object relation that emerges in the search for an adequate criterion of truth in the first two chapters of the *Phenomenology*, we see a complicated theory of truth emerging within the system of Hegel's thought. From direct apprehension of truth as object we have gone to a criterion of truth that oscillates between subject and object. Although the oscillation between the two has not yet become apparent to the experiencing consciousness, "we" can see that the "truth" at stake here is one that emerges from a complex relationship between subject and object. "We" can also see that such a truth is affected by the self-understanding of the knowing subject that comes to know it.

It is clear that Nietzsche strongly objects to the kind of system-building endemic in Hegel's philosophy. However, Nietzsche too will make problematic the status of "truth" by challenging traditional notions about its relationship to the knowing subject.

Nietzsche

There has been an upsurge of contemporary interest in Nietzsche,[7] stemming in part from the decentering of self that Nietzsche deliberately provokes in his texts. Refusing to build a system or to allow his philosophy to be systematized, he writes in aphorisms. Rather than presenting extended philosophical arguments to support his views, he gives us discontinuous passages, each of which demands interpretation in order to be comprehensible. In the interpretation of his texts, he deliberately discourages "closure." Closure would imply the definitive reading of a text, the reading that finally unravelled all the significance the text had to offer and that let one get to the "real" self that spoke the text. The attempt to achieve closure implies that there was such a self who intended to impart to the reader the significance that the reader's definitive reading finally revealed.

The work of people like Gadamer in hermeneutical philosophy and Derrida in deconstruction[8] has shattered the notion that a text is the product of a unified self with a definitively "correct" interpretation—the significance intended by the author. In proclaiming such concepts as "substance" and the "self" as fictions,[9] Nietzsche laid the groundwork for the idea of the decentered self. We think we are people with a personal identity extending over time to which we refer our experiences. We think we have selves—a sense of who we are, a personality with a history, a unified self that provides the basis for our knowledge and our actions. When we give increasing attention to a decentered notion of self we undermine the notion that a person has a unified self that provides a central perspective for knowledge and agency.

On Nietzsche's view, the self is a fiction, something we impose on a wide and conflicting range of forces that make up who we are. In calling such a self a fiction, he underlines the fiction that we are unified and coherent agents. If we have a unified sense of self, it is only because we have succeeded in subordinating our instincts in such a way that consistency and coherence appear to reign.   It is through mastering a conflicting torrent of impulses and, by setting up ruling instincts, bringing the rest into a hierarchy obedient to the ruling instincts that we are able to preserve the illusion of a unified self.[10]

The self, then, is not a thing, not a substance that we carry around with us.   There is nothing stable about us. We are an intersection of forces that are forever in the process of becoming.[11]   If there is anything stable about us, it is the fictional self in accordance with which we constrain those forces to act.   But this self is a dream, an illusion by which we attempt to veil the reality of our constant change and becoming—the chaos that we really are.   Just as, with regard to external reality, we need illusions to mask Dionysian flux, so we need the illusion of the self to mask the terror of a complete loss of identity.

If, as Nietzsche says, self and substance are but fictions that we impose upon Dionysian process and if, as Hegel suggests, the act of experiencing is a double act in which we constitute both self and object, then how we see ourselves will be inextricably linked with how we see the world.   Our views both of ourselves and of the world will be interpretations rather than essential truths, and these interpretations will be the creations of an activity that constitutes self and world simultaneously.   Investigation of how self-constitution is accomplished and the conditions under which it is possible will also illuminate how object-constitution is achieved and the constraints under which our conception of reality is put if we are to have selves at all.

Nietzsche introduced into Hegelian thought antisystemic strands which poststructuralists later picked up.   It was Heidegger, however, who emphasized the social web of forces that converge to form a self.

Heidegger

Heidegger felt that the problem of skepticism arises from the presupposition of a distinction between inner experiences and external-world objects.   He believed that the

Cartesian model presents a false view of ourselves. The self as a *res cogitans*, a thinking thing, is an objectified description of the self obtained by focusing on ourselves as passive spectators. But our fundamental mode of being is one of active engagement in the world. On this view, being human is treated as a relation in which a stand is taken on one's Being in one's everyday activities. Furthermore, to be human is to be a placeholder in a network of internal relations, constituted by a public language, of the communal world into which Dasein (human existence, or the human self as a relation—see Guignon 1983, 86) is thrown. It is the cultural context that provides Dasein with meaningful possibilities for its concrete ways of being engaged in the world. Because language is the medium in which both self and world can first be discovered, there is no distinction to be drawn between a private bundle of internal impressions and the public ways that Dasein manifests itself in the world (see Guignon 1983, chap. 3).

Thus, Heidegger, like Hegel, refuses to isolate the self from its relation to the world. In fact, the self is considered to be a relation—the active process of taking a particular stance vis-à-vis one's own Being. Human beings are the kind of entities that care about what it is to be human. In living out their lives they are "Being-toward-death"— that is, living with an eye to the significance that their lives as a whole will have when it is complete (Heidegger 1962, #51-52). Because language is the medium by which we create significance, it will be crucial to both our self-interpretations and our interpretations of the world.

In *Being and Time*, Heidegger takes Being-in-the-world as his starting point for investigating Dasein's Being. Thus, his analytic of Dasein emphasizes the unitary wholeness of Dasein and its environment. This in turn shifts attention from a world of entities in isolation from the Being that questions their ontology to a world of entities whose meaning arises in the particular context of Dasein's concern. We find ourselves thrown into a world in which we are already involved, but we are free to make something of our lives as a whole within the confines of the factical situation into which we are thrown. To take a stand with respect to my life requires a certain competence in getting along within the interrelated system of

my culture. I do not have a "true" self private to me: The
way I act and the roles I take on are the acts and roles of
the "they" (Heidegger 1962, #27). Insofar as my acts have
meaning it is a public meaning made available by the possibilities for action presented to me by my culture. That
my life is mine means that I choose the possibilities available to me in a particular way, but those meaningful possibilities are also available to anyone else.

In approaching the question of human existence (as a
preliminary to the question of being in general) without
preconceptions of what constitutes a human being,
Heidegger develops a vocabulary of his own that indicates
processes rather than occurrences that have already taken
place and that are now being examined after the fact.
Such an approach focuses attention on the dynamic nature
of meanings and the shifting frame of reference from
which each one of us, as our concerns change, makes
sense of the world. By bringing back into the picture the
questioning entity that traditional ontology overlooks,
Heidegger prepares the way for a conception of knowledge
that focuses on the totality of the questioning subject and
the object questioned. He does not try to explicate knowledge in terms of an object in isolation from the knowing
subject.

Anything that I attend to is brought to my attention
within the context of my immediate interests, which are in
turn meaningful to me within the context of who I understand myself to be. Thus, how the world presents itself to
me and how I understand myself are inextricably linked.
Furthermore, the range of possibilities for self-understanding is made available to me by my culture. My self is
therefore not a private entity but an intersection of interrelating cultural systems.

A Problematic for Constructing a Theory of Self

In keeping with the thoughts presented here, I want to
propose a new problematic for constructing a theory of
self, a problematic that adopts the Hegelian notion of self-
certainty. Not only are there various forms of selfhood,
but also each form is a response to the problem of estab-

lishing self-certainty. That human beings are subjects of experiences with selves that constitute the locus of those experiences (at least on an experiential level) is not simply a reality: It is the human response to the problem of intentional agency. To be an intentional agent requires more than being a conscious subject of experience. It requires a subject that perceives itself as having some degree of autonomy and efficacy in the world—in short, a self. Selfhood could thus be seen as the human solution to the problem of effective agency. Our actions have meaning because we are responsible agents who carry them out with a purpose in mind. What we do, think, and say has significance within the broader framework of social significance of which we form a part. An important feature of the ability to be an effective agent is self-awareness—a sense of one's place in the broader social framework and of how one's words and actions will affect one's world from that place.

For Hegel, Nietzsche, and Heidegger the pure "I" of Cartesian philosophy is at best a static abstraction of our experience of being selves, which cannot be described in terms of an object. Instead it is a process, a relating of subject to object, an interpreting activity that constitutes both self and world at once. Hegel and Heidegger stress the connection between the interpretation of self and the interpretation of world. Nietzsche does not stress the link between self- and world-constitution. Both are a product of the same activity, but it is not clear that in producing the one, one is also producing the other. In undermining the notion of essential truth, however, Nietzsche also undermines the notion of an essential self. He deliberately works against falling into ready-made patterns of significance by insisting on playing with many masks—many selves from which he can proclaim conflicting truths. From each self comes a different perspective. A decentered self entails a perspective that no longer privileges its viewpoint as the "correct" one. Thus, Nietzsche underlines our creative power in playing with masks, in taking up selves only to put them down again. If the self is a fiction, it is also not the constraint we once thought—we are not bound to our selves as if they were givens from which we cannot escape. The self as a relating process is an activity that may choose to change its orientation, with profound results for both self and world. Thus, a self could be seen as an orienting activity, a stance vis-à-vis the world, a perspective that interprets. In urging us to play, to make our words dance,[12] Nietzsche is urging us to take risks in our interpretations—to risk the loss of self that a breakdown in significance entails in order to create significance anew.

Heidegger introduces a note of caution into the Nietzschean dance with his notion of the self, in the form of the They, as a "crossing point" of cultural systems. Not only is the self that I am not an object, but, in the sense that the interpretations that make up my consciousness are drawn from a public realm of the interpretive possibilities in my culture, the self that I am is not even "my" self. Although my interpretations *may* be my own, they are constrained by the possibilities my culture makes available to me.

Because of the grammar of our language it is hard to talk about the self that I am referring to here in terms that are not misleading. The "self" implies a substance, not a process or relation. When I describe myself I tend to list attributes about someone that I hope has coherence and consistency—something that remains the same over time. Subjectivity might be a better term for the self as process or activity, but it is often awkward grammatically. Also, there is a difference between talking about the activity or experience of being selves and the selves that we consider ourselves to be. In the latter case I would probably be referring to what in psychoanalytic terms might be called a "self-representation." Self-representations are ideas we have about who we are that guide our thinking and behavior. They change over time as our goals change, but they are static in the sense that they are images we refer to rather than active processes.

If we take the Heideggerian notion that there is no distinction between inner and outer, that our selves are the words we speak, the thoughts we think, and the actions we take, then these words, thoughts, and actions are testimony to the self as a relation or process. They are self-representations we present to the world that tend to guide further processing activity as we attempt to make sense of our lives as a whole. Although Nietzsche emphasizes the creative possibilities in self- and world-constitution,[13] we would be hard put to create interpretations in a vacuum. No matter how much we may push at the bounds of the language and social structures at our disposal, we are constrained by the limits of what they can express.

Feminists have attempted to theorize about the relationship of a specifically female self to the world. In doing so, some have attempted to characterize what might distinguish distinctively feminist self- and world-constituting activity from "masculinist" self- and world-constituting activity. In the next section I will review some of these attempts as well as some of the problems they present.

The Feminist Context for a Gender-sensitive Approach to the Self

Gender identity is "one way of representing ourselves. By labeling myself a "man" or a "woman" I am also conjuring up a range of possibilities presented to me in my culture and language. If I stay within conventional bounds I will create a self on the basis of what is offered me. If I am more adventurous, I will push beyond conventional bounds, thus adding to my culture or language new possibilities of what a man or woman could be. Caring about the significance of my life as a whole means creating self and world interpretations that work for me.

In our society gender identity is a key element in our self-representations, a stable and important feature by which we orient our actions. In the process of being selves we tend to orient ourselves differently according to our gender. Gender is thus an interesting feature to consider when we ask how we orient ourselves. Differences in orientation due to sexual difference may give us further clues as to how subjectivity is possible. If selves are fictions and every perspective is no more than that—a perspective—then what clues can sexual difference give us to how a perspective is created?

Sandra Harding, in "Is Gender a Variable in Conceptions of Rationality?" (1982), discusses the implications of feminist gender theory for gender identity and perspectives informed by that identity. Gender theory developed by

Dorothy Dinnerstein (1977), Jane Flax (1978, 1983), Nancy Chodorow (1978), and others draws on post-Freudian psychoanalytic object-relations theory (e.g., Margaret Mahler, Harry Guntrip, and Donald Winnicott). Traditional psychological theories attributed the formation of gendered personalities to nature, sex, or "social learning" after the age of three. In contrast, gender theory attributes such formation to the same social and physical processes within which androgynous infants become human persons (Harding 1982, 50).

Harding argues that the importance of gender theory is due to the centrality of gender identity to personality formation[14] and to gender theory's ability to provide a causal account of gender that is both "materialist" and nondeterministic: "The account is materialist because the form of the actual psychosocial-physical environment with which the infant interacts is the variable determining whether or not gender will be produced. The account suggests that if, societywide, men shared equally in infant caretaking and the day-to-day maintenance of self and others, and if women shared equally in the labor of ruling, gender would not be produced at all" (1982, 53). On this view, we can trace variations in gender formation to historically specific psychosocial conditions and we can entertain the possibility that gender could be "eliminated through political processes" (p. 54).

On the basis of gender theory and additional feminist literature that examines gendered perspectives arising from the divisions of labor by sex/gender, Harding offers two gendered perspectives on rationality:

> A rational person, for women, values highly her abilities to empathize and "connect" with particular others and wants to learn more complex and satisfying ways to take the role of the particular other in relationships. . . . For men, in contrast, a rational person values highly his ability to separate himself from others and to make decisions independent of what others think—to develop "autonomy." And he wants to learn more complex and satisfying ways to take the role of the generalized other (Harding 1982, 53-54).

The contrast of a feminine, relational point of view that emphasizes empathy and connectedness to a masculine, oppositional point of view that emphasizes autonomy and separation is a recurrent theme of gender-theory literature.[15]   Emerging from this literature is the possibility of what some feminists have called a "feminist standpoint"— that is, a distinctively feminist perspective based in distinctively feminine experience, a perspective that posits an alternative theory of knowledge to go with it. Because feminist standpoint epistemology holds that epistemology is a product of particular social relations, it rejects the notion of an "objective" epistemology: "Not just knowledge, or what we know, is shaped by particular experience and the relations we have to others, but *how* we know and how we conceive of knowledge are also similarly shaped" (Hirschmann 1987, 251).   On this view, a feminist perspective would involve not only experiencing aspects of life a masculinist perspective would not (knowing different things); a feminist perspective would also involve experiencing aspects of life differently (knowing in a different way).   To give this difference in perspective justice, we would have to present a thoroughgoing critique of the conceptual frameworks of dominant (masculinist) discourse.

Harding, in *The Science Question in Feminism* (1986), describes feminists such as Jane Flax, Hilary Rose, Nancy Hartsock, and Dorothy Smith as being engaged in the work of developing a feminist standpoint approach, a proposal to transform the perspective of women into an advantaged "standpoint" for social and natural science.   This standpoint would be grounded in a feminist perspective on the universal features of women's experience and would be epistemologically privileged, according to this view, because "men's dominating position in social life results in partial and perverse understandings, whereas women's subjugated position provides the possibility of more complete and less perverse understandings" (p. 26).   In Chapter 6 Harding reviews some of the specifics of the work of Flax, Rose, Hartsock, and Smith.   All are concerned with locating a gendered difference in perspective based in gender theory and/or in divisions of labor by sex/gender.   Hilary Rose (1983) focuses on the unification of the manual, the mental, and the emotional ("hand, brain, and heart") that she claims is typical of women's work (and atypical of men's work). Nancy Hartsock (1983, 1984), in addition to drawing on gender theory, discusses the implications for a feminist perspective of engaging in "subsistence" work (cooking, cleaning, clothing maintenance, etc.) and child rearing. Jane Flax (1983) emphasizes the repercussions of a "defensive," masculine self versus a less defensive, feminine self, first formed in early childhood and then reaffirmed by patriarchal culture.[16] Dorothy Smith (1974, 1979) examines how women's work "relieves men of the need to take care of their bodies or of the local places where they exist, freeing them to immerse themselves in the world of abstract concepts" (Harding 1986, 156). In addition to arguing that women's labor shapes male concepts in specific ways, she claims that women's experience of their own labor is "incomprehensible and inexpressible within the distorted abstractions of men's conceptual schemes" (p. 156).

All four attempt to make generalizations on the basis of gender theory and/or on the basis of relatively rigid divisions of labor by sex/gender in our society that could ground a unified feminist perspective. Clearly, there are problems with this approach. Despite the obvious advantages of a unified perspective for collective political action, the differences among women disallow such a perspective. As Harding, after characterizing the feminist standpoint approach, goes on to ask: "Can there be a feminist standpoint if women's . . . social experience is divided by class, race, and culture?" (Harding 1986, 26). She argues for "feminist postmodernism," an approach that would be profoundly skeptical toward any universal or universalizing claims about "the existence, nature and powers of reason, progress, science, language and the 'subject/self' " (quoted by Harding 1986, from Flax 1986, 3).

Terry Winant deals with this problem by introducing a distinction between a feminist philosophical stance and a feminist standpoint, arguing that there is one of the former and many of the latter. She defines "standpoints" as locations in the political and cultural world that carry with them specific commitments to projects for political and cultural transformation. Obviously, these will vary from feminist to feminist according to her specific location. The adoption of the feminist philosophical stance, however, entails a commitment to taking responsibility for a variety of philosophical positions, each of which could be established by an individual epistemic subject only on the basis of that subject's place "in the whole net of human interdependency" (Winant 1987, 143). In addition to being competent in the dominant discourse, women are competent in the marginal discourses of their marginal identities as women, blacks, Jews, and so forth. Their epistemic competence in multiple forms of life depends on the specific marginal discourses at their disposal owing to their specific background. Thus the feminist standpoint is never complete but is rather a "flexibly developing standpoint that can handle whatever emerges in the process of eliminating sexism." Feminist concerns would be articulated in any idiom deemed appropriate. As feminists we would draw on the resources of all the languages we know "including a multiplicity of 'mother tongues'—or, as I shall dub such resources, 'cultural and discursive birthplaces'" (Winant 1987, 127).

Ann Ferguson has expressed a similar point in her article "A Feminist Aspect Theory of the Self " (1987). To counter the essentializing tendencies of a feminist theory that makes universal claims about the experience of being women, she proposes an "aspect theory of self." This theory rejects the idea that the self is an unchanging, unified consciousness: "Rather, conscious selfhood is an ongoing process in which both unique individual priorities and social constraints vie in limiting and defining one's self-identity" (p. 350). Gender is only one aspect of a self that has many aspects, none of which can be determined to be prior, more fundamental, or more or less authentic than other aspects of the self. Instead "aspects of our selves are developed by participating in social practices which insist on certain skills and values" (p. 351). If the skills and values developed by engaging in different social practices conflict, those participating in these practices "will develop conflicting aspects of self" (p. 351).

Just as Winant points to competence in marginal discourses as a resource for women, Ferguson points to competence in what we could call "marginal" social practices.

Competence in both dominant and marginal discourses and social practices can push women to a feminist viewpoint that attempts to resolve the conflicts in self-identity such competence entails. Whereas Winant does not discuss the content of categories like "masculine" or "feminine," Ferguson's article implies that we can make some general, historically specific claims about these categories. Thus, because of a "developing conflict in gender roles" (p. 353), men and women "will have both so-called masculine and feminine aspects of self as developed by their ongoing social practices" (p. 351). Although we cannot look at men to determine what so-called masculine aspects of self are, or at women to determine the so-called feminine aspects of self, we can attempt to fill out the content of these gender categories by investigating how they operate in our discourses and social practices.

In the subsequent chapters I will develop a theory of self that views the self as a process engaged in a continuous struggle to maintain itself within and through the discourses and social practices at its disposal. As a feminist, I am interested in the role that gender categories play in any process of self-constitution. I delineate the content of these categories in the light of that interest. In keeping with the views presented here by Harding, Winant, and Ferguson, however, I try to move beyond any essentialist notions about gender by moving beyond essentialist notions about the self. My investigation of gender categories must thus be taken as an investigation of socially constructed categories that currently play a role in the constitution of selves and identities. I believe that along the lines of feminist-standpoint literature, some generalizations about these categories can be made, based on an examination of gendered social structures. But my purpose in building on this literature is not to make the line between genders any clearer. Rather, I would like to articulate gender categories as still useful categories for expressing different aspects of human experience and modes of experiencing in the hopes of moving beyond those categories and making a richer range of experience available to us all.

I draw upon psychoanalysis because I believe that it is an important and influential discourse by which people have come to understand themselves and their personal histories and because I believe that feminist revisions of this discourse can provide politically useful transformations of our conceptions of self, gender, sexuality, and desire. I deliberately develop my "masculine" and "feminine" self-strategies as theoretical tools for examining gender categories as they manifest themselves in particular texts for two reasons. First, I want to underline the arbitrary nature of any attempt to dichotomize self-strategies into two genders. Second, I want to promote a notion of self that involves a continuous activity of positioning in and through social practices and meaning structures—thus emphasizing possibilities for individual and social change that traditional psychoanalysis omits.

Notes

1. "I shall now close my eyes, I shall stop my ears, I shall call away all my senses . . . and thus . . . I shall try little by little to reach a better knowledge of . . . myself" (Meditation III of *Meditations* [Descartes 1977, 157]).

2. "I never can catch *myself* at any time without a perception, and never can observe anything but the perception. . . . I may venture to affirm of the rest of mankind that they are nothing but a bundle or collection of different perceptions" (*A Treatise of Human Nature*, bk. I, pt. IV, sect. VI [Hume 1978, 252]).

3. For a discussion of how philosophical debate turned from a "self-approach" that took the experience of being a self into account (represented by philosophers like Descartes and Hume) to questions about personal identity that no longer considered the subjective experience of being a self, see C. O. Evans (1970).

4. For a review of different responses to a breakdown in this way of thinking rooted in various philosophical traditions, see Baynes, Bohman, and McCarthy (1987).

5. See, for example, Habermas (1971).

6. For a discussion of the French reception of Hegel and its influence on French poststructuralist thought, see Descombes (1982) and Butler (1987b).

7. See, for example, Allison (1985), O'Hara (1985), and Lorraine (1986). Also, for the French reception of Nietzsche and the reception's influence on poststructuralist thought, see Descombes (1982), Deleuze (1983), and Kofman (1972).

8. See, for example, Gadamer (1982) and Derrida (1978).

9. " . . . the basic presuppositions of the metaphysics of language, in plain talk, the presuppositions of reason. Everywhere it sees a doer and doing; it believes in will as *the* cause; it believes in the ego, in the ego as being, in the ego as substance, and it projects this faith in the ego-substance upon all things—only thereby does it first *create* the concept of 'thing'" *(Twilight of the Idols* [Nietzsche 1968a, 483]).

10. "I taught them all *my* creating and striving, to create and carry into One what in man is fragment and riddle and dreadful accident" *(Thus Spoke Zarathustra* [Nietzsche 1966, 198]). See also my discussion of Nietzsche in Chapter 4.

11. See Deleuze (1983) for a discussion in the poststructuralist tradition of Nietzsche's concept of force.

12. "Thinking wants to be learned like dancing, *as* a kind of dancing" *(Twilight of the Idols* [Nietzsche 1968a, 512]).

13. For an interpretation that emphasizes this aspect of Nietzsche's thought, see Nehemas (1985).

14. "Of all social characteristics, gender is the earliest to be solidified in the individual, the hardest to change, and the most inextricably connected with how we conceptualize and relate to ourselves, to others, and to nature" (Harding 1982, 49).

15. See, for example, Bordo (1986), DiStefano (1983), Gilligan (1982), Harding and Hintikka (1983), Lloyd (1984), O'Brien (1981), Trebilcot (1983), and Wawrytko (1981).

16. "Flax is arguing that infantile dilemmas are more appropriately resolved, less problematic, for women than for men. This small gap between the genders prefigures a larger gap between the defensive gendered selves produced in patriarchal modes of child rearing and the reciprocal, degendered selves that *could* exist were men as well as women primary caretakers of infants, and women as well as men responsible for public life" (Harding 1986, 153).

2

Lacan and Object Relations

Introduction

Psychoanalysis, because it explores the development of a self and the problems that can arise in such development, is useful to an approach to a theory of self that emphasizes the self's contingency. Created to "cure" people whose functioning as socially acceptable persons was impaired, psychoanalysis explores possible breakdowns in the attempts made by individuals to find a solution to the problem of effective human agency. Thus, rather than taking the self for granted, psychoanalysis has made problematic the development of a self and theorized about the conditions that make selfhood possible. According to psychoanalytic theory, the self is first formed in the relational context of the family, and a self formed in that context is a process that can disintegrate (e.g., into psychosis or schizophrenia) at a later time. In addition, psychoanalysis is particularly useful for a feminist theory of self owing to its emphasis on sexuality and the sensitivity to gender this emphasis entails.

In Chapter 1, I showed that the Hegelian tradition was congenial to an approach to the self that argues for the dialectical interaction of self and world. Philosophers like Nietzsche and Heidegger have extended this tradition by exploring the relationship of human consciousness to the world it "knows" and desires. The French psychoanalyst Jacques Lacan draws on this tradition[1] and extends it into the terrain opened up by Freud with the help of

Saussurian linguistics (see below).   The Hegelian tradition
emphasizes the effects of concepts and symbols on human
consciousness and human reality.   In keeping with this
emphasis, Lacan downplays the biological determinism of
classical Freudian theory and instead posits human behavior as the effect of a broader context of social significance.
In this way, an individual's behavior can be explained as
the result of both personal and social networks of meaning
that interact in complicated ways.

Lacan's relationship to more orthodox branches of psychoanalysis has not been unproblematic.   The *Société
française de psychanalyse* was formed by analysts and stu-
dents led by Lacan and Daniel Lagache who seceded from
the *Société psychanalytique de Paris* and thus were no
longer affiliated with the International Psychoanalytical
Association.   (Although Lacan himself was never recon-
ciled with the International Association, the other members of the *Société française de psychanalyse* have since
rejoined it under a new affiliation.)   One of the important
points of contention that led to the secession was Lacan's
emphasis on the question of the status of human discourse
in analysis.   Lacan was opposed to the tendency to reduce
analysis to a study of behavior, a quasi-biological theory of
instincts, or a "medical therapy inclined to reduce the
subject's psychical life to a series of symptoms to be interpreted by the (all-knowing) analyst in the way that a doctor interprets the symptoms of physiological disease"
(Wilden 1968, xxv).   Lacan felt that people had turned away
from Freud's more radical insights and that these insights
could be put into more modern terms with the help of
structural linguistics.

According to Ferdinand de Saussure, there is no one-to-
one correlation between words and things, between signifiers and signified, and any relationship between the two
is arbitrary.   Saussure represented the relationship of a
signifier (psychic imprint of an acoustic image) to the
signified (concept) as S/s with an ellipse around it.   The
ellipse emphasizes the relationship of a particular signifier to its signified (Lemaire 1977, chap. 1).   Lacan removed
the ellipse to emphasize the bar between the two.   On his
view, a signifier signifies only by virtue of its relationship
to the whole chain (system) of signifiers.   This produces

the constant sliding of the signified under the signifier—signifieds, rather than staying put vis-à-vis any particular signifier, tend to slip under the bar. For the production of meaning to take place, for signifiers to generate the signified (the meaning) there must be a third term to witness the meaning produced: the subject. The subject that intends meaning constructs itself in relation to meaning and thus completes the signifying chain by finding a place for itself in that chain (Lemaire 1977, chap. 3, and Coward and Ellis 1977, chap. 6).

On this view, the process of self-construction can be traced in our use of language. It is with our entry into language that we first take up the position of subject. In order to utter meaningful sentences I must come to grasp my position as a speaker. If I say "snow is white," I must have some notion of the snow as the subject of the ascription of a property and I must have some notion that the snow I am describing is not me. In other words, a meaningful utterance locates the speaker as well as what is spoken about. "Lacan calls the domain of the signifier, in which this perpetual restructuring of the subject takes place, the Symbolic order" (Bowie 1979, 132). The "domain of the signifier" in its broadest form includes all the symbolic orders by which we represent reality in meaning structures that operate via opposition, i.e., mathematical symbolism, language, and social and cultural symbolism (Lemaire 1977, 55). The "Symbolic" constitutes the possibilities for being able to take up any position in language at all. The particular relations an individual adopts with respect to the particular set of social relations she finds herself in are fixed in the same process by which she produces herself as a subject. The prevalent ideologies of the culture will determine possibilities for particular manifestations of positioning oneself in one's culture. An awareness of the unconscious—that is, the "gap" between the coherent subject that is perfectly suited to a position in society and the contradictions within the subject that work against that position—reveals the price one must pay to perpetuate the illusion of a unified self (Coward and Ellis 1977, 93-94). The conscious understanding we have of ourselves and the words we utter does not give a full account of the meaning of our words. Any signifier that is actually

enunciated by a subject of speech has significance only in
the context of a whole "battery" of signifiers, unconscious
as well as conscious, of those who hear it, including the
speaker. Lacanian psychoanalysis is interested in investigating the "unconscious" subject of speech—the effects of
signifiers at play in meaning making that are not readily
accessible to the conscious subject of speech.

Lacanian theory thus explores the various meaning
structures within which and by which human subjects
position themselves with respect to the world and one another. Like Hegel, Lacan posits human consciousness as
always searching for self-certainty and transforming itself and its world in its attempts to achieve such certainty.
Like Nietzsche, Lacan posits a fictional self always on the
verge of disintegration, a self that desires the illusion of
wholeness. Like Heidegger, Lacan posits a self formed in
and from a social matrix of meaning. What Lacan adds to
this tradition is a linguistic rereading of Freud that situates
the origins of individual selves within the social matrix of
meaning and that further explores the strategies by which
selves are created and maintained. Because the strategies
Lacan explores are linguistic and representational strategies humans use in order to be persons that can function
in a social whole, he reorients psychoanalytic explana-
tions of human behavior. Whereas previously such expla-
nations tended to be restricted to the individual, his or her
biological drives, and their interaction with the environment within the limited context of the family and important others, Lacanian theory extends that context to society
as a whole. This impetus, in turn, gives social theory new
insights into how individual selves negotiate larger social
structures.

Although I am not in complete agreement with all of
Lacanian theory, I believe it deserves serious attention. As
we take our identities and our world less for granted, we
are confronted with the complicated ways in which the
two interact. Lacanian theory addresses the question of
how our social meaning structures inform our identities
and how those identities negotiate those meaning structures. Lacan's linguistic turn brings the question of the
relationship of self and other, self and world, into arenas
already staked out by the contemporary philosophical in-

terest in language. With the help of Lacanian theory we can read individual philosophical texts as meaning structures that make sense only within a broader context of social significance. We can also unravel those texts as individual answers to the problem of effective human agency. This way of reading philosophical texts can give us insight into how concerns about human identity within social networks of significance inform and shape the content of those texts.

On the Lacanian view that the meaning produced by a subject of speech is the effect not only of that subject's conscious discourse but also of a range of signifying chains that operate beyond the subject's awareness, the traditional approach to philosophical texts (interpretations constrained by some notion of the author's conscious intentions) reveals only a small part of the signifying activity actually at work. Furthermore, any production of meaning is also an act of self-constitution. For example, a philosophical text, in addition to having a meaningful "content"—the thoughts it communicates (or miscommunicates)—also represents a self in process: the evolving relationship of the authorial voice to the meaning structures evoked in and by the text. An examination of Lacanian psychoanalysis will therefore assist in developing my thesis that philosophical texts represent a form of self-construction. In addition, Lacan feels that taking up a position with respect to meaning structures is inextricably gender-linked. Thus, his views on sexual difference will help establish the role that gender plays in that process of self-construction.

Lacan and the Fictional Self

To understand the Lacanian view of a "split" subject unaware of much of the signifying activity motivating her words, we must be familiar with Lacan's terminology, in particular, premirror, mirror, and postmirror stages of early childhood development. I will describe those stages and outline Lacan's notions about the dialectical aspect of subjectivity and the distinction he makes between the Imaginary and the Symbolic realms. I will then characterize the adult human subject via Lacan's "schema L" and summarize the interrelationships of a split subject—the "effect" of signifying chains that operate in various realms (the unconscious and consciousness) and self/other dialectics (me/other, I/Other, Other/me)—that make any production of meaning an overdetermined and inherently conflictual process.

Lacan's linguistic rereading of Freud presents the unconscious as primarily symbolic and relational. Lacan maintains a careful distinction between Freud's notions of "instinct" (*Instinkt*) and "drive" (*Trieb*). We will see that on Lacan's reading "drive" (in French, *pulsion*) takes a representational form with the goal of maintaining self-constancy and has very little connection with innate instincts. Tracing out Lacan's views on the initial formation of identity as it unfolds in early childhood will give us a better sense of Lacan's rereading of Freud as a structural theory about human motivation rather than as a biological theory about innate instincts. The stages I am going to describe are not developmental stages in the sense of Piaget—they are not genetically encoded in the biological organism. Instead, they are culturally encoded. Becoming a subject within the cultural context of the meaning structures of language and symbolic codes as we know them requires a developmental process wherein the subject takes her place in those codes.

The Premirror or Prespecular Stage

The infant is born without subjectivity—no unconscious, no identity, no sense of "self." He[2] has a highly developed perceptual system but very little muscular coordination because of his prematuration at birth. Lacan describes this organic insufficiency as a "lack of coordination of his own motility . . . intra-organic and relational discordance during the first six months" (Lacan 1977, 18-19). Although the infant has neither individuality nor subjectivity and cannot walk, talk, or obtain food on his own, he watches and listens to the world around him. Lacan calls this stage the "premirror" stage. It extends from roughly birth to six

months, and it is marked by the experience of fragmentation. During this stage, drive takes its primary form and is
synonymous with "need," aiming at the suppression of all
tension and thus keeping the organism constant through
the satisfaction of physical needs (Ragland-Sullivan 1986,
70). The infant, unable to actively take charge of satisfying his needs, strives to maintain constancy through the
introjection of part-objects. That is, as a primary representational energy, drive mentally represents part-objects
that satisfy. The voice and gaze of the primordial Other—
the Other that satisfies his needs—are introjected as part-
objects to sooth the infant whose prematuration makes him
unable to maintain the organism in a tensionless state of
constancy.

These elemental signifiers—the voice, the gaze, part-objects—are recorded by the infant in his link with the Other
(i.e., the primary caretaker) who maintains the organism's
constancy. Because the infant cannot place himself in the
array of representations of lived experience that he
records, he merges with them, becoming, for example, the
part-object of breast, the gaze of his mother, or his own
gaze. Phonemes, bits and pieces of the language spoken to
and around him, are taken in along with other images. At
this stage these images are fragmentary and fleeting;
there is no underlying continuity to perception.

Freud describes this early stage of human existence in
"Instincts and Their Vicissitudes" (Freud 1957). The infant's "pleasure-ego" absorbs objects that are sources of
pleasure and "thrusts forth upon the external world whatever within itself gives rise to pain" (p. 82). The pleasure
ego is so named because the criterion for distinguishing
the ego from the external world is a subjective one based
on what gives the infant pleasure.

This premirror stage, along with the next, are both
narcissistic stages where the infant has as yet made no
distinction between himself and the pleasurable objects
that are (in actuality) distinct from him. He is self-sufficient; he is his world insofar as he makes no distinction
between himself and the objects that give him pleasure.

The Mirror Stage

The "mirror stage," Lacan's term for the final phase of narcissism that precedes the object stage, is crucial for the development of subjectivity. It occurs roughly between six and eighteen months and is marked by the infant's *jouissance* (joy) of fusion with a Gestalt of the human form when, for example, he gazes into a mirror. In the primary narcissism of the mirror stage the infant feels himself to be ideal—his jubilation at the sight of his reflection is not yet marred by any suspicion of lack. The infant takes pleasure in his reflection because it presents him with "the total form of the body by which the subject anticipates in a mirage the maturation of his power" (Lacan 1977, 2). The Gestalt reflected in the mirror is a pregnant one that will give birth to the self to come. It "symbolizes the mental permanence of the I, at the same time as it prefigures its alienating destination" (p. 2). The infant assumes the image of the total body (representing the mental permanence of the I) in contrast to "the turbulent movements that the subject feels are animating him" (p. 2). This first encounter with one's reflection sets in motion in the Imaginary realm a dialectic that prefigures the dialectic between self and other.

The image of the total form of the body is an anticipation of the mastery over motor locomotion that is yet to come. Hence, even the primordial I, the prefiguration of the ego, is a fiction that is based on a projection of what has not yet occurred. The infant assumes the image because it is more pleasurable to feel one's self to be a functioning whole than a random array of discrete movements and sensations. But to assume this image from the outside is to internalize something that comes from the external world. At the pleasure-ego phase this internalization is natural; however, the primordial I will emerge in the object-stage as the ego, still carrying with it the fiction of an object (the image) absorbed into itself on the basis of the subjective criterion of pleasure.

The dialectic between actual ego and ego-ideal is prefigured here in primordial form. Freud discusses the interplay of the actual ego and the ego-ideals by which an adult measures herself in "On Narcissism" (Freud 1957). In the transition from primary narcissism to the object stage a sort of dialectic between the actual ego and the ego-ideal comes into play: "To this ideal ego is now directed the self love which the real ego enjoyed in childhood. The narcissism seems to be now displaced on to this new ideal ego, which, like the infantile ego, deems itself the possessor of all perfections. . . . That which he projects ahead of him as his ideal is merely his substitute for the lost narcissism of his childhood, the time when he was his own ideal" (p. 116). On Lacan's account, the dialectic between self and other is founded on the assumption of an image in the form of a totality that belies the fragmented movements and responses the infant actually feels himself to be. Thus, at the irreducible core of the self (if one could call it a core) lies a fiction of totality assumed from the outside that is later elaborated layer by layer in the dialectic of identification with the other.

The gap in the primordial me initiates the rivalry between these two "selves" (the inner sense of fragmentation versus the whole image of the human form) and the aggressivity of the me who defends against the feeling of disintegration by identifying with an alien object. Whereas drive at the prespecular stage aims at satisfaction of physical need, drive at the mirror stage takes the form of desire. There is a growing awareness of differentiation and otherness along with psychic awareness, although the "pleasure-ego" still reigns. The infant still feels himself to be what gives him pleasure, but rather than merging with the part-objects of the prespecular stage, he wants to merge with the mother as a whole object. To feel that he and his mother are one, the infant must gain the mother's recognition. Pleasure becomes linked with responses from the mother that demonstrate his effect on the mother as a whole. Desire in its primary form is the desire to be desired by the (m)Other in order to fuse with her; it is this recognition of the (m)Other that desires him that allows identificatory merging to occur (Ragland-Sullivan 1986, 72-73).

Thus need matures into desire via the recognition of the (m)Other. To be desired, the infant must conform to the desire of the m(Other) and forfeit certain pleasures. Need in its original undifferentiated form is recorded as primal

repression as the infant becomes increasingly aware of
him-"self" as an object of the voice and gaze of the other.
The infant identifies with the mother, fusing with her so
as to retain the sense of stability and continuity he would
not otherwise feel.   At some point (given all the frustra-
tions his mother causes him) he comes to realize that not
only is he not omnipotent (that is, he is not the whole
world that matters to him—the mother that supplies his
needs) but his mother also is imperfect.   She wants more
than catering to his needs; she has desires of her own.
However, the infant still wants to fuse with the mother (as
in the mirror stage proper), and he becomes increasingly
aware of his separateness.   The realization that the mother
is lacking (i.e., has desires of her own) brings on the castration complex, which marks the end of the mirror stage.
With the advent of this complex the primordial ego formed
through identificatory merging with the (m)Other suc-
cumbs to secondary repression.   The child displaces his
desire for (m)Other-fusion onto cultural substitutions that
disallow such fusion, and the ego will be built up by layers
of identifications.   But representations of identificatory
mergings with the (m)Other that originally desired one in
very specific ways, although repressed, will continue to
exert an effect.

The Postmirror Stage

For Lacan, the transition from narcissism to the object
stage is marked by loss; the tie between mother and child is
lost and the child is confronted with his existential negativity.   That is, the child realizes that he is not self-sufficient and that objects important to him (such as the
mother) can absent themselves and thus are separate from
him.
At this point the father and language step in with the
Law-of-the-Father that forbids incest (fusion with the
mother) and give the child something to compensate him
for his terrible loss: the symbolizing power of language.
Words, because of their power to represent what is absent,
help the child to compensate for the pain of separation
from his mother.   In the famous Fort! Da! game of the baby

observed by Freud (in *Beyond the Pleasure Principle*), the baby throws a spool of cotton out of his crib, saying "ooo" (*fort*, "gone"), and reeling it back, saying "*da*" (there), thus mastering (according to Freud) the comings and goings of his mother by representing them with the help of the spool and words that will eventually come to represent desired objects that are absent in and of themselves. By soothing the pain of absence, words allow the child to defer his desires, to articulate them as representations that he can keep until such time as satisfaction is possible.

In the desire to be desired the child identifies with the object the mother seems to desire, i.e., the father. Thus, in much the same way as the infant assumes the mirror image, the child assumes an image that anticipates the power that is not yet his. This identification, however, is modified by the restrictions placed upon the child in the Symbolic matrix that encodes kinship relations (and prohibits incest). Hence, a dialectic between the actual ego, with all its inadequacies in getting its desires satisfied, and the ego-ideal that the ego compares itself to (the ego-ideal incorporating ever more of the restrictions the actual ego is confronted with) is mediated through successive identifications with the other within the Symbolic matrix.

The castration complex is the moment in which the subject finds his signifying place and completes the detachment from the dependency on the mother as the source of need satisfaction. In the postmirror stage the desire to be desired so that identificatory fusion can occur is displaced from the mother. The child attempts to fill in his lack through fusions with cultural substitutions instead of the spontaneous fusions of the narcissistic premirror and mirror stages (Ragland-Sullivan 1986, 79). Thus, desire at this stage, while still linked to the Imaginary, manifests itself in the Symbolic. The transition from the Imaginary to the Symbolic is forced by the assumption of castration, which creates the lack "through which desire is produced in a way organized to cultural ends" (Coward and Ellis 1977, 120).

In the primary processes of the unconscious system, psychical energy flows freely by means of displacement and condensation. These processes are at work both in the fleeting and fragmentary mergings of the infant in the prespecular stage and the narcissistic identifications of the mirror stage. In the secondary processes, "satisfaction is delayed while the mind tries different ways to satisfaction" (Coward and Ellis 1977, 100). In the postmirror stage the subject acquires the ability to exercise the secondary processes of conscious thought. The subject first splits itself off from "its sense of continuum with the mother's body, then it splits itself off from the ideal ego of the mirror stage, and finally it separates itself in order to find itself a place in symbolisation" (Coward and Ellis 1977, 100). Thus, the process that constitutes a subject of speech who can place itself with respect to its world constitutes the unconscious in the same movement (Coward and Ellis 1977, 115).

The Schema L

For Lacan, a theory of "self" is a misnomer if what we mean by a self is a unified subject of experience. Lacan's theory of self is better termed a "theory of the human subject." Rather than about how an ego develops and maintains itself, it is a theory about a structure of signification that can maintain itself only by repeatedly reconstituting these significations in the present.

With the help of Lacan's famous schema L,[3] we can summarize our characterization of the premirror, mirror, and postmirror stages:

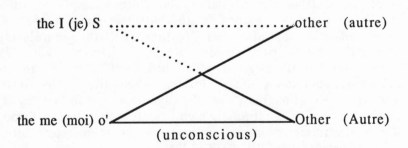

The diagram represents four poles of subjectivity through which an individual's signification oscillates. The split subject of the "me" (*moi*) of narcissistic identifications and the "I" (the subject, S, or *je*) of speech makes the project of self-identity and self-constitution a continuous one: trying to find equilibrium between conflicting aspects of the subject in order to maintain the illusion that the subject is a unified self. The place of the "Other" (*Autre*) is the place of both lived representations not incorporated into the me/other dialectic and of meaning structures of the Symbolic (i.e., language) not incorporated by the "I" into the conscious signifying chains of the subject. The "I" is the locus of significance as determined by the rules of language. The "me" is the ideal ego first formed through identification with the mother (or primary caretaker) and then diverted into a series of identifications with ego ideals. The "other" (with a lowercase *o* — *autre* with a lowercase *a* in French) is the other that one addresses in the Imaginary realm of narcissistic identifications—it functions as a screen onto which the identity drama is projected. Although the me/other dialectic of narcissistic identifications originates in the mirror stage, its origins have been relegated to the place of the Other. This dialectic operates in the realm of the Imaginary where the "me" seeks to maintain the illusion that it is without lack by repeating self/other identifications reminiscent of mother-fusion.

The I/Other dialectic originates in the postmirror stage where the subject is introduced into the realm of language and the Symbolic order. The taking on of sexual identity and the subjectivity of a language speaker creates a split in the subject between the me of narcissistic identifications and the I that submits desire to the paternal law. In the Symbolic realm the I positions itself with respect to the social categories of the Symbolic order, activating signifying chains by placing itself as a signifier with respect to those chains. It is continually deflected from a dialectical relationship with the Other by the me, which wants to dictate the position the I takes with respect to an other. The me, in its search for a sense of cohesiveness, a stable, continuous identity, enlists the aid of the I to "translate" its identificatory needs by adding to the speaking subject the additional, intentional aim of tracing out the desire of the me.

The unconscious is the discourse of the Other. It speaks in the individual's dreams, slips of the tongue, and so forth. This speech will have an ostensible listener, the other, to whom one is speaking, but will actually be addressed to one's own Other, the source of unconscious truth. The truth sought by what Lacan calls the "true" subject is the truth that the me evades with every narcissistic trick of identification that it has at its disposal. It is the truth of the subject's radical lack of being, the primordial gap that marks it.

The me is a function of the Imaginary, whereas the I operates in the Symbolic. The identifications of the me are crucial to subjectivity, but they also lead to the alienation of one's truth in illusion. The strategies of the me were put into place in the preoedipal stage and lost to consciousness with the resolution of the Oedipus complex. Others are searched for that will mirror back the wholeness the me can identify with. These Imaginary "lures" motivate a person's view of reality, putting that person's range of available signifying possibilities into the service of a limited repertoire of narcissistic identifications. Since the me is not a thing but a dialectical structure dependent on the other to maintain the fiction that it exists, libidinal energy is unceasingly motivating the I, another dialectical structure, to find and recreate the identificatory relationships it needs for its survival.

At the same time, signifiers first repressed because of the "no" of the father and one's insertion into the Symbolic and then repressed because of one's subjugation to that Symbolic order still exert pressure from the place of the Other. The illusions of the me are belied by the signifiers that represent aspects of lived experience the me has had to deny. The "truths" of the Symbolic order, reality as it is officially sanctioned by socially imposed meaning structures, are also belied by aspects of one's lived experience repressed in deference to those structures.

The truth of the unconscious points to what Lacan calls the Real—the realm beyond language, the ineffable, that which slips away when we try to speak it.[4] The Real of the subject's lived present activates the signifiers that operate on both conscious and unconscious levels in the Imaginary and Symbolic realms but finally eludes all attempts at definitive signification. Because of the elusive nature of the Real and the split nature of the subject, the desire to take one's place in the Symbolic as the person one "really" is, is forever thwarted by the inadequacy of the signifier by which one must represent oneself. It is inevitable that any self-signification is partial and incomplete. Thus, the subject is doomed to "castration." As there is nothing that can fill in the subject's lack making the subject whole, the object of desire as such is impossible to attain. The subject will never reach the wholeness it seeks by deferring its desire through Symbolic signifying chains. Without such an object one might expect desire as well to be impossible. But oedipal rivalry dissimulates the impossibility of mother-fusion, leaving one with the illusion that one can find the absolute object that will replace the lost (m)Other and fill in one's gap. The absolute object or "*objet a*" (the desired object)[5] is the "lure" that makes desire possible despite its futility. Thus, the signifier and speech create both the law of castration imposed on the one who speaks as well as the subject that desires.

The subject as a signifier and the self as the effect (that is, the signified) are linked through the discourse of the Other, the unconscious. A changing array of signifiers at both the conscious and the unconscious levels will effect changes in the signified. Thus, my identity is the outcome of a signifying network at various levels (conscious, preconscious, and unconscious) and in three realms (the Imaginary, the Symbolic, and the Real) that play themselves out in a zigzag between the four poles of the Schema L.

Self-construction and the Production of Meaning: Take 1

In the foregoing section we saw that in the act of speaking or writing, the Lacanian subject is not merely attempting to communicate information to his audience. Instead, there is an oscillation of meaning between the four poles that make up the Lacanian quadrature. The human subject is therefore not a unified entity transmitting information to another unified entity; it is a quadrature in complicated communication with itself that only incidentally transmits information to another.

Such a view of the human subject requires us to change our interpretations of philosophical texts. The assumption that there is a unified self with a unified set of intentions behind the text leads the interpreter to cancel out contradictions and discrepancies in the text to conjure up a picture of what the author "really" meant. The assumption that the author is a split subject, a decentered self of signifying chains that oscillate between four poles, renders reductionistic interpretations that assume such a unified subjectivity. A reading that cancels out the contradictory and equally valid meanings the text yields does not do justice to its complexity.

Desire—the desire to fill in the primordial gap in being—is the motivating force of enunciation. The speaking I strings together signifying chains according to socially acceptable codes of meaning. The me directs these chains in keeping with its desire to maintain the illusion of wholeness and continuity. The I in enunciating a signifying chain signifies the self by taking up a position in the signifying chains enunciated. This position is motivated by the me, which ceaselessly reconstitutes its position with respect to the other according to old patterns. If the subject cannot reconstitute itself with respect to the other—that is, put into play the signifying chains that have represented it in the past—the subject will be threatened with disintegration: loss of continuity, loss of meaning, loss of self.

Although the me attempts to direct the speaking I in its interest, the subject's "truth," which has its location in the place of the Other, subverts those attempts. We thus have the picture of a subject at odds with herself, a subject with two sources of "truth": the "truth" of the ego that would dissimulate its lack with illusion and the "truth" of the unconscious subject who would subvert that truth by bringing into play the unanticipated meaning of signifiers not yet incorporated into the me/other dialectic. The gaps and contradictions of a text can be seen as the collision of these two orders of "truth"—the self-certainty of the me (based on illusion) and the unanticipated meaning of the unconscious forever trying to subvert that truth and confront the individual with its irreducible lack.

Therefore, the very act of writing theory is simultaneously an act of self-construction in which the subject constructs signifying chains that position it as a signifier. In the act of writing theory, the writer is attempting to assimilate experience in accordance with rules of conventional language as well as in accordance with the identity themes that give coherence to that writer's experience. To do only the first would result in arbitrary strings of words that have meaning but no impetus. When there is no speaking "self" that informs words with intentionality, significance beyond the conventional meaning of the words is missing, leaving us with the feeling that we are just reading arbitrary strings of words. What gives language impact is the drive of a me to reconstitute a relation to an other in continuity with an endless series of such relations extending back to earliest infancy. Through this drive the me attempts to communicate something beyond the conventional meaning of the words: the message of who the speaker is, what he is about, what his relationship to the words spoken is.

Thus theory is simultaneously about the subject who is writing it and about the object under examination. We can read theory for the story it conveys about the positions a subject took in constructing self-identity as well as for the meaning it conveys in terms of a social pool of meaning. In the philosophical texts considered in this book, I will examine the play of the me and the unconscious subject of truth as two levels of meaning in a text—the identifications translated by the I and the "symptoms" of the text that subvert those identifications.

On a Lacanian view, a theorist wants to find the lost object, that which will fill his lack and make him whole. That object has been truth. There are times when theory pushes at the boundaries of meaning in order to incorporate more of the lived experience that evades current (Symbolic) meaning structures, and there are times when language is put into the service of maintaining old, if comforting, illusions. Lacan gives us a way of reading out both. Any "self"-conception is going to be inadequate because it is based on a fiction; analogously, no theory is ever

going to be whole. The illusion of the theorist is that she
has finally found closure, finally gotten the "whole" theory, the "whole" truth. She wants to maintain the illusion
of that wholeness, just as she wants to maintain the illusion of her own wholeness, by evading the truth that
would subvert that illusion—the meaning that eludes her
theory. The desire of the theorist is finally to take on the
image of the whole theorist, the theorist who is whole, who
knows all, who has filled in the gap in self, the gap in
knowledge. Lacan suggests that achieving that is impossible but also that the desire motivating such a quest is
inextricably bound with the quest for wholeness of self,
for self-identity. We will be forever searching for the
"lost" *objet a*, which we never had to begin with. And, in
fact, Lacan does not advocate giving up the quest for
wholeness—the "cure" consists, not in giving up the quest,
but in adhering to it more rigorously, in a less alienated
way, by escaping the lures of the me that would delude us
into thinking that we have already gotten what we were
looking for.[6]

Whereas Lacan emphasizes the illusory nature of the
me's quest for wholeness, object-relations theory offers a
different reading of the me's activity. After reviewing the
work of Donald W. Winnicott and Margaret S. Mahler, presented in the next section, we will be able to evaluate
Lacan's conceptions of the mirror stage and of the radically fictional nature of the me. This critique will allow us,
in the final section of this chapter, to conceptualize an alternative to the strategy for self-constitution characterized by Lacan's schema L. This alternative will allow us to
formulate a different strategy in the production of meaning.

Object Relations and a Critique
of the Fictional Self

Although Lacanian psychoanalysis is attractive in light
of my project, I believe that it can be enriched with insights taken from object-relations theory. Lacan, with his
notion of the Imaginary, makes room for the preoedipal
experiences of the mother/child dyad that object-relations

theory tends to emphasize. But on Lacan's view, one takes up one's Symbolic position in language by accepting the paternal law (forbidding the child sexual access to the mother) and the father as legislator of that law. Positionality in the Symbolic order, although it is influenced by effects of the Imaginary, has more to do with the father (or the paternal law) than the mother. On my view, Lacan's emphasis on the Symbolic leads him to overlook intricacies of relationships in the Imaginary that could further illuminate how positioning in the Symbolic is affected. The question of sexual difference and the role of gender in self-construction will be considered in Chapter 3; there we will see that the treatment of such relationships in object-relations theory suggests possibilities overlooked by Lacan.

Lacan's quadrature provides an illuminating conceptual framework for understanding how the kinds of preverbal identifications made in early childhood can interact with identifications rooted in the Symbolic, e.g., the taking on of a particular role in life (doctor, lawyer, or plumber). The latter involves inserting oneself into the Symbolic code, taking one's place in a network of kinship relationships within the family (e.g., daughter/sister or son/brother) and in the broader network of social relationships (black and rich or white and poor, for example). These positions are encoded in language—marked out by the signifying chains connected with each position (for example, it sounds "funny" for me to say "I'm a menace to society" if "I" refers to an upper-middle-class doctor and perfectly natural if "I" refers to a poor car thief). The preverbal identifications of the Imaginary involve identifications based on symbiotic fusion with the primary caretaker. As such fusion involves a more "direct" form of identification than one mediated by Symbolic representation, it is less accessible to Symbolic understanding. That is, analyzing what my uncle represents to me as my role model is more straightforward than analyzing the wordless fusion experiences I had with my primary caretaker as an infant. Lacan's interrelating of the Imaginary and Symbolic realms underlines the unconscious effects my original fusion has in any later identifications that take place on a more conscious level. On his account,

Imaginary effects are playing into the Symbolic identifications I later make, and these Imaginary effects remain
unconscious for the most part. The me enlists the I in the
attempts to repeat its original identifications and so to
maintain "self"-continuity. Thus the preoedipal experiences that constitute the Imaginary have a lasting effect
throughout one's life, no matter how much they are modified and diverted by the Oedipal complex and the diversion
of desire through the Symbolic chain.

It is to Lacan's credit that he stresses the interplay of
the Imaginary and Symbolic realms throughout life—the
preoedipal realm where the mother predominates and the
Symbolic realm of the father introduced by the Oedipus
complex. In this way we can see how both the mother and
the father (taken in the traditional sense) can exert a continuing influence on one's self-identity, and we can un-
tangle some of the mechanisms involved in such an identity. Lacan emphasizes the "lures" of the Imaginary and
the "illusion" of wholeness that fusion gives one—an illusion that we must shatter if we are to uncover "truth." His
technique of analysis and the "short session" emphasizes
the father role of rupture—breaking off the analysand's
session at arbitrary moments in order to reveal the illusory nature of any Imaginary identifications the
analysand may be in the course of carrying out.[7] We could
contrast this kind of technique to that of the object-
relations theorist, Winnicott, who prefers sessions longer
than the traditional fifty minutes, sessions that foster trust
and the creation of a "holding environment" for the
analysand. This technique would seem to be more in
keeping with the analyst as mother.

I agree with Lacan that Imaginary fixations leading one
to ignore or deny aspects of one's experience, aspects that
conflict with the maintenance of illusory wholeness, can
unnecessarily restrict one. Because of these fixations, one
becomes alienated from the "Real," which eludes one's
rigidified structures of meaning. Lacan's technique, by
involving the analysand in the "death work" necessary to
break one out of restricted meaning structures, certainly
has a place in liberating one from such fixations. His own
"flight from mother engulfment," however, led him to un-
deremphasize the more positive aspects of the Imaginary—

aspects that can be revealed with the help of object-relations theory.

Whereas Lacan emphasizes the primordial gap in one's "self"—the gap between one's own inner sense of fragmentation and the alien mirror image one identifies with in order to feel whole—object-relations theory seeks a more complete account of the origins of self. An important feature of identification in the Imaginary for an object-relations theorist is the "match" between infant and primary caretaker that makes identification possible. Of course, Lacan recognizes the necessity of adequate mothering for the origins of self, but object-relations theorists trace out more completely just what "adequate" might mean. In so doing, they draw attention to a feature of primary identification that Lacan overlooks: the necessity for an adaptation by both infant and primary caretaker in order to achieve the particular kind of connectedness that allows identification to occur. This leads me to question the completely illusory quality of such identifications. True, the infant's belief that caretaker and infant are one is an illusion that will be destroyed, compensated for, and protected against in various ways by the infant throughout his life. But contrary to Lacan's claim that most communication is "mis"-communication, it seems crucial to me that the feeling of identification (which for the infant amounts to an experience of fusion) is based on a very real adaptation of two entities, one to another. In Lacan's terms, one might say that identification involves actual experiences of a match between two human beings with respect to their desire to be desired. That is, for periods of time at least, the infant *is* what the caretaker wants and the caretaker *is* what the infant wants. Thus, identification involves the felt experience, for a period of time, of actually being all to each other, with no need to defer one's desire through the Symbolic chain. The infant can feel at one with its caretaker because the caretaker identifies with the needs of the infant. From reading Winnicott and Mahler, we can get some sense of what a fusion experience involves, of what such a "match" between two human beings might mean.

Winnicott felt that Freud presupposed the "separateness of the self and a structuring of the ego" (Winnicott 1965,

41). Because Freud assumed that the patient was a person, he overlooked factors involving the emergence of personhood. Winnicott, in his work with psychotics, became interested in the early developmental processes that facilitate the emergence of personhood. Psychotics are not "persons" in our usual meaning of the term. Why not? What is the process of becoming a person? Where did it break down in the case of his patients who never fully emerged as persons?

According to Winnicott, it is the mother who provides the infant with the experiences necessary for the emergence of a self.[8] At birth the infant is in a state of "unintegration." The infant has no self that can act as the subject of his experiences. Instead there are only fragmented experiences, which correspond to the experiences of Lacan's premirror stage. The organization of the infant's experience is preceded by and draws upon the mother's organized perceptions of him. As a result of "primary maternal preoccupation," the mother offers herself as an attentive medium for the infant's growth. She provides a holding environment for the infant in his quiescent states and "brings the world to the child" in response to his needs. The mother, in the case of "good-enough-mothering," is attentive enough to her baby that she anticipates his needs, presenting him with the object (e.g., the breast) that will satisfy him just as the infant craves that object. This creates a situation of infantile omnipotence in which the infant experiences himself as the source of all creation—the objects that the infant hallucinate appear, leading him to believe that it was he who created them. This infantile omnipotence is the basis for the healthy development and solidity of the self: "The simultaneity of infantile hallucination and maternal presentation provides the repetitive experiential basis for the child's sense of contact with and power over external reality" (Greenberg and Mitchell 1983, 192).

The mother's responsiveness to her baby's needs creates a mirroring effect that allows the baby to become attuned to his own bodily functions and impulses, which become the basis for his slowly evolving sense of self. One of the needs to which the mother must be responsive for "good-enough-mothering" is for a nondemanding presence. That will enable the infant to experience a state of "going-on-being" of needlessness and complete unintegration; out of this state needs and spontaneous gestures can emerge.

Just as Lacan stresses the infant's need to turn to an external object for the feeling of wholeness that constitutes the primordial self, so Winnicott stresses the importance of a whole external object to which the infant can turn.[9] Winnicott, however, gives a more detailed account than Lacan of what this mirroring effect involves. The infant's identifications with its mother, the fusion experience of feeling at one with its mother (and therefore omnipotent, or in Lacan's terms, free of lack), require certain conditions. When the infant feels a need and hallucinates the object that will fulfill that need (e.g., the need of hunger and the breast that will satisfy it), the actual object must appear for fusion to occur. Without this "good-enough-mothering," the infant will not be able to make the identifications of the mirror stage. He will have no sense of creative mastery, no sense that what he hallucinates is real—and therefore no confidence that the mirror image of himself, which he adopts as his own to maintain constancy in the face of felt fragmentation, is actually his. Thus, the mirror image is traced in his memory as a primordial self-representation—the first in a complicated series of signifying representations that will make up his self-identity, what it means to him to be him—because of a nurturing context where his needs were attended to by the other "good-enough" to tune in to and anticipate those needs. This primordial self-representation allows the ordering of a series of representations that hitherto were the fragmented experiences of a being with no self. It gave those fragmented images order by grouping them (e.g., my hand waving, my foot kicking) into the gestalt of a whole human form.

Once hallucinatory omnipotence is established, the child needs to learn the limits of his power. "Good-enough-mothering" involves a shift from the all-consuming attentiveness of the new mother to a mother who no longer anticipates her infant's every need. Thus, maternal responsiveness decreases in synchrony with the increase in the infant's ability to communicate his needs. Now, rather than having his every wish anticipated, the infant ex-

presses his needs through gestures and signals that the
mother responds to. The mother's "graduated failure of
adaptation" (Winnicott 1958, 246) is essential to the development of separation, differentiation, and realization
(Greenberg and Mitchell 1983, 194).

Just as Winnicott stresses the role of the infant's frustration in leading it to confront the need for symbolic representation (gestures and signals to an outside world
rather than hallucinations), Lacan stresses the role of the
infant's felt lack that leads it to the desire to be desired
(being what will draw the mother into fusion with one)
and to symbolization that will master lack by making the
absent present. Again, however, note the attention
Winnicott gives to a decrease in maternal responsiveness
that is in "synchrony" with the infant's needs. In other
words, a continuous, real synchronization of infant and
caretaker is needed if the illusory identifications the infant makes are to continue.

Two kinds of maternal deficiencies are "experienced by
the child as a terrifying interference with the continuity
of his own personal existence" (Greenberg and Mitchell
1983, 194) and result in the experience of the "annihilation
of the infant's self" (Winnicott 1958, 304). One is the failure to actualize the infant's hallucinations; the other is
interference with the infant's quiescent states of formlessness. In "good-enough-mothering," the mother acts as
both the medium for formlessness and the instrument of
omnipotence. Failure to provide such a medium results in
the fragmentation of the infant's experience into a "true
self" and a "false self." The former is the source of spontaneous needs, images, and gestures. The true self goes into
hiding to avoid the psychic annihilation caused by expressing itself without being able to get a response. The
content of the false self rises out of maternal expectations
and claims. The child thus becomes the mother's image of
him: "The false self draws on cognitive functions in its
anticipations of and reactions to environmental impinge-
ments, resulting in an overactivity of mind and a separation of cognitive processes from any affective or somatic
grounding."[10]

Winnicott here makes a distinction between two kinds of
possible identifications, both of which go into the layering

of identifications that make up the self. In Lacanian terms, the "true self" refers to those identifications made with a caretaker whose desires are in synch with the child's felt needs. That is, in the desire to be desired by the caretaker, the child meshes with the desire on the part of the caretaker to be desired by the child. There is a meeting ground where the desires of both fuse. The "false self" refers to those identifications made when no such mutuality of desire occurs. The child tunes in to the caretaker's desire, but the caretaker does not tune in to the child's desire. This distinction can help us better understand when Imaginary identifications may (by allowing new gestalts of representations of lived experience) generate new understandings of the self and the world that do not merely repeat past identifications with one's caretaker.

The interesting feature about Winnicott's account that Lacan glosses over is the particular context required for the emerging significance of the self. Whereas Lacan emphasizes the fictional character of the self, Winnicott emphasizes the space created between infant and caretaker that allows new significance for the infant to emerge. In *Playing and Reality* he introduces the notions of the transitional object and playing and discusses this space further. The emergence of the person involves the movement from a state of illusory omnipotence to a state of objective perception; of solipsistic subjectivity to objective perception; of the inner world to the world of outer reality. "Relations with transitional objects constitute a third, intermediary, and transitional realm between these two worlds" (Greenberg and Mitchell 1983, 195). Such transitional objects are allocated to neither of the two realms, thus allowing the baby to gradually shift from the experience of himself as the center of a subjective world to the experience of himself as a person among other persons: "In transitional experience, we maintain access to the most private wellspring of our thoughts and imagery, without being held accountable for them in the clear and harsh light of objective reality" (Greenberg and Mitchell 1983, 196).

The transitional object of a young child can be many things, for example a soft rag or blanket the child clings to. Winnicott believes that such objects relate to the pro-

cess a child (as well as the rest of us throughout life) un-
dergoes in relating inner to outer reality. The parent who
does not challenge the importance of the object to the
child is agreeing to a neutral area of experience, an area
where the question whether the child conceived of the
object or whether the object was presented to the child
from the outside will not be asked (Winnicott 1971, 12). In
a neutral area of experience one does not have to make a
final decision on whether an object is my own creation or
part of an external reality. According to Winnicott, this
area between inner and outer reality of transitional phenomena continues to play a role throughout our lives.
"There is a direct development from transitional phenomena to playing, and from playing to shared playing, and
from this to cultural experiences" (Winnicott 1971, 51). It
is this feature of existence that for Winnicott allows us the
capacity for creative living that makes life worthwhile,
and it is in the overlap of the playing together of two people that real communication occurs.

The "playful" space in which the infant first originates
a self is crucial for the layering of identifications necessary to taking one's place in the Symbolic order. Lacan
would, of course, agree. However, Winnicott chooses to underline the creative aspects of a holding environment
based on trust and the reliability of the caretaker in which
new gestalts can spontaneously emerge, whereas Lacan
emphasizes the dangers of Imaginary "lures." Winnicott
emphasizes the need for mutual attunement in an overlap
of two play areas—in which neither the infant nor the
caretaker makes the final decision on what is and what is
not—as the appropriate environment for the emergence of
new significance. Such "play" can lead to fusion-like experiences. In creative play (for example, two children
fantasizing together or two jazz musicians improvising together), two people play off one another by anticipating
where the other is headed (in Lacanian terms, anticipating
the desire of the other and attempting to satisfy it in advance—even if the other player could not have predicted in
advance what the next move desired was). The "fun" comes
in the attunements of one to another that lead to confusion
in the end about who contributed what to the playing. In
contrast, Lacan emphasizes the "no" of the father that

would have us forever defer fusion through the Symbolic chain.

Mahler's work corroborates and complements Winnicott's by giving us specifics about the attunement of the mother-child dyad. For Mahler, the child must struggle to reconcile his longing for autonomy with the equally intense longing to "surrender and reimmerse himself in the enveloping fusion from which he has come" (Greenberg and Mitchell 1983, 273). She distinguishes three phases of development in the child's preoedipal development, the second of which is further divided into three subphases. In the first phase, the "normal autistic phase," the infant is concerned only with the satisfaction of his needs and does not associate that satisfaction with its source in the external world. The second phase is the "normal symbiotic phase." At three to four weeks of age an infant's enhanced responsiveness results in a dim awareness of the mother as an external object. The infant continues to behave, however, as if he and the mother form a symbiotic, omnipotent unit. "Islands of 'good' and 'bad' memory traces form within the undifferentiated matrix of ego and id" (Greenberg and Mitchell 1983, 275).

From four to ten months there is a "differentiation subphase" in which the infant becomes increasingly aware of his mother as an external object. In the "practicing subphase" the infant begins to express an increasing interest in exploring his world, but an interest in mother still takes precedence over interest in the world of things. It is in this subphase that Mahler locates the occurrence of "psychological birth." When the child achieves upright locomotion his horizons widen, and he concentrates on his expanding abilities, which are perceived by him as omnipotence. In the "rapprochement subphase," which usually starts between fifteen and eighteen months of age, the child experiences a kind of separation anxiety due to the deflation of his illusion of omnipotence. This subphase includes what Mahler terms the "rapprochement crisis": From approximately eighteen to twenty-four months of age, the child, to consolidate his separation from the mother, denies that he needs help from another person at the same time that he experiences the need for such help. "This leads to a behavioral picture in which intense neediness and clinging to the mother alternates with equally intense negativity and battling with her" (Greenberg and Mitchell 1983, 278). Mahler sees the successful resolution of this stage as crucial for the avoidance of the more severe psychopathologies, just as Freud felt that the successful resolution of the Oedipus complex was crucial for avoiding neurosis.

The next phase is the phase of libidinal object constancy. It normally takes place during the third year of life, and its major task is to form stable concepts of the self and of the other. In this phase, the child establishes emotional object constancy by consolidating the internalization of a constant, inner image of the mother that was gradually developed in the previous phases. Mahler stresses that the establishment of a reliable internal image necessary for a stable sense of self is not possible without the trust and confidence developed in the child's relationship with the primary caretaker. Trust and confidence is developed through the "regularly occurring relief of need tension provided by the need-satisfying agency," which over the course of the subphases of phase two described above "is gradually attributed to the need-satisfying whole object (the mother) and is then transferred by means of internalization to the intrapsychic representation of the mother" (Mahler, Pine, and Bergman 1975, 101). In other words, for the child to internalize a "good" representation of the mother, a representation that will soothe the emotional distress caused by the inability to maintain an omnipotent duality of mother and child, something must occur in the real interactions of the caretaker/child's relationship. This something involves "need-satisfying."

Mahler, in delineating the various phases and subphases of mother/child interactions, stresses that this "need-satisfying" cannot occur without what she calls "mutual cuing." As is obvious, the child has different needs at different times. In the autistic phase the infant needs to sleep. In the differentiation subphase of the symbiotic phase he needs to be cuddled and engaged by eye contact. In the practicing subphase, increased motor coordination (i.e., the ability to crawl) allows him more opportunity for leaving the mother behind. At this point the kind of maternal behavior appropriate in the previous

subphase becomes a liability for the infant's need to separate from the mother. In the rapprochement subphase,
the now-walking toddler needs emotional support from his
mother to calm his fears about separation and loss of omnipotence and yet encourage further separation.

The mothers Mahler observed also had needs. Some
mothers were much more comfortable with a nursing baby
and resented their growing child's increased independence. These mothers found it harder to give their child
the freedom to crawl at will or the emotional support he
needed as a toddler to explore. Other mothers felt overwhelmed at an infant's dependency needs and disrupted
early symbiosis by encouraging their child to be independent before he was ready. All these infants did become
healthy children with intact self-identity. Mahler stresses
the "mutual cuing" of each mother/child pair that allowed
this to come about. A child whose mother preferred a dependent infant tended to remain a "lap-baby" longer or
reacted by refusing to meld his body into the mother's. A
child who did not get the reassurance he needed at the
rapprochement subphase tended to become clingy, revert-
ing to an earlier phase where he got what he needed, or
found tactics that would get his mother's attention.

Thus, we can fill out, with the mutual adaptation of
mother and child that Mahler observed, Winnicott's picture of the mother who adapts herself to the child's needs.
Winnicott talks about "good-enough-mothering," Mahler
of "mutual cuing." For both, the infant forms and stabi-
lizes an identity in the context of a loving other attentive
to the bodily cues of the infant; but the infant also attends
to the bodily cues of the loving other, meeting her needs
in order to get his own needs met.

Through attentive tuning in to the gestalt of the cues
given by the other (as opposed, for example, to the meaning content of speech) and the anticipation of the desires
of the other, a bond of communication is formed where
who wants what becomes blurred—where the self/other
distinction breaks down in a mutual recognition of desire.
This forms a moment of contact between two people, a moment when one's own desire is in synch with the desire of
the other in such a way that the two become mutually satisfying and fuse into a place of no lack. For this to happen,

each must be prepared to anticipate the other's desire, willing to desire that the other's desire be satisfied rather than insisting that the other satisfy one's own (fixated) desire. It is through this mutual adaptation of desire that fusion is born. As a self becomes more fixed, such moments become extremely rare because of the need to repeat past identificatory patterns for self-continuity. The trick becomes finding a meeting ground for fusion between two people—a place where, for moments of time, they "connect" through the fusion of mutually satisfying desire at the same time that each maintains self-integrity—that is, continuity with the layers of signification that they feel themselves to be. Of course, an infant—starting out fresh so to speak—is much less restricted by that need than is an adult, making fusion that much easier. For an infant, physical need will provide the departure point for "authentic" contact. This point of contact, then, is the meeting ground in an area in which the appearance of an object is a satisfying one. Through mutual cuing and adaptation to the other of one's own desire within the range of what would satisfy that desire given one's physical needs (the infant) or given the network of signifiers that make up one's conscious and unconscious systems (the mother), one can find those points where meaning connects—where both find something that satisfies in the unanticipated Real that eludes current meaning structures.

In light of Winnicott's and Mahler's rendering of the origins of the me, we can evaluate Lacan's characterization of the mirror stage. According to Lacan, the self precipitated in symbiotic fusion is a "fiction." The image with which the infant identified was outside of him. It was an illegitimate, if necessary, move to take on this image of wholeness as his own when he actually felt fragmented and out of control—not whole at all. To maintain this identification he was forced into the dialectic of desire that led him to identify with his father and the position of phallic power and to deny the loss of the mother by upholding the paternal law that will provide him with substitutes for that loss.

We can explain this misreading of the mirror stage with Lacan's own views on the me's denial of its lack to perpetuate the illusion that it is self-sufficient. From the start the mother is no more than a vehicle for the infant's self-constituting activity. What occurs in fusion is a fiction. The infant is actually self-sufficient, using his mother to reflect himself back to him. The feeling of wholeness is an illusion—a necessary illusion, but an illusion nevertheless. The loss of the mother is thus not really a loss because the infant never had the mother to begin with—he just used his mother as the first image he identified with. This image, owing to the nature of early child care, carried with it many intensely felt representations of the sensations of bodily contact with the mother, but the feeling of fusion with the mother was still illusory.

The Lacanian theorist looking back on such early experiences sees the infant and mother as two distinct entities with clear-cut boundaries. The self the me maintains must be one, whole, and phallic—the self of the me without lack. In reading the phallic self back into this early childhood experience, the sense of connectedness, of feeling one with another—the two as one of fusion—is discounted as an illusion. The self that is maintained is reconstituted in experiences that repeat this conception of the mirror stage—a me that projects what I need onto an other in order to repeat an identification with something outside of myself. These identifications are always illusions, always to be looked upon with suspicion as "lures" we project upon the world to evade our primordial lack of being. Thus, on a Lacanian view, self-insufficiency becomes synonymous with the illusory nature of connectedness with others.

Lacan breaks down the illusion of a unified self in favor of a split subject that is continually reconstituting itself in a dialectic of self and other. But he assumes that if subjectivity is to occur, this dialectic must be purely specular in nature: No real connection between the me and an other ever occurs. Thus, he assumes that the self is entirely fictional, although in fact the concrete connections in which it is based are real. The mirror image is not merely identified with, an image taken on from the outside; it is created in connectedness with another in a space where two are one, a place where desire is satiated and becomes pleasure. Fusion with another is truly experienced—as truly experienced as the experiences of fragmentation. It is within fusion that one experiences oneself in responsiveness to another who also responds. These experiences are recorded in representations that may never reach consciousness or play into the repetition of narcissistic identifications. To feel that responsiveness one needs connection, one needs more than an image projected by the me to identify with. For meaning to be created, for the original images to be formed, the subject must be in a state of responsiveness to a world that responds to it. Thus the illusion of the mirror stage is not that one was whole in connectedness with an other, but that one does not need an other for such connectedness.

Self-construction and the Production of Meaning: Take 2

Lacan's "cure" consists in freeing the subject from the me's lures so that the I can address the Other of unconscious truth. Lacan seems to think that this truth will always be that the subject is primordially lacking and therefore doomed to a futile search for the lost "*objet a*" that would complete it. The truth the unconscious lets slip as the me attempts to maintain the illusion of a whole self is that there is no object that will satisfy Desire.

The me Lacan characterizes in the schema L is the me of the postmirror stage who has repressed mother-fusion, modifying its self/other identifications in accordance with paternal law. This me represents the objects of its Desire via Symbolic categories. Satisfaction is continually deferred since Symbolic representations can never fill in the subject's gap. On Lacan's reading of the mirror stage, there is no alternative to a self-constituting activity that subjects itself to the Symbolic order, as mother-fusion was an illusion. This means that the Lacanian subject is the effect of the battery of signifiers in which and by which it places itself. The subject is subjected to and constructed by language. The me, being inherently fictional in nature, provides only arbitrary guidance to the speaking subject. The me is necessary for the continuance of subjectivity, but the "truth" of the subject is that it is an arbitrary effect of the linguistic signifiers at play through the four poles of the schema L. Lacan's "cure" therefore emphasizes the negative moment of undermining the subject at any point it may find peace or repose in a sense of wholeness.

Adapting what we have learned from Winnicott and Mahler to Lacan's schema L, we might posit another me with an alternative self-constituting activity. Assuming that what the subject Desired was the *kind* of contact (m)Other-fusion provided, rather than an identity that could take a fixed position within the Symbolic, we would say that the subject could choose to reexperience that contact. That is, rather than defer Desire by representing objects of Desire via Symbolic categories, the me could seek fusion with another in its lived present. The "truth" of a subject with such a me would be not that its primordial gap dooms it to a futile search for satisfaction but rather that it is forever "doomed" to seek its satisfaction in connectedness with others. Such a subject would accept that it could never be whole in and of itself and would continually reconstitute itself through contact with others.

A theorist who engaged in such self-constituting activity would have a different attitude toward the concepts at her disposal than the theorist I described in "Take 1" in the light of Lacan's schema L. The theorist depicted by Lacan's schema would evade the "truth" that no matter how masterful his theory, no matter how well he wields words in keeping with paternal law, he will never find the lost *objet a* that would complete him. Instead he will be captured by the lures of a me that structures reality via fixed imagos it projects upon the Real of lived experience. Such theory will say more about the particular theorist's identity fixations than the Real that continually eludes our attempts to symbolize it. The theorist who has taken Lacanian analysis to heart will refuse to become captured by the identity fixations of his me. Instead, he will pay attention to the Other that his I attempts to address. The unconscious—the discourse of the Other—will subvert the subject's every attempt to pronounce a truth, be it about himself or the world, that can stand for all time in an enduring edifice of Truth. The Lacanian theorist will thus deliberately tease his reader by refusing to make any final pronouncements. He will attempt to follow the twists and turns of the discourse of the Other—thus demonstrating his prowess in evading capture by his me.[11]

The theorist who engages in the self-constituting activity that seeks fusion will neither evade the "truth" of her inability to find the lost *objet a* nor demonstrate her prowess by forever evading the lures of her me. Instead, she will engage in the playful open-endedness we saw in our discussion of Winnicott's transitional object. This kind of theorist will hold in suspension any final decision on the existential status (real or imagined) of the objects her words represent. Her desire is not for *the* object (e.g., a truth about herself) that will complete her but for a particular kind of contact with the other (the reader) as well as her own Other (which speaks from the unconscious). She is not looking for an object that will fill in her gap and allow her to take up a final position in a timeless Symbolic order of fixed positions but for the word that will enable contact with another.

It is not what the word refers to that matters so much as the feeling it evokes in the Other. Contact is made when the word (or words) sets off a chain of associations that reverberate in the unconscious, activating representations of experiences not yet integrated into the me's structure. Through receptive attentiveness this theorist tries first one word and then another, listening for the Other's response, until the right word is found—the word that "fits." This theorist's desire for psychic wholeness manifests itself both in the desire to maintain the me's structural coherence and in the desire for contact with an other that will allow new meaning to emerge. She creates a play space in which the question of the word's viability as a substitute for Desire (i.e., as a stand-in for the *objet a* in accordance with paternal law) is left open. In her willingness to respond to the desire of the Other she holds her narcissistic identifications in suspension, looking for the word that will stimulate a yes from the Other. In these moments of contact, resolution and integration can occur. The me, rather than seeking to obscure the subject's lack, seeks to compensate for lack by incorporating new meaning into its dialectical structure. This, in turn, allows the subject to make sense of a broader range of sensations. Receptivity to the other's (the reader's) Desire and to one's own Other's Desire (what the Other wants the me to be) allows the theorist to play with words and generate new meaning. This theorist will not merely tease her reader but will allow moments of fullness—moments of integration when both she and (one hopes) her reader discover a word or category that characterizes hitherto inarticulate sensations in a satisfying way. Just as the infant's sensations were originally given meaning in contact with the caretaker who articulated the infant's desire for the infant by supplying him with objects that satisfied him, this theorist finds a "fit" between inarticulated experience and the word that could symbolize it.

For example, I could be developing a theory about childhood development. As I contemplate the process of separation/individuation I may have feelings and sensations that I cannot articulate. I could choose to ignore them, cranking out my theory according to familiar views I have long held about children, or I could attend to those feelings until I found words that made sense of them. If, say, I felt queasy every time I thought of the child's first step away from mother, I might finally connect that queasiness to anxiety about separation I had myself experienced. This could affect not only my theory but also my view of myself as someone who could easily leave people behind. Thus, to incorporate this insight into my theory would require incorporating a new aspect of my experience into my self-system.[12] If I chose not to change my self/other pattern, I could, for example, continue to hold the view that the process of separation/individuation is an automatic, relatively painless experience. For the theorist to allow insights that such vague feelings and "intuitions" can give, she must be willing to create a space in which she holds both her conceptions of herself and her "reality" in suspension.

By emphasizing the negative aspects of a me that evades confrontation of loss with identifications based in the "Imaginary," Lacan underestimates the positive moment of a me who seeks integrative contact based in lived experience. To counter the danger of the former, Lacan would have us unravel the me entirely. Although I agree that the danger of the me who alienates the subject ever further from the "truth" of unconscious desire is real, I do not agree that human subjectivity entails the continual deferment of satisfaction. Lacan describes one approach to subjectivity, but there is an alternative approach, which we could characterize as an alternative self-strategy for the me. We would then have two self-strategies that could enable human subjectivity—one that forever deferred desire through Symbolic signifying chains (Lacan's version) and one that sought to reexperience "Imaginary" fusion (the alternative derived from our look at object-relations theory). In Chapter 3 I will link those two self-strategies to gender categories and develop them further through a critique of Lacan from a feminist perspective. I will then discuss the role of gender in the self-constituting activity of writing philosophical texts.

Notes

1. For discussions of Lacan's relationship to this tradition, see Dews (1987, chap. 2); Juranville (1984); Ragland-Sullivan (1986); and Edward S. Casey and J. Melvin Woody's "Hegel, Heidegger, Lacan: The Dialectic of Desire" and Wilfried Ver Eecke's "Hegel as Lacan's Source for Necessity in Psychoanalytic Theory," both in Smith and Kerrigan (1983).

2. After trying out just about every conceivable combination of pronouns for referring to the infant, I decided to refer to the infant/child as "he" for the following reasons: (1) although at this point in the infant's development he has no gender identity (on a Lacanian reading), this makes no difference to the people who care for him (whether he knows it or not, he is gender-labeled from birth, and even before), (2) despite my preference for the generic "she," using "he" for the generic is less confusing because "she" can then refer to the mother without ambiguity, and (3) Lacanian theory, like Freudian theory, tends to assume that the primary caretaker is female and tends to take masculine development as the paradigm for human development.

3. "He [the subject] is stretched over the four corners of the schema: namely, S, his ineffable, stupid existence, *o*, his objects, *o'*, his ego, that is, that which is reflected of his form in his objects, and O, the locus from which the question of his existence may be

presented to him" ("On a Question Preliminary to Any Possible Treatment of Psychosis" [Lacan 1977, 193-194]). Lacan also discusses his schema L in "Le Seminaire sur *La Lettre Volée*" (Lacan 1966, 53). My discussion is informed by these essays, the exposition of Lacan given thus far in this section, and discussions of the schema L in Benvenuto and Kennedy (1986, 100-101, 130, 146), André Green (1966), Ragland-Sullivan (1986, 2-3, 46-47, 196-197), and Wilden (1968, 106-108).

4. I do not have space here to do full justice to Lacan's realm of the "Real." For discussions of this important concept see Benvenuto and Kennedy (1986), Juranville (1984, 84-86), Lemaire (1977), Ragland-Sullivan (1986, 183-195), and Wilden (1968, 197-200).

5. "The full term in Lacan is usually *objet petit a*, where the 'little "a"' in question derives from *autre* (other)" (Kerrigan 1983, xx).

6. See Ragland-Sullivan's discussion of transference and resistance (1986, 119-129) and Juranville's remarks on the analytic cure (1984, 95-96).

7. Schneiderman (1983) discusses both the controversy Lacan's short session caused in the psychoanalytic community and, from the personal perspective of the analysand, its effects.

8. For my discussion of Winnicott and Mahler I am indebted to Greenberg and Mitchell's clear account of Winnicott's views on the emergence of the self (1983, 190-210).

9. For some discussion of the relationship of object-relations theory to Lacanian theory see Ragland-Sullivan (1986).

10. Greenberg and Mitchell (1983, 194-195). They cite Winnicott (1958, 191-192) as the source for this information.

11. Gallop gives a playful account of Lacan's stylistic prowess in *The Daughter's Seduction* (Gallop 1982).

12. The concept of "self-system" as developed in Epstein (1973) is similar in many respects to the version of the self as a process that I am developing in this work. I have generally chosen to use the term "self-strategy" since it speaks to the problematic I set for selfhood as the solution to human agency.

3

Lacan and the Feminist
Perspective

Introduction

Much psychoanalytic theory today still minimizes the problem of gender. Of course, the Oedipus complex cannot be the same for girls as for boys, but this distinction has been accounted for in traditional psychoanalysis by the somewhat deviant depiction of the feminine path to self-hood. The full-blown self is that of the male adult—if the path to that self is different, even more difficult, for women, masculine identity is still the norm to which both the sexes are compared.[1] Thus, there is often no systematic effort to account for gender differences. The tendency since Freud has been to posit woman as a sort of negative reflection or complement to man. Psychoanalytic theory, rather than providing a positive account of the category "woman," made that category the repository of everything that is not "man."

Irigaray, a French psychoanalyst in the Lacanian tradition, and Chodorow, an American sociologist interested in object-relations theory, have taken steps to rectify this situation.[2] Both attempt—in very different ways—to give a positive rendering of the feminine that goes beyond relegating woman to the inverse image of man, beyond doctoring Freudian theory here and there to fit in women. Instead they present a systematic account of just where Freudian theory fails. Irigaray offers a radical critique of the Freudian approach to femininity that reduces woman into the polar opposite, the specular image, of man.[3] Chodorow addresses the question of gender in the preoedipal stage.

The question of woman in psychoanalysis, then, involves not only accounting for the path of feminine development but also exploring sexual difference and the validity of the masculine model of selfhood as *the* model. If we take gender into account in a systematic way in the course of developing a theory of self, we see that there are two different strategies for constructing and maintaining a self. All psychoanalysts agree that certain key turning points for the developing child—the discovery of anatomical difference, resolution of the Oedipus complex—present different problems for the different sexes. What has not been fully addressed is how the solutions to these different problems represent different strategies for evolving a self, strategies that have ramifications lasting for the individual's life. Freudian theory has tended to presume that the paradigm for normal adulthood must be the same for both sexes—if women are not as "mature" or "adult" as men, it is because certain obstacles, not faced by males, have blocked their development.[4] The possibility that a woman has faced the problems presented her and overcome them, achieving maturity in her own right, has been overlooked.

A theory of self that takes gender seriously makes problematic the norm for "mature" selfhood. If both sexes equally successfully navigate the problems set for them and yet one sex somehow achieves a "maturity" that the other sex does not, then we should ask whether it is a "lack" on women's part (perhaps biologically based) or a misconstrual of the ideal paradigm of selfhood that is at fault.

In Chapter 2 I developed a self-strategy as an alternative to the Lacanian-based self-strategy. The "standard" self-strategy defers desire through the signifying chains of the Symbolic. The alternative self-strategy seeks fusion. In this chapter I will explore the ways that gender affects self-constituting activity. The lacuna in Lacanian theory that I pointed to in Chapter 2 has interesting implications when put in context with Lacan's account of gender differences. The "standard" self-strategy will turn out, from a

Lacanian point of view, to be a "masculine" one—leaving the very possibility of a truly feminine subject in doubt. With the help of feminist critiques of psychoanalysis that bring the question of gender to the fore, I will further develop both self-strategies and differentiate them according to gender, correlating the "standard" Lacanian account with a "masculine" self-strategy and the alternative account with a "feminine" one. That I characterize two kinds of gendered self-strategies implies that men may make more use of one and women of the other—but I am not presuming that this gender-differentiated characterization of self-strategies is either universal or necessary. The gender differences explored here are social constructions that have had influence in certain mainstream discourses. By articulating them as strategies for positioning oneself, I hope to break down constraints on positioning that are related to socially constructed definitions of what it means to be a man or a woman.

Lacan and the Gendered Self

As we saw in Chapter 2, the castration complex introduces the child to sexual difference and the Symbolic realm. The mother/infant dyad is, in a certain sense, static. In the world of symbiosis where nothing lacks, no positioning with respect to difference need take place. The phallic signifier represents sexual difference.[5] The mother is not complete unto herself, but desires the phallus, which becomes the signifier of lack and establishes substitutive desire. Rather than desiring the mother, the child first identifies with what the mother wants—the phallus—and then relinquishes desire for fusion in order to take up a position with respect to the phallus. The power of the phallic signifier comes from its representing difference and lack, which introduces the child into the public realm of individuation and language. Exchange and communication occur in this realm through a complex network of social relations. Whereas identification with the mother provided the infant a victory over fragmentation, identification with the father reaffirms the split in the human subject. Identificatory fusion with the mother in the Imaginary dissimulated the primordial gap between the fragmentary experience of prematuration and the gaze of the mother that reflected one back as whole. Identification with the father reaffirms that gap by disallowing fusion and stipulating the search for the object that will fill in the infant's gap in accordance with rules laid out by the Symbolic order. Henceforth the child cannot settle for Imaginary "illusion" but must continually defer desire for fusion by accepting Symbolic substitutions for the objects of Desire.

Thus, in "normal" development, the child will ultimately identify with the phallic signifier—the male child by embodying it and the female child by associating with it (Ragland-Sullivan 1986, 293)—that is, both sexes will accept castration. They will accept that they cannot remain in the world of symbiotic fusion with the mother, that they will instead have to take up a position in a network of social positions that are different from one another. The boy accepts castration with the understanding that he is heir to the paternal law—although now he is subject to it, he will one day embody the phallus himself and have a mother-substitute for his own. The girl accepts castration by turning to the father. Her loss of the mother as a love object is complete—she will never have the phallus, never have her mother back. Her compensation is to turn to her father, who does have the phallus. By association with men, she will vicariously experience some of the power they possess and may also receive from a man one day the child that can be her phallus.

Feminists interested in developing Lacan's work have emphasized that according to him both men and women are castrated: We are all split subjects with a primordial gap in our being; we all "lack"; we are all motivated by the Desire to compensate for our lack.[6] Ragland-Sullivan has argued that the inferior position of women stems from a "secondary castration" (1986, 298). In addition to acceding to the castration complex, women have been subjected to the myths perpetrated by the Symbolic order that veil man's lack by symbolizing him as the "*tout*," the whole that can fill in the hole, and symbolize woman as lack.[7] Thus, the mother symbolizes loss that is relegated to the unconscious—lack, the nether side of conscious existence—

whereas the father is privileged because he symbolizes the opposite of need or loss. But this symbolization of man and the father is based on an illusion that veils the primordial gap in our being, which all human subjects share.

Thus, from a Lacanian perspective, the truth is that we are all castrated. We can, of course, differentiate the positions of the standard and the alternative self-strategies vis-à-vis that truth by referring to the phallus—the signifier of sexual difference and lack. The "haves" (those who identify as male) flee that truth in the Symbolic. The "have-nots" (those who identify as female) deal with that truth in the Imaginary. By further delineating these two strategies we may find some means to transcending the impasse of this sexual polarization. A characterization of the masculine and feminine positions of Lacanian theory follows.[8]

The Masculine Position. The boy learns that although the paternal law forbids him to fuse with his mother, he will one day have a woman of his own if he identifies with his father and upholds the paternal law. That is, he "has" the phallus; he is not castrated after all; he has what his mother desires. The Symbolic order represents paternal law. It lays out the social hierarchy determined by the Name-of-the-Father. It decides what the relationship of all the beings of the society is according to socially sanctioned codes. As heir to the paternal law, he will wield its phallic power: making judgments about the form relationships should take according to his desire. To identify with the father he will deny the loss of his mother—deny castration—and displace his desire for his mother onto cultural substitutes represented within the Symbolic order. By displacing his desire along the signifying chain in keeping with narcissistic identifications, he will continually defer the fusion sought. What was gained in fusion was a sense of wholeness more pleasurable than the feelings of fragmentation that preceded it. It is this feeling of wholeness, of mastery, that he strives to maintain with the repetition of narcissistic identifications. The Symbolic order assures him he can maintain his self through the repetition of positions first established in the Oedipus complex.

The masculine position thus involves the repetition of a self through the Symbolic that translates and transposes the same self precipitated in early childhood throughout life according to the rules of the Symbolic. In doing so he will deny the (m)Other within in order to find the substitutes for his primordial Desire (the mother of fusion) that are in keeping with the Symbolic order and paternal law.

The Feminine Position. The girl learns that not only is she not allowed fusion with the mother but also that she will never gain a woman-substitute for the mother. That is, she doesn't "have" the phallus. She is castrated; she lacks; the loss she is currently experiencing is final, her compensations inferior to those of the boy. Instead of identifying with the father, with phallic power, with the wielder of the paternal law, she can only passively enjoy phallic power through association with a man. The paternal law does not interest her the same way it interests a man because it guarantees her nothing. She will never be what is desired by the other and thereby regain the fusion she lost. She can only be the other for some man, can only vicariously enjoy his phallic pleasure at being the whole. Being passive, she can never create the paternal law that orders social relationships. She is an object of exchange, waiting to be exchanged by those who wield phallic power, those who have the right to say where and when fusion can occur. Thus, she cannot speak with the same authority as a man. She can only parody a power that is really not hers to wield. The self that she lost with the loss of fusion can be maintained only passively by her finding subjects to whom she can be an other. Instead of actively repeating the self she formed in fusion in a layering of identifications according to the rules of the Symbolic order, she will take on the position of the sex that lacks. Instead of maintaining the experience of wholeness she had in the mirror stage in a layering of repetitions where she repeatedly plays the phallic whole that is mirrored in others' responses to her, she will find her identity by mirroring others' wholeness back to them, letting them define her by being the lack, the hole, that their "wholeness" fills.

Despite the drawbacks with respect to social power such a position entails, woman does have a certain compensation: "There is woman only as excluded by the nature of things which is the nature of words. . . . It none the less remains that if she is excluded by the nature of things, it is precisely that in being not all (*pas-toute*), she has, in relation to what the phallic function designates of *jouissance*, a supplementary *jouissance*" (Mitchell and Rose 1985, 144).[9]

On a Lacanian reading, it is not clear whether or not woman as woman can be a subject, playing out her own desire in the same way a man does. Given that she is of the sex that does not have the phallus, she cannot want in the way a man does. A man desires objects that are substitutes for the mother. He desires to reconstitute himself by re-playing the dialectic of being desired by the other (originally his mother) according to the rules of the Symbolic order. A woman cannot, properly speaking, desire at all. Because she is of the sex that lacks, she cannot hope to find substitutes for the mother. She will never be able to regain the desire of an other, a substitute for the mother, in some dialectic of identifications that, through the transformation rules of the Symbolic, represents the other as the other that can reflect her back to herself as a whole. What then, as a woman, can she do?

Ragland-Sullivan says that woman is closer than is man to the personal and the narcissistic (1986, 296-297); because she is not allowed to find substitutes for the mother in the same way as a man, she is closer to the primordial Desire of the mother whose messages she received into the unconscious in symbiotic fusion. Lacking the man's phallic power to find substitutes for the Desire to satisfy this primordial Desire, she is closer to the loss of the mother, the loss of the feeling of fusion when mother was satisfied by the infant and mother and infant were one. Because she is confronted with this loss in a way that someone who "has" the phallus is not, she does not have the masculine option of reconstituting the situation of fusion in identifications with images that replace objects associated with the mother. That is, she cannot maintain the self of fusion by finding others to mirror back to her that she is desired in a way analogous to the way she was desired as an infant.

On the Lacanian view, this means that she has no possibility of subjectivity at all. Unable to find the reflection in an other that will repeat and thus reconfirm her primordial self in a layering of identifications, she is reduced to being the other, the mirror, for the self-representations

of men.   Unable to wield the phallus herself, she can
maintain what little identity she has only by being a
screen for the imagoes that men project upon her.   By conforming to their desire, responding to their need to see
themselves as forever the same, always the same self, she
can gain vicarious pleasure in phallic power through association.

Although one can assume that Lacan intended the
schema L (discussed in Chapter 2) to represent the self-
constituting process of both the men and the women that
went to him for analysis, it is clear that his notion of pure
femininity excludes woman from this process.   Rather
than projecting her imago onto others and thus reaffirm-
ing herself through narcissistic identifications, she is
man's other.   It is thus that Lacan comes to say that as a
category woman does not exist,[10] that in fact if she were
actually to exist there would be no man.   For man to maintain himself he must be able to find others that will support the repetitions of self and other needed to provide him
with continuity.   For this to occur, an other that will conform to his imago is needed.   Woman, having no identity of
her own as woman, being defined as lack, is eminently
suited for this purpose.   To ask what woman wants, then,
and be prepared to hear her speak, would actually threaten
this whole project of self-constitution.[11]   Because Lacan
himself is writing from the masculine position, using the
masculine strategy of self-constitution, he cannot really
ask the question of what woman wants.   To hear the answer
would undermine his own project of self-construction in a
way that would threaten him with loss of mastery and loss
of self.   Thus, although he asks the question, and although
he admits to some perplexity about the answer, he is not, in
fact, able to hear the reply.

Since the masculine position requires evasion of
Imaginary fusion by finding Symbolic substitutes for
Desire in accordance with the paternal law that veils his
lack, any rendering of the feminine could only undermine
his own strategy by unveiling it.   Masculine satisfaction
does not include the *jouissance* of a genuine fusion experience because preference has been given to the Symbolic—
the other is not the Real other in her specificity but a
projection screen upon which one can play out one's fan-

tasies. Preference is given to representations that replace concrete objects of desire—abstract images that stand in for what was lost and will be forever deferred through the Symbolic chain. Once the category of woman is unveiled as a different strategy, a different way of dealing with lack, rather than lack itself that only the phallic male can fill, the masculine strategy of displacing loss and lack onto woman will no longer work. Instead, men will have to find other ways of dealing with lack. Articulation of the feminine position, although undermining the tenability of the masculine position, could open the door to a new relationship to origin and lack.

The girl, because she has to mourn the loss of the mother in a way the boy does not, is forced to maintain the self formed in fusion in other ways (Ragland-Sullivan 1986, 297). Instead of basing her self on the fiction of whole self-sufficiency, that is, instead of assuming that the self she formed in fusion with the mother can continue without the mother, she accepts the loss of that fusion state and is open to finding that fusion state, or something like it, elsewhere. That is, she accepts that the self formed in fusion with mother is not her own self but is the two of them—she and the mother—as one. Thus, to rediscover that feeling of wholeness, she will need to connect with others the way that she once connected with mother. Instead of deferring substitutions for the mother through the Symbolic chain, she will adhere less strictly than her brothers to the paternal law (which after all guarantees her nothing) and allow fusion to occur: moments when through connection with another she can feel whole. What she takes away from such fusion is, not an identification with an image that is actually outside of herself (and thus not actually her at all), but the concrete feelings and sensations of having been close to another. These feelings she cannot necessarily repeat in other interactions à la the schema L; they reside in her unconscious in a fluid manner, ready to be activated by other encounters that evoke them.

The feminine self-strategy is thus less subjected to the Symbolic and the paternal law and more inclined toward "Imaginary" fusion than the masculine self-strategy. With no promise of inheriting the paternal law to inhibit her,

she deals with loss in ways that subvert that law. Fusion is
not as taboo for her as for her brothers. She is closer to
the primordial unconscious, less afraid that fusion experiences will confront her with castration. She thus has a
different attitude toward Imaginary fusion—an attitude that
cannot be allowed full expression in the Symbolic if the
paternal law is to stand unchallenged. Contrary to Lacan's
view, however, the feminine does not have to be any more
ineffable or mysterious than the masculine. That it has
not yet found full expression in the Symbolic does not
mean that it cannot be expressed. The task is not to veil the
"mysterious" feminine in more veils than already cover it
but to reveal the feminine as a particular strategy, different from the masculine strategy, for dealing with the
problem of subjectivity.[12]
    Thus, Lacan gives a one-sided view of the picture.
Although his insistence on the castration that we all share
is an important feature of his theory, undermining phallic
power by rendering its illusions more visible, Lacan has
not succeeded in stepping outside of the masculine position
enough to be able to characterize the feminine position as
anything but the negative counterpart, the other, of the
masculine position. In the next section I will present a
more positive characterization of the feminine position
with a discussion of Luce Irigaray's book *Speculum*
(Irigaray 1985a).

Irigaray: Woman as the Specular Other

    Luce Irigaray was excommunicated from the Lacanian
community for writing *Speculum*. Her critique of Lacan
and her valorization of the feminine was too radical to be
embraced by the Lacanian psychoanalytic community
(Moi 1985, 127). I will argue that Irigaray's position with
respect to femininity, radical as it is, falls into some of the
same assumptions she tries to avoid. Her work is still useful, however, for delineating the feminine position.
    On the basis of my presentation of Winnicott and Mahler
in Chapter 2 and of gender with respect to Lacan in the
previous section of this chapter, I will make some preliminary claims for the theoretical framework I am developing

here before amplifying them with an examination of Irigaray's work. My first claim is that the category woman is a projection screen for playing out a masculine fantasy of wholeness that is finally untenable as well as a category representative of the lost joy (*jouissance*) of fusion experiences. My second claim is that the feminine strategy involves accepting the original loss and compensating for it by repeating fusion experiences with others.

The masculine strategy denies the loss of mother-fusion and continues to evade confronting it by finding Symbolic substitutes that forever defer satisfaction. The loss, not being dealt with, is displaced onto woman. "Woman" is thus a category associated with loss, fusion experiences, and the possibility of confronting that loss along with the threat of complete disintegration of self such a possibility brings. It is the fear of this disintegration that makes confrontation of "woman" so difficult from a masculine position. And yet even from the masculine position, the experiences of fusion and the possibility they hold for another way of dealing with lack still remain in the unconscious. The "death work" of Lacanian analysis is one way of unraveling the layers of identification built up on symbolic identifications leading further and further away from the concrete objects that originally satisfied in symbiotic fusion. But fusion experiences in the present—saying yes to fusion rather than rigidly adhering to the no of the father—is another.

The principal function of the Symbolic is to mediate between the Imaginary and the Real: to process experience as it is lived into meaningful form, given the narcissistic layers of identifications previously enacted by the self. The unanticipated of the Real—the specificity of concrete experience, that which has not yet been made articulate according to current meaning structures (Juranville 1984, 84-86)—is continually being made sense of. On the basis of my critique of Lacanian theory in Chapter 2, we can give the Imaginary a more important role to play in this process than Lacan does. Imaginary fusion does not happen just once and then play itself out in repetition through Symbolic substitutions. Not only do Imaginary narcissistic identifications of the self motivate the speech of the I, but at the Imaginary level fusion can continue to occur, allowing new gestalts to form and providing fresh impetus for narcissistic identifications. For self-continuity to be maintained, fusion has to be contained within the context of one's past identity, but within given parameters fusion can still occur.

Irigaray questions the paternal law in a way Lacan does not. Instead of assuming that the father's law, the phallus, the Symbolic, represent features of subjectivity that, unfortunately or not, lead to the subordination of women, Irigaray valorizes the feminine position. In order to characterize the feminine position positively, she wrenches it out of the negative role of other to the phallic position. I will make use of her characterization to fill out what Lacan has missed. Irigaray counters Lacan's blind spot by depicting the masculine and feminine positions in the extreme of their polarization. On the one hand, there is masculine specularization and the logic of the same (the rules of analogy and similarity);[13] on the other, there is feminine pleasure and heterogeneity.[14] Like Lacan, Irigaray does not believe that the feminine can be spoken. Language is masculine: It operates according to a masculine economy of representation. For women to speak as women, language would have to change.

Thus, Irigaray believes that there are two distinct economies—one masculine, one feminine.[15] The masculine economy, because it requires the category of woman to be the negative inverse of "man" if it is to function, disallows the feminine economy. By filling out what Irigaray means by this masculine economy of representation that operates according to the logic of the same, we can fill out our picture of the masculine strategy for self-constitution. By examining Irigaray's views on feminine pleasure, heterogeneity, and the possibility of woman's language, we will get some clues as to how to break through Lacan's impasse of feminine subjectivity.

Irigaray begins her book *Speculum* with a discussion of Freud's views on female sexuality. In the style of mimicry she developed to speak the feminine without reducing it to the logic of the same of typical theory, she questions Freud's rendering of female development as an aberration from "normal" male development. Irigaray suggests that instead of one relationship to one's origins, there are two—

but the feminine relationship has been reduced to the masculine one, because of the blind spot of the masculine position. According to Irigaray this blind spot comes from the dream of symmetry (Irigaray 1985a, 13-129). The nature of the masculine economy of self-representation makes it blind to another economy that takes a fundamentally different approach.

Lacan and Irigaray agree that an infant is born from the body of another, and that the primordial self of the infant is first precipitated in symbiotic fusion with the primary caretaker. Where Lacan and Irigaray disagree is on the nature of each individual's relation to this origin of the self. Whereas Lacan accepts the representation of that relation according to what Irigaray terms the "logic of the same," Irigaray is convinced that there is another way of representing that relation. Because representing that relation according to another, a feminine, logic would disrupt and undermine masculine logic, it cannot yet be done (Irigaray 1985a, 42-44). Yet Irigaray holds out the possibility that through attempting to speak the feminine in ways that subvert the masculine logic of language, women could finally dispel the illusions of the masculine position.

We could therefore say that Irigaray's rendering of the logic of the same, of the masculine economy of representation, is the economy played out in Lacan's schema L. On Irigaray's view, the masculine subject desires the same, the self-identical. He denies his origin in the mother and determines his relation to origin himself: The origin of his primordial self in fusion with the mother is relegated to the unconscious. The layers of identifications built up on those unconscious representations are linked to that self through the signifying chains of the conscious and unconscious systems, but this primordial origin of the conscious self is veiled. The self is reconstituted in the dialectic of self/other identifications that continue to occur, but the subject has lost sight of the active role played by a real other that originally helped create him. He projects imagoes that will confirm his identity. To do this, he needs real people upon which to project those imagoes—people who will not challenge them, thereby threatening his identity. Woman is the socially sanctioned other; by conforming to the masculine subject's imagoes, she ensures the maintenance of his identity as the same. He is thus free to continue to believe in the illusion that he is whole, that he is the phallus that the other desires, that his identity is not contingent upon the mother that gave birth to him or upon the other that reflects him back to himself. The feminine "subject" has abandoned her own relation to the origin, to her birth, her self, in order to allow masculine subjects to inscribe upon her their relation to their origin, their desire, their self-representations.

Thus, woman is required by the masculine position to be silent, to be the other that will support the repetition of his self-representations as the same. The primordial self formed in mother-fusion is translated and transposed into the Symbolic order through a layering of identifications sanctioned by the paternal law. Anything that would upset this economy of representation, which repeats the masculine subject as having the same self, is relegated to the unconscious. In this way a stable, socially functioning identity is formed and maintained despite the constant onslaught of chaotic experience that besieges it. Anything that does not fit, that cannot be ordered according to the Symbolic rules of analogy, resemblance, and identity is dismissed. Experience is ordered according to repetitions of identifications that support the self as self-identical. Woman comes to be associated with the unconscious, the fusion experiences of infancy, and the chaotic flux of experience that the self has mastered through this logic of the same. In the puzzlement men express to one another with respect to the question of what woman wants lies the dim awareness that the masculine strategy is based on an illusion—the illusion that man seeks in the other recognition of what he already is. If woman were to speak, to articulate her feminine desire for contact, the connectedness with an other that represents her relationship to her origin, the masculine subject could no longer posit himself as self-identical. Instead, he would be forced to realize that he was created in and by contact with another—that the other that recognized him in fusion not only saw him as he was but, at least in part, also created him through the contact of that recognition.

According to Irigaray, that women do not have the phallus, that they have instead a "nothing" where there should be something, is threatening to men because it represents a hole in men's signifying economy (Irigaray 1985a, 50). She suggests that this "nothing" might have been interpreted as the symptom of another libidinal economy, one that would recall heterogeneity rather than the identical or identifiable. We can delineate the two economies that she opposes to each other as her versions of the masculine and feminine positions. In rendering these positions into the "phallic" language of typical theory, I am flying in the face of Irigaray's insistence on the ineffability of the feminine position—at least in language as it stands. Irigaray feels that attempting to represent feminine desire and sexuality in typical theoretical language can only reduce the feminine to the masculine logic of the same and so deprive it of its specificity. If there is no system of representations to assist the girl in her conflictual relationship to her mother and to her sex/organ (Irigaray 1985a, 68), it is for a reason. The girl's relationship would have to be expressed in an economy of representations other than that of the schema L.

I believe that this holds only if we accept the extreme polarization of the sexes as Irigaray depicts them. Just as there are times when men relate to women as more than their mirror reflection of men, there are times when women represent themselves according to the logic of the same. If we take Irigaray's two positions as the extremes, with room for varying shades of gray in between, we may see beyond the polarization of the sexes. Just as it is helpful to relate Irigaray's logic of the same to Lacan's schema L, it is also helpful to relate Irigaray's notion of heterogeneity to my earlier discussion of the deficiencies of Lacan's account of the Imaginary and fusion experiences. I will characterize Irigaray's version of the masculine and feminine positions from that perspective.

The Masculine Position. The child, upon discovering that he and his mother are not one and that the self formed in fusion is thus at risk, makes "the very place and space of being his own" (Irigaray 1985a, 137). That is, he denies the mother's contribution to the self of fusion and makes his existence as a human being one of his own making. He then "becomes a prisoner of effects of symmetry that know no limit" (p. 137). Barred from fusion experiences because of his denial of the other's part in the making of his self, he is doomed to repeat forever that same self by setting up narcissistic identifications of self with the other. For the masculine subject, these identifications must exclude activating any representations of primordial connectedness with an other so that he can maintain a self in separation from others. This means that the other must repeat past identifications and anything about the other that might subvert these identifications must be relegated to the unconscious. Nothing that would challenge the boundaries of his self can be admitted. Instead the self of the Imaginary will push the I of speech to organize all experience in conformity with the Symbolic rules of analogy and resemblance. Boundaries remain fixed. The Real is made intelligible by his repeating the same self/other relationship over and over again according to transformation rules that relate the multiplicity of experience without endangering his layering of self-representations. Thus, "everywhere he runs into the walls of his palace of mirrors" (p. 137).

In "Plato's Hystera" Irigaray rereads Plato's cave analogy as representative of the masculine position: The cave is the womb, the empirical connection with the mother, and the phantasmic images that lie at the subject's origins. In leaving the cave, the subject is denying these origins lost in "fluid darkness" and the "shimmering imprecision of reflections" in order to replace them with "the neat, clear cut, immutable, unambiguous categories that characterize, divide up, classify, and order everything, every 'being,' according to rational intuition" (Irigaray 1985a, 281). The subject denies his origins in the mother in order to represent his relationship to his origins as that of the son to the Father. The Father is represented by the sun— "the keystone supporting the whole—phallic—edifice of representation that it dominates, illumines, warms, makes fertile, and regulates by scattering its beams everywhere" (p. 267).

Thus, the shadowy reflections of mother-fusion are relegated to the unconscious and denied, to be replaced with the clear-cut categories and interdictions of the Symbolic order. Through the chain of associations created in repetitions of the self that "pivot the scene around axes of symmetry" (p. 259), the most recent layer of self-representation maintains a link with the primordial self of mother-fusion. But the shadows of the subject's origins are denied so that he can maintain the illusion of a self that was never merged with an other, a self that is forever self-identical, able to take its place in the Symbolic order of "being," where everything already is what it is and every-thing already has a place.

The Feminine Position. Upon the loss of mother-fusion the girl is coerced by the Symbolic order into abandoning her own relation to her origins—which is different from that of the boy. Because the masculine subject needs a co-operative other, she is forced into the position of having "nothing" and submitted to the "projects and projections of masculine consciousness" (Irigaray 1985a, 141). Thus, "by resubmitting herself to the established order, in this role of delirious double, she abandons, even denies, the pre-rogative historically granted her: unconsciousness" (p. 141). The prerogative of unconsciousness belongs to the sex associated with fusion and loss, with representations relegated to the unconscious because they are sunk in shadows—dreams and fantasies that do not conform to any of the categories of the Symbolic (the realm of the clear-cut and already known). It is the specificity of women's relationships to other women that allow this prerogative, something about the nature of a girl's relationship to her mother that is different from that of a boy. Owing to this special relationship she is unconsciousness, "but not for herself, not with a subjectivity that might take cognizance of it, recognize it as her own" (p. 141). Thus, she is the "reserve of 'sensuality' for the elevation of intelligence," the "matter used for the imprint of forms" (p. 141). Instead of activating unconscious representations by associating them according to the dictates of her own desire, she al-lows herself to take on the identity of the other that will fulfill masculine desire. That is, the layering of identifi-cations a woman builds up in the self/other dialectic will have more to do with the dictates of some masculine sub-ject's search for lost objects associated with his mother than with her own search.

What is the special relationship to the mother and her own origins that grants her the prerogative of uncon-sciousness? What does it mean to have this prerogative?

How could it be represented if it were not co-opted by man? Although Irigaray is wary of giving it expression in language that operates according to the masculine economy of representation, she gives us some clues.   In "La Mysterique" Irigaray "mimics" mystical literature to articulate a way of relating not based on the masculine logic of the same.   This kind of relating constitutes a "marriage of the unknowable" where "everything is relentlessly immediate" (Irigaray 1985a, 196).   Here two (whether it is a human subject and God or two human subjects is not entirely clear) who have no "possessions" are "wedded only in the abolition of all power, all having, all being, that is founded elsewhere" (p. 196).   The ranking of social positions as laid out by the Symbolic order is left behind.   Two come together without the attributes assigned them by the place they take as speaking subjects.   Rather than placing themselves vis-à-vis each other according to the self/other relationships laid out by the Symbolic—relationships where the boundaries between self and other are fixed—"each becomes the other in consumption."

> Each will not in fact have known the identity of the other, has thus lost self-identity except for a hint of an imprint that each keeps in order the better to intertwine in a union already, finally at hand.   Thus I am to you as you are to me, mine is yours and yours mine, I know you as you know me, you take pleasure with me as with you I take pleasure in the rejoicing of this reciprocal living—and identifying—together. (p. 196)

If we take this passage as an attempt to articulate the desire specific to woman, we can contrast this feminine desire to masculine desire.   Masculine desire motivates the narcissistic identifications of the schema L.   The desire for the desire of the mother is replaced by the desire for the desire of objects offered by the paternal law as substitutes, i.e., recognition from others taken as ego-ideals in the self/other dialectic.   For the speaking subject, the I of speech has translated the desire of the me of narcissistic identifications into the Symbolic order of language, which stakes out the social network of positions.   The kind of desire expressed in the above passage has nothing to do with obtaining the desire of an other who has a given place in a social network. In fact, this "feminine" desire is a desire for another kind of connection, one where the boundaries of self and other as laid out by the Symbolic melt and two become one in a fusion experience reminiscent of mother-fusion.

The passage under discussion can be compared to the treatment of fusion experience based on Winnicott and Mahler (Chapter 2). Fusion experiences involve the melting of self/other boundaries—a way of relatedness that does not abide by the rules of the Symbolic. The desire for the desire of an other from its position as laid out by the Symbolic is not what is at issue. Instead, the desire is for contact, for connectedness—the kind of connectedness where the self/other boundary breaks down and two desire as one. Through a reciprocal attentiveness to the specificity of the other—a specificity that defies all categorization by the Symbolic, that eludes any articulation one could give it in terms of attributes, properties, and possessions available in the Symbolic order—the two merge their desire by desiring exactly what the other is in all his/her specificity. This is a kind of attentiveness beyond language in the sense that it is two bodies' reciprocal responsiveness that may or may not find expression in conscious thought.

Just as the primordial fusion of primary caretaker and child resulted in phantasmic images associated with bodily sensations eventually relegated to the unconscious, later fusion experiences based in body sensations can activate earlier sensations in a dialogue that may not be immediately translatable into language. This reciprocal responsiveness of two bodies allows the self/other boundary to break down and the two to become one organism. Just as an organism instantaneously communicates sensation from one area to another, so do these "two" bodies. Just as an organism acts as one, moving with a single goal or desire, so does the desire of these "two" converge into one. In the desire for the desire of the other in his/her specificity, the pleasure of the other rather than recognition is the goal. The pleasure of each is instantaneously communicated to the other via subtle body cues, and the desire of

the two become one as the mutual goal of giving pleasure
to the other is satisfied and communicated.

Thus, the Imaginary realm is not merely a function of
"illusory" identifications with objects outside of oneself. It
is a real arena where body sensations are communicated
and where desire is not for a particular "lost" object but for
the pleasure of merged desire. The "nonknowledge" of this
realm may find partial, and perhaps subversive, translation into the Symbolic in the mode of sensation-ideas—
"half" thoughts, thoughts that are connected with the
indistinct meaning of body sensation and have not yet attained the clarity of the clear-cut distinctions laid out by
the positions of the Symbolic. These body sensations are
retained in the body (and activated by experiences that recall earlier experiences evoking such sensations); that is,
because of the signifying chains of representations associated with them, they can be recalled by experiences that
reevoke them. These representations of body sensations
are part of the unconscious and are therefore grouped according to the laws of primary process (condensation and
displacement) rather than those of secondary process.
They are connected with words, images, and other representations that are associated with the earlier experience
that they represent.

Body sensations reevoked in the present can be given
conscious significance if attended to. The attunement of
another to one's body sensations can activate them more
intensely. Thus, the body has a sort of language of its
own—one that is neither distinct from nor synonymous
with actual speech. Feminine subjects, with their desire
for the connectedness that makes two one organism, are
more conversant with the language of the body than are
masculine subjects. Whereas masculine subjects vie for
the recognition that will place them within the social network, feminine subjects attune themselves to the more
subtle body signals that each in his/her specificity con-
tinuously sends out. Just as the mother learns to "read" her
infant's signals—the slight grimace that means he is about
to cry, the restlessness that means he will soon be hun-
gry—the feminine subject learns to read the body cues of
those around her. And because of the lack of representation for the desire for such connectedness, this communi-

cation will usually take place on an unconscious level—
without mother, child, or man bringing this kind of connectedness to conscious awareness. Furthermore, this kind
of connectedness is not peculiar to mothers. Every infant
who has desired the desire of its mother has had to learn
the same kind of responsiveness to the body sensations of
an other. It is this kind of "nonknowledge" that is so difficult to represent in terms of the logic of the same, for instead of a placing of two with respect to one another, it involves the fusion of two into an organism that desires the
same pleasure. This pleasure of connectedness where two
become one and where the pleasure of the one is the pleasure of the other is *jouissance*—a pleasure that transcends
boundaries and revels in immediate, "naive" sensation, a
pleasure that is unmediated by the social network of positions of the Symbolic.

This kind of connectedness, however, despite the difficulty of translating it into Symbolic language, has trace-
able effects. In leaving the cave of his empirical origins
in the mother, the masculine subject has "left the place,
still based in the senses, where the traces of his desires
were inscribed." But the effects of the body-based connectedness of mother-fusion are still felt: "The wound suf-
fered by being thus torn away might leave scars in the
memory. Reminders, rejoinders. Passages, and hemor-
rhages, between sensible and intelligible. Resulting in
sensation-ideas, ideal sensations. Any self-respecting
philosopher avoids confusion like that" (Irigaray 1985a,
299). The masculine position disallows the blurred boundaries of the masculine subject's childhood. Instead, he
must leave the cave of shimmering reflections and rediscover his "true" origin in the bright light of the sun.
People and things are more or less perfect copies of ideal
forms whose boundaries are unambiguous and immutable.
"Eclipse of the mother, of the place (of) becoming, whose
non-representation or even disavowal upholds the absolute being attributed to the father. He no longer has any
foundation, he is beyond all beginnings" (p. 307).

"Sensation-ideas" or anything hearkening back to the
subject's foundation in mother-matter and sense experience that respected no boundaries would threaten the logic
of the same. For a person to maintain the self/other rela-

tionship of separateness, where loss of the mother no longer poses the threat of loss of self, experience must conform to fixed categories. Woman, due to her different relationship to her origins, is capable of a different kind of language. When she is not co-opted by masculine speech, she has a different way of speaking. "Hers are contradictory words, somewhat mad from the standpoint of reason, inaudible for whoever listens to them with ready-made grids, with a fully elaborated code in hand. For in what she says, too, at least when she dares, woman is constantly touching herself" (Irigaray 1985b, 29).

The self that motivates the I of feminine speech, owing to that self's different relationship to the primordial self of mother-fusion, is not bound by the need to repeat the same relationship of self and other in layers of narcissistic identifications. Rather than translating that primordial self into the Symbolic network of positions via the transformation rules of analogy and resemblance, she is "constantly touching herself." Identification with an image outside of herself does not give her the contact she craves. What she wants is the pleasure of connectedness, the spontaneous response of her body to sensed experience that defies all categorization. As her identity does not depend on the logic of the same, she uses words differently. The self that motivates her speech has less respect than a masculine self for the paternal law. It therefore makes less difference to her whether or not she upholds it, whether or not her words make "sense" according to the socially sanctioned Symbolic code. Her self is closer to the narcissistic self of the unconscious—the self that remembers mother-fusion and connectedness, that refuses to accept Symbolic substitutions. Instead of repeating self/other relationships that hearken back to a precipitation of self in mother-fusion she no longer remembers, she wants to feel again the physical response of her body to an other or to the discourse of her Other that would re-evoke such forgotten responses. When the I translates this self into the Symbolic, it is not with the intention of finding that self's position in the larger network of social positions. The feminine intent is that of representing the spontaneous response of the body to a concrete situation in order to give it a local position with respect to other such responses she may have had.

It is unclear why Irigaray thinks that woman's relation to her origins is different from man's. If both precipitated a primordial self in fusion with a woman, then the origins for both would seem to be the same. From her discussion of the masculine denial of his origins in "Plato's Hystera," Irigaray seems to grant this. And yet woman is coerced through submission to the Symbolic order to abandon feminine desire and a peculiarly feminine relation to origins. On a Lacanian account, what makes women different from men is the different position they take with respect to the phallus. Each has to resolve the crisis of the castration complex, but their ways of resolving that crisis will differ. On Irigaray's account, woman seems already to have a different relation to the mother. Because she is coerced into playing man's "delirious double" by the Symbolic order, she is unable to represent this relation to the mother and she does not know herself the way a man does (Irigaray 1985a, 141). She is denied the economy of representation that would reflect feminine desire and sexuality. This suggests that feminine desire and sexuality are essentially different from man's. Although some have argued that Irigaray is not advocating an essentialist view of sexual difference, there are certainly strains in her work that can be given an essentialist reading. Unless some explanation is given of why a girl's relation to her origins is different from that of a boy, one could gather from Irigaray's valorization of female genitals (two lips—the sex that is not one)[16] that sexual difference is based in anatomy, that is, that one has specifically female desire and sexuality because of having female genitals.

The limitations Irigaray points to in the masculine position are important ones; there are, however, equally debilitating limitations to the feminine position as Irigaray depicts it. If wielding phallic power involves defining social relationships, then it is time women wielded more of that power themselves. If we women were to take Irigaray's advice, we might experience more of the feminine *jouissance* that from the masculine position eludes our grasp, but we would also have no more power than before. I see no point in valorizing one position over the

other. We need to articulate the feminine position and explore its possibilities. It is my belief that doing so will get
us past the impasse that both Lacan and Irigaray leave us
with: how to make sense of a "feminine" subjectivity that is
the counterpart of the Lacanian "masculine" one.

If we read Irigaray in light of Lacan's Symbolic and
Imaginary realms, we can find a way of accounting for the
difference in masculine and feminine desire that is contingent upon the position one takes up with respect to the
phallus—regardless of one's anatomy. This leaves open the
possibility that not only are both positions open to both
sexes but also they remain open throughout one's life.
Both men and women have had the experiences necessary
for taking up either position—whether those experiences
have been relegated to the unconscious or not. Thus, the
question becomes one of why women tend to develop a different strategy for maintaining the self in the face of loss
of mother-fusion and what that strategy is.

With respect to why a girl's relation to her mother is
different from boy's, Chodorow gives us some clues that
allow us to avoid a biological explanation. Although there
are some problems with using her work to fill out
Irigaray's story because of differences in their theoretical
frameworks, it can be done. In the next section I will discuss Chodorow from this perspective and offer my own
view of a feminine position—one that does not make problematic the possibility of feminine subjectivity in the same
way that Lacan and Irigaray do. By theorizing sexual difference as a difference in strategies with respect to the
problem of subjectivity, as opposed to a difference in
anatomy, I will pave the way for examining how a conflict
in strategies is manifested in philosophical texts.

Chodorow: Woman as Nurturer

Nancy Chodorow, in her book *The Reproduction of
Mothering* (1978), uses object-relations theory in the attempt to answer the question of how women today come to
mother. Because Chodorow is by training a sociologist, her
perspective on psychoanalysis and object-relations theory
is that of an outsider. She uses psychoanalysis to answer a

question that concerns her as a sociologist. By asking how women come to mother, Chodorow opens not only the question of how the nurturing qualities of the primary caretaker of children are reproduced but also the question of how women as a gender, in contrast to men, are socially reproduced with the personalities requisite to mothering. Thus, the issue of the gender difference of selves is introduced, and the question of the material conditions for the creation of gendered selves becomes important.[17]

That there are two genders and a sexual division of labor points to two kinds of subjectivity, two kinds of possibility for selfhood. Thus far, men have been privileged in cultural accounts and manifestations of self—at least in dominant discourses. Taking mothering as a legitimate expression of self and exploring the conditions that allow this kind of self to evolve are steps toward opening up other possibilities of selfhood. As long as the masculine self is considered the paradigm of selfhood proper, we lose sight of the fact that the masculine self is only one possibility for selfhood—and not the only one. The feminine self as a socially reproduced gender, that is, a socially created category, is a self deserving of a richer and more appreciative account. Women are not "failed" men but human beings with selves that tend to be socially constructed differently from those of men. Chodorow's book is one attempt to account for the material conditions of that difference in the context of the family where it is first produced.

According to Chodorow's reading of object-relations theory, the mother acts as an external ego for the infant, providing holding and nourishment. In the earliest stages the infant does not experience the mother as separate and uses defensive mechanisms such as introjection to retain primary identification. "Separateness during this early period threatens not only anxiety at possible loss, but the infant's very sense of existence" (Chodorow 1978, 60).

The self originates in the inner physical experience of body integrity and the demarcation of that body from the object world. This demarcation is achieved, as we saw in our earlier discussion of Winnicott, through frustration. As the infant is confronted with the mother's failure to anticipate and satisfy its every need, anxiety spurs the development of ego capacities. The infant internalizes representations of aspects of its mother to counter the anxiety of frustration. It comes to define aspects of its self in relation to these representations. As the mother must help the child achieve separation, she also evokes the child's ambivalence. The process of separation and individuation thus provokes in relation to the mother frustration and anxiety that the infant must cope with if it is to achieve a stable sense of self.

Chodorow suggests that preoedipal experience is likely to differ for boys and girls. In addition to resolving the castration crisis differently, girls have a different relationship to their mother, based on the mother's unconscious attitudes toward her same-sex offspring. "A woman identifies with her own mother, and through identification with her child, she (re)experiences herself as a cared-for child" (Chodorow 1974, 47). A mother is more likely to experience her daughter as an extension of herself. Thus, she discourages her daughter's process of separation and individuation. In contrast, she is more likely to emphasize her son's masculinity in opposition to herself, thus pushing him to individuate at an early age.

Both girls and boys develop a deep personal identification with the mother during their early years. Girls can maintain continuity with this identification based on daily, continuous, concrete contact with someone who is the same sex as they are. Boys must replace this early identification with a masculine one. Because fathers usually work outside the home the concrete nature of their day-to-day activities is a mystery, and the boy must identify with a fantasized masculine role. This often leads him to define masculinity as that which is not feminine or involved with women. He tries to deny primary identification with the mother by repressing the feminine inside himself and by denigrating and devaluing whatever he considers to be feminine in the outside world.

The development of a girl's gender identity does not involve this kind of rejection of her primary identification with the mother. "Feminine identification is based not on fantasied or externally defined characteristics and negative identification, but on the gradual learning of a way of being familiar in everyday life, and exemplified by the person . . . with whom she has been most involved. It is continuous with her early childhood identifications and attachments" (Chodorow 1974, 51). Furthermore, taking the father as her primary love object does not mean the girl completely rejects her mother. In fact, she usually continues her relationship of dependence upon and attachment to her. "The care and socialization of girls by women ensures the production of feminine personalities founded on relation and connection, with flexible rather than rigid ego boundaries, and with a comparatively secure sense of gender identity" (Chodorow 1974, 58). Because the mother was also a girl, she tends to have grown up without having established adequate ego boundaries or a firm sense of self. This leads her to experience the same boundary confusion with her daughter that she experienced with her mother.

Chodorow suggests that from the start, male and female infants learn different ways of handling the emergence and maintenance of self because of the different problems in separating from an opposed-sex or same-sex primary caretaker and because of unconscious attitudes of the mother to the different sexes. "These object-relational differences, and their effect on defenses, splits, and repressions in the ego, better explain the important differences in masculine and feminine personality and the important aspects of feminine personality that emerge from the Oedipus complex than does the more conscious and intended identification with the same gender parent" (Chodorow 1978, 114).

The Lacanian reading of psychoanalysis emphasizes the linguistic aspect of the unconscious, thus suggesting that the unconscious is accessible in people's speech and writing. American psychoanalysis tends to rely on empirical data for confirmation of theories about the genetic development of people. Lacanian psychoanalysis looks at linguistic output to see how a self that is inherently contradictory and fictional is currently maintaining its fictional unity. Chodorow, with her emphasis on genetic development, misses the revolutionary impact of the repressed feminine that Irigaray makes possible through a radicalized Lacanian reading of Freud. For Chodorow, women are finished products of their past—there is a certain closure to the process whereby their selves were formed. In

Irigaray's reading of Lacan and Freud, the self is always provisional, always subject to the conflict within it, thus leaving open the possibility for radical change. It is this questioning of the givenness of selfhood—whether one grants an initial formative period or not—that is exciting in French psychoanalysis.

Chodorow's analysis is empirical. She starts by asking how women come to be psychologically equipped to be mothers, assumes that there is a social/cultural explanation, and pulls together the empirical data as theorized by object-relations theorists to explain it. Her question is not how subjectivity is possible. She assumes the self is unproblematic; it is the formation of a particular kind of self in a social context that she wants to explain. She is not looking for the divided subject but seeking to understand why the unified subject we have is as it is.

The self that Chodorow describes is determined in early childhood and forever fixed in place. It develops and matures over time, but this development unfolds in the social setting according to the dictates of the original situation of early childhood. Instead of a system of signifying chains that, upon the shifting of a signifier, can result in a new configuration of meaning, we have a self whose internalized representations cohere in stable patterns. Thus, once the self is developed, it is not threatened with constant disintegration. The notion of reconstitution of the self in each meaningful word or act—with the implications this presents for the possibility of self-transformation—is lost.

This may be one reason why there is a pessimistic tone to Chodorow's polemic for change. She advocates coparenting; yet if it is women, and not men, who are psychologically equipped to become (or want to become) mothers, how are we to bring that change about? Although Chodorow reclaims the unconscious as the aspect of Freud that American psychoanalysis has tended to repress, she is still within the American tradition.

Chodorow, however, does something that Irigaray does not. She attempts to give an explanation for the material conditions under which two initial situations for internal object relations are formed—male and female. I do not believe that Chodorow's analysis can be used as a universal to explain patriarchy. The conditions she describes are those of a particular form of the nuclear family under capitalism. But if we are cautious in applying Chodorow's work, we could use it to illuminate the structures that Lacanian psychoanalysis tries to analyze.

The important part of Chodorow's analysis, from my point of view, is not that female selves end up being different from male selves but that a strategy for maintaining selfhood is put into operation differently according to gender. The interesting questions here are the material conditions under which one initially creates a self—and how those conditions still have ramifications in the way that we recreate ourselves in the process of being selves. Irigaray talks about the repressed feminine, but Chodorow fills out the picture of how that repression is first set into motion—and why it is that someone who can speak the feminine is more likely to be a woman than a man.

Developing Chodorow's work to bring it in line with the theory being developed here, we can characterize the masculine and feminine solutions to the problem of separation and individuation as two different strategies. Both males and females have to deal with the anxiety of loss of mother-fusion. My characterization of the masculine and feminine positions à la Irigaray supplied some clues as to how these strategies differ. Chodorow allows us to fill out the picture further by giving us some clues as to why and how the girl's relationship to the mother and her origins differs from a boy's.

The Masculine Position. In contrast to the mother's attitude to a daughter, the boy is pushed to individuation. Not only does the castration complex confront him with the no of the father, but the mother has already been discouraging symbiotic fusion. In the situation of fusion, two become one in the communication of body sensation that leads to the fusion of desire for the pleasurable body state of both. The mother's attitude toward an opposed-sex child makes her less apt to prolong this situation than with a same-sex child. She assumes the separateness of her child from herself at an earlier stage of his development—and thus assumes that the child's desires will be different from her own. She stops expecting the child to pick up on her body cues so intensely and starts expecting that he will become more difficult. His desires will no longer seem as accessible to her, or vice versa; she will expect less fluid communication and more conflict in the relationship. With the resolution of the Oedipus complex, the boy will take his position as "having" the phallus. The more subtle communication of fusion already having been discouraged, he will be quick to take up the compensation offered him—identification with the father, who upholds the Symbolic order.

Because of the abstract nature of a boy's masculine identity, the masculine position as we have already laid it out is natural to him. He is more comfortable building up layers of narcissistic identifications in keeping with the logic of the same than repeating fusion experiences because he is not entirely sure what masculinity means. The concrete, body-based contact with his mother is with a woman—the opposite, inferior sex. His experiences of her and mother-fusion cannot, therefore, be validated. Instead he must come to distrust his body-based self and turn for guidance to the abstract positions of being as laid out by the Symbolic. He must "be a man" and learn how to get an other to give him the recognition he needs to repeat his self/other pattern. Because he cannot allow connectedness reminiscent of fusion with his mother or other women, he adheres rigidly to the transposition of the same self throughout the conventional network of meaning encoded in language.

The Feminine Position. The mother is more likely to see her same-sex child than her son as an extension of herself. Instead of pushing her daughter away, she will continue to act as if she and her daughter are one—one organism, communicating body sensation instantaneously via subtle cues, with one desire. She expects not only that her desires will continue to be one with her daughter's but also that her daughter will continue to conform to her desires. Thus, instead of breaking fusion entirely, another kind of connectedness is developed that is reminiscent of the intense body-based communication of symbiotic fusion. To compensate for the loss of fusion the boy learns the strategy of obtaining recognition from others that fit his self/other pattern. The girl compensates for her loss by maintaining connectedness with others. Both feel terror at the prospect of finding themselves helplessly dependent and alone, cut off from the source of nourishment and the origins of self. The masculine strategy involves relying on the phallic power to obtain recognition to compensate for this break. The feminine strategy involves transferring to others the connectedness once felt only with the mother.

In taking on her position of "not having" the phallus, the girl accepts that she lacks, that she has been cut off from the mother, that she thus has a nothing waiting to be filled by another. With that acceptance comes a receptivity—an awareness of the other as subject, as desiring, and the desire to fill in her lack by listening to the other as desiring subject. When she accepts that she is not whole, not self-sufficient, she knows that mere repetition of the same self in a self/other dialectic based on recognition is insufficient. She wants more, wants to know what another's desire is, what another wants, and she wants to conform to that desire and satisfy it in order to regain the connectedness that she has lost. She is thus receptive to the other that will form her, that will tell her more about who she is by eliciting her desire to conform to his/her desire, to fit. She needs an other to tell her who she is because she admits that she does not yet know. When she can anticipate some unarticulated desire of the other, she also learns something about herself, something about where she fits, because of the response within herself such satisfaction evokes.

Symbolic layers of identification are stripped away in fusion experience, leaving only the actuality of the moment, of allowing a reciprocity to form that transcends all labeling, all attributes that define one, all signifying chains that conform to paternal law and one's position as laid out by that law in the social network. Instead of a voyage through all the circuits of one's Symbolic layering in order to place the other with respect to oneself à la the paternal law, there is a breakdown of that circuitry, resulting in fusion, a merging of positions. Instead of the desire for contact deferred through the signifying chains that determine one's position, there is the pleasure of immediate contact. In the Symbolic each signifier can signify only through the position it takes up in opposition to all other signifiers. In fusion there is contact. Through a heightened awareness of the other that involves minute adaptations to minute signals—signals that involve body movements, tone of voice, gaps and pauses in speech, and so forth that point to the other's desire, what would constitute the other's other, what would feel like a "fit" to the other, contact is made. Although the subject thinks he wants merely to repeat the relationships of identity where he was subjected to the law of the father and its rules of substitutiton, actually he wants to get all the way back to the kind of immediate identity he had with the mother, the one who helped him articulate his desire by anticipating it and giving him what satisfied before he asked for it.

Fusion can occur without the masculine subject realizing it because the feminine subject is conforming to his other: He gets sustenance without having to change his identity. When fusion is reciprocal, both are transformed; real fusion occurs as both realize that they both desire the same thing—to conform to the desire of the other and be one as two. Instead of the projection of an imago alone, the projection of an imago along with allowing oneself to be imprinted with the imago of another is allowed. There is a receptiveness to being the other for another that when reciprocated, allows one to transform each other's imagoes. The unconscious, the nether side, the other, holds suspended representational chains that work according to the logic of primary process and heterogeneity. Fusion experiences allow new meaning to emerge in a different manner than the logic of the same. Instead of translation of the self through repetition, transformation through mutual shaping is allowed. While some fusion experiences threaten self-disintegration by overwhelming all meaning structures, this transformation does not overwhelm; each self grounds the other, providing parameters (determined by what the self finds desirable) to which the other can conform. Instead of a fixed anchor point for one who repeats a self-representation, there are two beams orienting one another without the need for a fixed anchor. Self-representations become mutually adapting.

By unraveling identity layers through careful, reciprocal attention to the imago projected upon one and by patiently looking for the point of contact, the point where two imagoes can merge, one can have fusion occur without destroying self-identity. A point of contact is found where space for new meaning is made. If too much new material is released from the unconscious, then chaos ensues. But in the space of Imaginary fusion mutually bounded by the Symbolic layers of the other's other, only enough new material is released to become what another desires. Patterning of the logic of the same is maintained, but the self is transformed in the fusion with another's desire.

Just as the extreme of the masculine position assumes the imposition of a same self onto an other, the extreme of the feminine position assumes the complete conformity to that position of other. This is the feminine position that Lacan describes. Irigaray fills out what that position means in a more positive way than Lacan, without being able to make feminine subjectivity much more plausible. On her view, woman as woman is still unable to make herself understood.[18] I have used Chodorow, with her description of the female sex as the sex with "permeable ego boundaries," the sex that operates on the basis of relatedness rather than opposition, to fill out Irigaray's story in the light of two strategies—masculine and feminine. I think this can be extended to finding a way of envisioning feminine subjectivity—a feminine subject who can articulate feminine desire and feminine sexuality. Given that women learn language, that they are subjects who operate according to the logic of the same of language, then the question is, how is their use of the Symbolic different from that of a man? Irigaray has offered some clues, but she takes the extreme of the feminine position as her point of departure. Using Chodorow's notion of connectedness, we can see feminine subjectivity as a different position with respect to the Symbolic—one that allows the kind of Imaginary fusion that the extreme of the masculine position cannot tolerate. Thus, the description of fusion experience above is not necessarily of an experience that is and must forever remain ineffable. Rather, such experience involves the ability to suspend the Symbolic as a complete and closed system of signifiers, in order to articulate experience locally in a way that may contradict and even wreak havoc with the broader realm of positionality.

The feminine subject who, in addition to being the other for another, wants the power denied the mute feminine subject of Lacan's or Irigaray's characterization wants her desire taken into account as well. Besides being shaped by the desire of the other, she wants the other to be shaped by her own desire. She wants a receptivity to her desire, an attentiveness to her other that will allow her to see her reflection as well. Connection is made in the mutual overlap where each is stretching equally, reciprocally transformed, in order to fuse desire. Thus there is a merging of subject and object. One feels both that one is the other for the other and that the other is one's own other. In the space thus created, new meaning can arise—room is made in the suspension of old categories for new categories and patterns to form. In the play space, the rules of the Symbolic order are suspended and traveling along the path of the logic of the same is not required.

On the account being developed here, this process would not have to require a human other. It could happen any time the subject relinquishes the position of imposing objectivity on the other and allows the object the status of subject—that is, allows the "object" to set the boundaries on meaning. The subject allows herself to be shaped by the object: Repetition of self-representations is suspended in order to merge with the object-as-subject. Thus, one's own self of repetitive identifications is left behind, allowing the backlog of unconscious representations not yet brought into the self-system[19] to be activated by the object. Thus, on this view, the kind of process described in the mirror stage continues throughout life, not (as Lacan would have it) as a mere repetition, a buildup of layers—but in a buildup of fusion experiences where we are affecting and influencing through connectedness who we are.

On this account, the Symbolic order is composed of signifying chains that have been exchanged and communicated over the social network of individuals. Adhering to these chains, guaranteed by paternal law that by saying no to fusion ensures their stability, thus guarantees stable identity. The nether side of meaning, the storehouse of representations that do not fit the current Symbolic order, threatens this stability. To lose these meanings would be death, to unleash them would overwhelm. Imaginary fusion recognizes them without their having to be incorporated into conscious meaning structures or the Symbolic.

The feminine position allows for a different order of meaning, one that might conflict with the Symbolic order. It allows for a suspension of disbelief, for the nonjudgmental merging of two into one that requires a reciprocal shaping on the part of both in order to fit each other and make contact. This requires a suspension of the Symbolic order—not a "you are like (or unlike) me" but a "I am you and you are me" that takes place simultaneously; an oscillation of perspectives that finally ends in merging both without losing either. The Symbolic holds together representations in patterns that relate them in particular ways—relationships where they are laid out in time and space. The Imaginary suspends such relationships, allowing an "irrational" fusion of representations. Whereas the Symbolic sorts things out according to "reason," the Imaginary operates according to more local positionality. It can thus hold representations simultaneously, in a fullness that does not overwhelm because no attempt is made to sort it out.

Self-construction and the Production of Meaning: Take 3

Because both masculine and feminine subjects are "castrated," what masculine subjects project onto the other (woman) to maintain their own unity gives us a clue to the difficulties that we all face in trying to be subjects. Women are subjects also, but they have had to develop another strategy to maintain subjectivity. There are structural differences between a quintessentially "masculine" and a quintessentially "feminine" perspective. One way to illustrate such a difference is to characterize different relationships between the Symbolic and the Imaginary. The quadrature that Lacan describes is that of masculine identity. A "feminine" quadrature would place more emphasis on the Imaginary, allowing fusions to take place that would subvert layering of narcissistic identifications in the Symbolic. We can thus link the "masculine" perspective to the self-strategy that defers satisfaction through the Symbolic chain (see Chapter 2). In turn, we can link the "feminine" perspective to an alternate self-strategy that seeks fusion experience.

The theory of self developed here has offered some reasons for the difference between a feminine and a masculine strategy of creating and maintaining a sense of self. The problems presented to the female child are different problems, necessitating different solutions. Different kinds of experiences are repressed as inappropriate to the self-image one is attempting to construct. That we can delineate two gender-linked self-strategies in this way presents interesting questions for meaning-productive activity such as writing theory: How congenial is theoretic language to the expression of the repressed "feminine"? Does this "feminine" realm of experience threaten to emerge and subvert the works of the men who are represented in the philosophical tradition?

Woman as other represents a category that stands in for aspects of experience repressed by both men and women, but particularly by men. This repressed material is a threat to the constitution of selves and to the social order as we know it, and yet repressed material that needs release does get represented through symptoms. A reading of a philosophical text that examines its "symptoms," its gaps and contradictions, its blind spots and repetitiveness, what the text says as opposed to what it does, is a reading that attempts to "psychoanalyze" the text. How one positions oneself in one's production of meaning is motivated as much by the need to continually reconstitute one's identity as by the need to communicate information to one's reader. Thus, these gaps and contradictions can be read as conflicts in self-constitution. Such a reading assumes that the self is not a coherent unity, that any self presented on a conscious level is subverted by the unconscious in a way that threatens its very existence.

By attempting to articulate fusion experiences and a feminine position that does enable subjectivity, I have delineated a position that contradicts the masculine one. If, then, a text attempts to speak from both positions, it is bound to run into problems; it will seem contradictory and "irrational" from the perspective of "correct," i.e., masculine, theorizing. Fusion experiences have been relegated to the unconscious and woman in order to preserve order.

Through the building up of Symbolic meaning in a social context, individual experience is given meaning and selves are formed that can take effective action. If too much of the concrete experiences that evade such meaning structures at any one time were not filtered out via the unconscious, chaos would ensue. To lose these experiences, however, would impoverish life, leaving us only abstract categories with nothing to fill them. Fusion experiences provide a means for releasing some of this unconscious meaning into conscious meaning structures. Feminine subjects, being less attached to paternal law than masculine subjects, are more apt to enjoy these fusion experiences that tend to subvert the Symbolic order.

The masculine position involves denying fusion experience—even though it was through such experience that masculine primordial selves were formed—and instead takes flight into the Symbolic through the repetition of self in transposition that rigidly avoids fusion. Fusion experiences have to be denied due to the masculine fallacy that man is self-sufficient: the phallic whole that is desired by woman because he is whole and she lacks. If he were to uncover his own lack, to confront the fact that he is not the phallus his mother lacked, and that he certainly is not whole but in fact is confronted with lack himself, he would face loss of identity. He would be threatened with mother engulfment and chaos because the masculine position involves assuming that the self he had with the mother is his own self (which illusion he maintains in repetition of the self/other dialectic). Feminine subjects, who know they lack, are less threatened by the notion that they are only whole selves in relation to others, that it is in connectedness that they are whole.

An impasse between the two kinds of self-strategies can be shown in the symptoms of a text that speak to what cannot actually be said because of the limitations presented by gender categories. Aspects of the text can speak from the feminine position, thus pushing against the confines of the masculine position, only to cave in at certain pressure points. Looking at the text's version of "woman" and the "other" gives some idea of just how much in the way of fusion experience the subject signified in the text has relegated to the other. One of the "lures" of the me is "woman"—not women themselves, but the various ways that women are perceived. Lacanian theory gives us a way of understanding how talk about the other can be revealing of ourselves and our strategies of self-constitution—the repetition of identity fixations that we use to maintain our self-identity. What philosophers say about women can be shown to be indicative more of their own intrasubjective experience than any real truth about women. Woman as other, then, is a particularly interesting category for understanding how these men constitute themselves: the fixations that they repeat and the aggression that any threat to these fixations unleashes. This in turn can allow us to analyze what these fixations are trying to veil—the truth that an analysis of the gaps in the text can reveal. Thus, if the identity constituted by a text pushes against the boundaries of the masculine position, the extent and content of that pushing will be limited by the particular version of "woman" (which according to Lacanian theory and Irigaray is an unspecified category from the masculine position that takes the form of masculine fantasy) that the text represents. In Chapter 4 I will apply this interpretative strategy to examples from the work of three male philosophers who take up different versions of a masculine self-strategy.

Notes

1. In addition to Freud's depiction of the male path to selfhood as the norm (see my discussion of Irigaray's critique of this view in "Irigaray: Woman as the Specular Other"), women have been and still are denigrated for being less "developed" than men. There is a long tradition of this kind of treatment in philosophical literature (see Osborne 1979, Mahawald 1978, and Okin 1979) as well as in other forms of culture (literature, popular culture, religious institutions, etcetera).

2. The key works I deal with in the expositions of Irigaray and Chodorow will be Irigaray's *Speculum* and *This Sex Which Is Not*

One (Irigaray 1985a; 1985b) and Chodorow's *The Reproduction of Mothering* (1978).

3. "Disguised as reflections on the general conditions of man's Being, the philosopher's thinking depends for its effect on its specularity (its self-reflexivity); that which exceeds this reflective circularity is that which is *unthinkable*. It is this kind of specul(ariz)ation Irigaray has in mind when she argues that Western philosophical discourse is incapable of representing femininity/woman as other than as the negative of its *own* reflection" (Toril Moi on Irigaray [Moi 1985, 132]).

4. "For women the level of what is ethically normal is different from what it is in men. Their super-ego is never so inexorable, so impersonal, so independent of its emotional origins as we require it to be in men" ("Some Psychological Consequences of the Anatomical Distinction Between the Sexes" [Freud 1963, 193]). I will discuss Irigaray's critique of this bias in Freud's thought in "Irigaray: Woman as the Specular Other."

5. See Mitchell's "Introduction—1" and Rose's "Introduction—2" in Mitchell and Rose (1985), as well as the essays by Lacan on feminine sexuality that are gathered in that book.

6. See, for example, Mitchell and Rose (1985) and Ragland-Sullivan (1986, Chap. 5).

7. See also Gallop (1982, 22): "So the man is 'castrated' by not being total, just as the woman is 'castrated' by not being a man. Whatever relation of lack man feels, lack of wholeness, lack in/of being, is projected onto woman's lack of phallus, lack of maleness. Woman is then the figuration of phallic 'lack'; she is a hole."

8. In my discussion the masculine position is derived from my exposition of Lacan in Chapter 2 and the feminine position is derived from my earlier discussions of Lacan as well as discussions of "woman" in Lacan from the following sources: Benvenuto and Kennedy (1986, Chap. 10), Freeland (1986), Gallop (1982), Lacan (1975), Mitchell and Rose (1985), and Ragland-Sullivan (1986, Chap. 5).

9. Benvenuto and Kennedy make the following comment on Lacan's notion of woman's *jouissance* (enjoyment): "She has a surplus of enjoyment which cannot be integrated into language, unless it is placed under a prohibition, such as the law of castration. Might the woman, who after all does not risk much when faced by the threat of castration . . . be partly exempt from the pursuance of this law?" Also see Freeland (1986) on this point. We will see that Irigaray picks up this notion of feminine pleasure in positing a

logic different from the masculine "logic of the same" (see "Irigaray: Woman as the Specular Other").

10. "There is no such thing as *the* woman since [in] her essence . . . she is not all" (Mitchell and Rose 1985, 144). Also see Ragland-Sullivan (1986, 297), Gallop (1982, 23) and Irigaray's "Any Theory of the 'Subject' Has Always Been Appropriated by the 'Masculine'" (1985a, 133-146).

11. According to Gallop (1982, 43) Stephen Heath starts his article (Heath 1978/79) by informing us that "*Encore*, Lacan's 1972/73 seminar, [is] devoted to 'what Freud expressly left aside, the *Was will das Weib?* the What does woman want?'" Of course, to devote a seminar to this question implies that Lacan thinks he knows the answer to this, but strangely enough, he is not interested in encouraging women themselves to speak on the subject. For more on this point see Freeland (1986).

12. Cynthia Freeland, in "Woman: Revealed Or Reveiled?" criticizes Lacan for holding a romantic view of woman and comments that "Lacan leads the way not to women who voice their heart but to women who embrace their inability to do so, rejoicing in their own mysteriousness" (1986, 69).

13. In addition to Irigaray's *Speculum* (1985a), see also "The Power of Discourse" (Irigaray 1985b, 68-85). Also see Toril Moi's discussion of these concepts (Moi 1985, 131-143).

14. See *Speculum* (Irigaray 1985a, passim) and "Cosi Fan Tutti" (Irigaray 1985b, 86-105).

15. See "The Power of Discourse and the Subordination of the Feminine" and "The 'Mechanics' of Fluids," both in Irigaray (1985b), as well as "Any Theory of the 'Subject' Has Always Been Appropriated by the 'Masculine'" in Irigaray (1985a).

16. "Woman 'touches herself' all the time, and moreover no one can forbid her to do so, for her genitals are formed of two lips in continuous contact. Thus, within herself, she is already two—but not divisible into one(s)—that caress each other" ("This Sex Which Is Not One" [Irigaray 1985b, 24]).

17. See my exposition of Harding's account of feminist gender theory in Chapter 1, "The Feminist Context for a Gender-sensitive Approach to the Self," for a reiteration of this point.

18. "I can thus speak intelligently as sexualized male (whether I recognize this or not) or as asexualized. Otherwise, I shall succumb to the illogicality that is proverbially attributed to women. All the statements I make are thus either borrowed from a model that leaves my sex aside—implying a continuous discrepancy be-

tween the presuppositions of my enunciation and my utterances, and signifying furthermore that, mimicking what does not correspond to my own 'idea' or 'model' (which moreover I don't even have), I must be quite inferior to someone who has ideas or models on his own account—or else my utterances are unintelligible according to the code in force.   In that case they are likely to be labeled abnormal, even pathological" (Irigaray 1985a, 149).

19. The concept of "self-system" as developed in Epstein (1973) is similar in many respects to the version of the self as a process that I am developing in this work.   I have generally chosen to use the term "self-strategy" since it speaks to the problematic I set for selfhood as the solution to human agency.

4

Self-constituting Activity in Philosophical Texts: Three Examples

Introduction

According to one commonsense approach to the nature of the self, "I" am a unique individual with a relatively coherent worldview that I continually refine and correct as incoming facts require. Thus, as a child of five I might think that the car rather than the driver knows how to get where we want to go, but by the age of ten I learn that if the driver doesn't know the directions, we'll get lost. I am the same individual at ten that I was at five, but I know more about myself and the world in which I live.

This view posits the self as a substance whose attributes, such as bodily appearance and items of knowledge, may change over time but that endures from the moment of birth (or from some arguable time in the womb) to death. I have as a child relatively primitive categories in which I arrange the incoming data provided by my senses. These categories become more refined (allowing nuances in the breakdown of data) and more sophisticated (with respect to cross-referencing of data) as I become older. By the time I am five, cars are in the same category of animate objects as cats and dogs and human beings; at ten, I have moved them into the category of inanimate objects manipulated by people. This view of the self assumes that my knowledge of the world builds in a systematically meaningful way—that a subject who endures through time will orient herself with respect to the world that is the object of her knowledge and desire.

One feature of existentialist philosophy is an emphasis on concrete lived experience as opposed to the abstract categories in which we organize and generalize our particular experiences. On this view the self as an enduring substance is cast into doubt—my self is no more than an abstract category that I use to organize experiences that seem to belong to me. Any concrete particularity of experience that cannot be contained within the categories is threatening because it implies that there is always an excess of existence for which we cannot account. If there is no enduring substratum to ourselves, if we are no more than the series of concrete experiences located in bodies that continually change, then who are we? What kind of stability and coherence do we have? What kind of meaningful action can we take?

In the face of a growing awareness that we do not have immediate access to either the world or ourselves, philosophers such as Kierkegaard, Nietzsche, and Sartre struggled with the question of who we are and what makes our lives meaningful. With the emphasis on the concrete particular over the abstract came an emphasis on the self as action, rather than a self whose actions are mere attributes of an enduring substratum. The self came to be seen more as process itself than as an entity that processes. Thus it was less clear where the self ended and the world began.

Where does the self end and the world begin if the abstract category of "self" is no more than a construct we invent? How do we distinguish a subject that is a process from an entity outside the flux of experience? We are faced with, instead of a fixed subject processing input, the prospect of a self that is no more than a continuous stream of sensation on the verge of melting into a vast sea of sensations—a subject without background, without means for distinguishing her own outline in a chaos of bodily sensations. In such a chaos there can be no inner or outer, the ability to reflect upon a stable image that provides a centering point is lost, and subjectivity is swallowed in a ceaseless flood of sensation that is neither controlled nor directed.

The old dichotomies of subject/object and self/other are thus brought into question. In the texts of these existential philosophers a new kind of subjectivity struggles to emerge—subjectivity as the creative process of constituting a self from a superabundance of sensation; a self that is always in question, always contingent, always on the verge of disintegration; a self that cannot be taken as a given but that must be continually chosen; a self that must be held accountable for the choices it makes in choosing itself. But in the struggle to articulate a new kind of subjectivity that leaves behind the category of substance, old categories are used as landmarks. To stabilize a self that might otherwise be threatened with complete extinction, thus rendering human agency impossible, each of these philosophers finally reaffirms the very subject/object dichotomy that he had been undermining.

Chapters 2 and 3 developed the notion that there are two gender-linked strategies that take different approaches to the problem of organizing a self and a world out of a chaotic range of sensations. One strategy makes primary the abstract categories of a socially sanctioned Symbolic order, whereas the other makes primary the pleasure of connectedness with an embodied other. In a culture where psychoanalytic theory has explanatory force, the former strategy could be characterized as "masculine," and the latter strategy, "feminine." My characterizations of the two strategies draw upon the Hegelian idealist tradition as well as Lacan's psychoanalytic theory and feminist theories that make use of the Hegelian tradition and psychoanalysis. Whether these characterizations apply equally well in all situations for all philosophical traditions is a question that I leave open. This chapter will explore whether the theory of gender-linked self-strategies can be brought to bear in an interesting way on philosophical texts also based in the Hegelian tradition. Attempts to subvert abstract categories in favor of a connectedness that defies self/other dichotomies could thus be read as attempts to incorporate more fully a feminine self-strategy into one's theorizing, and reversions to self/other dichotomies could be read as the effects of a masculine self-strategy.

I have thus far given a polarized version of the difference in two gender-linked, self-constituting strategies.

Because of the correlativity of self and world (see Chapter 1), groups of people with fundamentally differing self-strategies live in different worlds—that is, they have different perspectives with their own epistemological standpoints. Thus, self-constituting activity is also world-constituting activity. Psychoanalytic theory, in addition to grounding the emergence of differing self-strategies in the child-rearing practices of Western society, offers the possibility that we all have both self-strategies available to us. As masculine identity is the "norm" for full-fledged personhood in Western society, the feminine self-strategy is culturally devalued. We have seen (Chapter 3) that this cultural devaluation and the masculine need to repress the primordial self of mother-fusion stifles development of a different kind of self-strategy. Self/world-constituting activity continually strives to make sense of a chaotic array of sensations and Symbolic input. For the theorist who attempts to enlarge his perspective to include as wide a range of his lived experience as possible, it is likely that the alternative, "feminine" self-strategy will be brought into play and that this alternative self-strategy will create problems for his masculine identity.

In Chapters 2 and 3 I delineated masculine and feminine self-strategies. In this chapter I will give examples of masculine and feminine positions from which a text can speak. That is, taking the production of theory as a self-constituting as well as a meaning-reproducing activity, we can say that the "voice" of a text situates itself with respect to a whole network of social positions. In Chapter 3 I showed what such positioning might mean with respect to gender. Having characterized "masculine" and "feminine" self-strategies that position one as male or female in the social hierarchy of positions (Lacan's Symbolic order), we can give a philosophical text a "gender-sensitive" reading, one that highlights how gender categories inform both the position from which the text speaks (the self the speaking I of the text puts forth) and the theoretical perspective the text presents. Given my assumption (taken from Lacanian theory) that any speaker of language is "decentered," I assume that there is no one position from which the I of the text speaks and that the text will manifest symptoms that speak to conflicts in positioning.

"Symptoms"—gaps, contradictions, puzzles—of the text can be read as a conflict between the position that the I attempts to construct and unconscious forces that undermine or subvert that position. We should be able to resolve some of the puzzles these symptoms present—explain their presence in the text—by analyzing the gender categories put forth by the text and by examining the puzzle in light of a conflict between two kinds of self-strategies.

The kind of reading I am proposing here is "deconstructive"[1] in the sense that rather than assuming textual integrity and explaining away contradictions as mere aberrations in what is presumed to be a coherent whole, it focuses on gaps and contradictions in the text. It is not deconstructive in the sense that it attempts to explain those contradictions via a coherent theory. My goal is to explain the "symptoms" of a text in a way that will render them intelligible via a theoretical framework that the author himself lacked. Thus, rather than proliferating the possible meanings of the text in an unbounded way, I will interpret symptoms of the text in the light of the broader project of understanding how gender informs our identities and our perspectives as theorists.

In addition to communicating meaningful content to the reader, a text tells the story of a subject in communication with himself or herself. Both positions outlined here are taken up by the text with respect to the other (the reader) and the Other (the site of representations of lived experience not incorporated into the conscious self-system). We can trace the strategy a subject utilizes in positioning him- or herself with respect to the reader as well as with respect to his or her unconscious by examining the text that that subject has produced. The masculine and feminine positions delineated here are related to polarized versions of the two self-strategies described in previous chapters.

The Masculine Position. The speaking I or grammatical subject of the text positions itself in keeping with two constraints: On the one hand what is articulated needs to make sense according to socially sanctioned codes; on the other, a self with some sort of continuity needs to be continually reconstituted. On the Lacanian view (see Chapter 2), this means that in addition to stringing together words in a way that will have some significance to other mem-

bers of the speaking community, the I is motivated by the
me to retain self-continuity and self-coherence. The primordial me is the ego originally precipitated out of identification with one's primary caretaker. A masculine self-
strategy maintains continuity with this ego by seeking
objects that will confirm his self by repeating past
self/other patterns. That is, the me is looking for the lost
"*objet a*" which is associated with the lost mother of
mother-fusion. Through a complicated series of substitutions this lost object of primordial fusion with another has
been translated into objects of current desire.

The child originally learns to compensate for the loss of
mother-fusion by using symbols to fill in for that loss and
by coming to desire the desire of the other. The boy, because he is of the sex that is not castrated, has, or rather
would inherit, what the mother wants—the phallus, primordial signifier of desire. He can be, or hope to be one
day, that which does not lack and therefore that which can
fill in his mother's lack. The gaze of the other is the gaze
that desires him, the gaze that confirms him as self-sufficient and whole. As upholder of the paternal law, he is
entitled to cultural substitutes for the lost mother, the
other that originally reflected him back to himself. To
maintain self-continuity he will find cultural substitutes
that will reflect back a self in keeping with the self of
mother-fusion. This means that the speaking I will always
be positioning itself with respect to an other that will
provide the me with the kind of recognition that it craves;
this other will confirm the same self by repeating a past
self/other pattern. Such a self-strategy assumes that the
self is self-sufficient—if it were not, it could not be what
the mother desired. This self must deny any dependence
on the other and posit the other's gaze as only affirming
what is already there—the same, self-sufficient self. For
this strategy to work, objects of desire must conform to the
other of the subject's self/other pattern. This positioning
of self with respect to an other may take many different
forms via complicated translation in keeping with
Symbolic codes, but the me will strive to maintain the same
relationship between self and other.

From this position there is reverence for and rigid adherence to what Lacan calls the Symbolic order—socially

accepted categories that generalize and universalize experience. The motivating force of the self-strategy associated with this position is the desire to repeat self/other positioning. Here, one seeks to position oneself with respect to an other within socially sanctioned codes in a way that retains associations with the self formed in mother-fusion. That is, for the other originally played by mother one seeks cultural substitutes that are sanctioned by paternal law within the Symbolic order. The speaking I of the text will position itself with respect to others explicitly or implicitly referred to in the text, to the reader as other, and to the subject's own Other—the unconscious. All such positioning will abide by preestablished categories of the Symbolic order.

The Feminine Position. Because the girl is already castrated and therefore does not have the same need to deny dependence on another, she has a different self-strategy open to her. Her relationship to her primordial self assumes that it takes two to make the pleasure of mother-fusion possible. The paternal law does not guarantee her objects to fill in for the lost mother in the same way it does for a boy; therefore, she tends toward another kind of compensation. Instead of needing to affirm the same self by finding an other to reflect back a self that she recognizes, she seeks to reexperience the pleasure of mother-fusion. She admits her dependence on the other and remains in a state of receptive responsiveness to the desire of the other. Thus, rather than seeking cultural substitutions for the lost mother in keeping with Symbolic codes, she seeks contact with an other that may require her to violate the demands of both the I that would produce meaning in conformance with Symbolic codes and the me that would add the additional constraint of conformance to past self/other patterning.

From this position there is a relative lack of regard for the Symbolic order. The socially sanctioned categories that encode experience are subverted, if need be, in deference to a spontaneous response to the specificity of experience that eludes those categories. The subject speaking from this position tends to subvert the Symbolic order—she is more concerned with maintaining responsive attentiveness to the desire of the other than she is with "making sense." What she attempts to communicate will have significance to the specific other she addresses, but this significance will take the form of shared pleasure with an other rather than positioning with respect to an other in the Symbolic order. The specific others she addresses are those explicitly or implicitly mentioned in the text, the reader as other, and the subject's own Other—the unconscious. Rather than repeating past self/other positioning via socially sanctioned categories, the speaking I will attempt to break down categories in order to respond to the other's desire to be recognized/reflected in all his/her specificity.

These characterizations represent two extremes. To investigate the effects of gender categories in a particular text we can examine the specific content the theorist gives to the category "woman." Woman, on the Lacanian view, is an empty category filled in by man.[2] She is man's other, what he is not, and can affirm his self-sufficiency. What he projects onto her is often what he feels he himself cannot be and still be a man and can thus give us clues as to the particular form the gender categories of the text take.

The "masculine" and "feminine" positions I sketched above are filled out differently by different theorists according to their particular gender categories. Each theorist, taking the above characterizations as two ends of a continuum, is able to conceive of a range of positions in between that falls under his categories of "masculine" or "feminine." The two self-strategies I described in a polarized, mutually exclusive form thus turn out to have varying degrees of overlap according to the gender categories that inform a text. That is, both self-strategies are available to both male and female persons. How far one can go in conceiving of a man using what I have called a "feminine" self-strategy or vice versa, and how far one can go in conceiving the possibility of a person's making full use of both self-strategies, hinge on the conceptual barrier posed by one's particular version of gender categories. How a particular text fills in the category of "woman" can give us a clue as to where the conceptual barrier for a given text is, which, in turn, can help explain why the attempt to use two self-strategies in a text runs into conflict: The speaking I needs to maintain a masculine identity.

For each philosopher I focus on a specific text to under-line the particular way I link gender, identity, and the production of meaning. I am not trying to psychoanalyze the author of the text—the flesh-and-blood philosopher who, if put on a couch, might free-associate far beyond the confines of a particular text. I am taking a specific text as a particular attempt on the part of the flesh-and-blood philosopher to create both a self and to produce meaning. I am thus interested in the particular identity put forth in the production of meaning of a text. And I want to examine how gender affects this identity and the content of the text. One could, of course, then correlate the various identities put forth in the various texts of a given author and ask, do all those identities speak from the same posi-tion? What factors play into any shifts in position that may occur from text to text? But for the purposes of this work I will put those problems aside.

The analysis of each text is divided into four parts. The introduction outlines the masculine and feminine posi-tions of the text—identifies where the I of the text is using a masculine self-strategy and where it is using a feminine self-strategy—according to the general characterizations of these two strategies given in Chapters 2 and 3. This means establishing that philosopher's terminology for his version of what Lacan calls the Symbolic order and for the "feminine" forces that threaten that order. The second part, "The Puzzle," delineates the textual puzzle that will be addressed. The puzzle will be some problem in the text that challenges our notion that the text was written by a com-pletely unified, rational subject whose intentions and mo-tivations were transparent to him. Rather than dismissing the puzzle as an aberration and then explaining what the author "really" meant to say, I will use the puzzle as an indication of conflict in the position from which the I of the text attempts to speak.

The third part, "Woman," describes the content the text gives to the category "woman." This will help us to locate the conceptual barrier presented by the particular form gender categories take in the text, the barrier that pre-vents further overlap of the two extreme positions into

one. I leave it open whether we ever could completely incorporate the two positions (thus leading us beyond gender
distinctions entirely?), but I am interested in how far a
particular text goes in using both self-strategies and
where use of the feminine self-strategy is curtailed because of gender categories.

The fourth part, "The Positions," makes use of the analysis of the text's category "woman" to fill out specific content of the two positions and their self-strategies according
to the particular gender categories of the text. The puzzle
described in the first part is seen as a conflict in these
self-strategies. The use of a feminine self-strategy, despite
"unconscious" forces that emerge in the symptoms of the
text, must be curtailed in order to maintain a "masculine" I.
Thus, although this feminine self-strategy continues to exert effects (the symptoms of the text), it cannot be incorporated into the self put forth by the speaking I. I then
make some suggestions about the kinds of self and theoretical content that might have emerged as a solution to the
puzzle if the conceptual barrier presented by the particular gender categories informing the text had been broken
down.

My goal in this kind of reading is to understand how our
gender categories affect our identities and our perspective
in the world. Do philosophical texts espouse timeless truths
that are gender-neutral, or does the presence of a male-
identified voice create certain limitations in perspective
that we can articulate and explore? Using a self-strategy
that is alternative to the typical "masculine" strategy of
our traditional views of theory allows us to release the repressed "feminine" of a text.

The explorations of particular texts written by
Kierkegaard, Nietzsche, and Sartre are not meant as a
definitive response to the question of how gender categories inform the production of meaning but as initial for-
ays into possible approaches to philosophical texts that
could take this question into account. These "gender-sensitive" readings are examples of how the account of self-
constitution developed in Chapters 1, 2, and 3 could be ap-
plied in the interpretation of philosophical texts. Perhaps
the most "radical" claim of my reading is that the theoretical content of the text might have been different if the

speaking I had not been motivated by the need to maintain a masculine identity. When a particular line of thought in the text has been released from the conceptual barrier of the text's gender categories, the further development of that line of thought—unavailable to its author—becomes possible. To highlight this particular perspective, I have chosen to relegate references to pertinent secondary literature to endnotes. The interpretations I give here can be supported and complemented by other interpretations extant in the literature. Because my concern with gender categories, however, is not in keeping with most of that literature, I will restrict the main body of my text to clarifying the kinds of questions and insights a gender-sensitive perspective might elicit.

Kierkegaard: *Fear and Trembling*

Introduction

Kierkegaard's pseudonymous authorship is particularly interesting in light of my project. In adopting various authorial personae, Kierkegaard tries on, and discards, several positions in the masculine spectrum. In doing so he underlines the active positing that goes on in taking up any position. In the leap that can come only from a personal decision made in the concrete setting of a particular situation, one takes up a position in the aesthetic, ethical, or religious spheres.[3] Kierkegaard does not refer to this positioning with respect to gender categories. But by looking at, in the light of my discussion, one of his personae, we can relate his positioning with respect to his spheres of human existence to our positioning with respect to the extremes of the masculine and feminine positions.[4]

In what follows I will place Johannes de Silentio, the pseudonymous author of *Fear and Trembling* (Kierkegaard 1983), in the spectrum of masculine positions. I will examine his position as a rendering of a male position pushing against the gender barrier. Although the whole question of the relationship of Kierkegaard's pseudonymous works

to himself is an interesting one,[5] here I am exploring a
possibility in masculine positioning.

Silentio's perspective in *Fear and Trembling* is that of
an ethical man with enough understanding of the religious sphere to attempt to articulate its perspective,[6] thus
one that he knows is beyond his own.   The exact nature of
the relationship between the perspectives of the ethical
and religious spheres is still debated in the literature on
Kierkegaard, but it is generally agreed that Kierkegaard
considered the religious perspective more "advanced" than
the perspective of the aesthete or the ethicist.   To approach
the religious perspective, Silentio makes use of two terms
that we can apply to our polarized schema of masculine
and feminine positions.   First, there is the "universal"—the
universal, socially accepted categories that encode values
and communicate experience in a way that is readily understood by other members of society.[7]   This term can be
correlated with Lacan's Symbolic order—both concern socially accepted categories of thought to which members of
the society must defer in order to position themselves with
respect to others.   The ethical realm, for Silentio, is the
realm in which one situates oneself with respect to others
in regard both to one's ethical responsibility and to one's
production of meaning.[8]   This dual meaning can be compared to Lacan's use of the term "Symbolic order" to refer
to a hierarchy of social positions that involve taking up
certain responsibilities to others in that hierarchy, as well
as to the order of language and the communication of experience.[9]

Second, there is the "paradox of faith"—a movement of
faith that takes one out of the ethical sphere into a religious realm where the categories of the universal can be
suspended when faith demands.   The paradox of faith
constitutes what I call a feminine position.   That is, the
person in this position will defy Symbolic categories in the
concrete context of a relationship with another.   This
paradox can take one not only beyond the duties encoded
in the universal but also beyond language itself when socially acceptable categories become inadequate for expressing the experience of the religious person.   We can
correlate this terminology with "feminine" forces, those

that defer to concrete relationships and experiences that cannot be captured in the general categories of language.

Silentio himself, of course, does not qualify these terms with adjectives like "masculine" or "feminine." I will show that correlating his terminology with the two gender-linked self-strategies in light of an examination of his category of "woman" will help us resolve a puzzle in this text in an interesting way.

The Puzzle

In *Fear and Trembling* Silentio discusses the paradox of faith in the context of the story of Abraham and Isaac. In this story God commands Abraham to sacrifice his only son. Abraham proceeds to obey but is reprieved by God at the last moment.[10] Whereas most accounts of the story emphasize Abraham's willingness to obey God's incomprehensible demand,[11] Silentio emphasizes the double movement of Abraham's faith. Not only does he resign himself to Isaac's death in obeying God, but "by virtue of the absurd" he never stops believing that God will keep his promise of making him the father of nations through Isaac.

Silentio repeatedly says that he could not achieve Abraham's movement of faith: "I cannot make the movement of faith, I cannot shut my eyes and plunge confidently into the absurd" (p. 34). Silentio can only marvel at Abraham's greatness without making the movement himself. To help us, his readers, do the work of understanding just how great Abraham was, he presents some poetic sketches in the "Preliminary Expectoration" and in "Problema III" that suggest the incomprehensibility of Abraham's faith. None of the stories are meant as analogies to Abraham. They are told "only in order that in their moment of deviation they could, as it were, indicate the boundary of the unknown territory" (p. 112). In these sketches Silentio explores the difficulties of relationships that would take one beyond the universal of the ethical realm. The single individual has the ethical task of annuling his singularity in order to express himself in the universal which applies to everyone (p. 54). Asserting him-

self in his singularity before the universal is a sin. The
impulse to do so puts the individual into a spiritual trial
"from which he can work himself only by repentantly
surrendering as the single individual in the universal" (p.
54). In each sketch a lover feels the impulse to defy the
universal because of a relationship with a loved one.[12]

Why is it that Silentio digresses, giving a series of
sketches of unconsummated male/female relationships,
before returning to his discussion of Abraham's God relationship? One could respond that the comparison of love
relationships and God relationships is a "natural" one because of its history in the Christian tradition and the
deeply personal nature of such relationships. But in the
context of my concern with the importance of the other to
self-constituting activity, Silentio's use of these sketches to
intimate Abraham's faith bears further attention. First,
there is the series of self/other, lover/beloved, relationships that Silentio abandons one by one with no solution.
A God relationship is the only one with a solution to the
problem of connection—even if Silentio still despairs of
understanding how such a connection was effected. In his
struggle to understand a position (the religious one) beyond his own, he struggles to understand positions vis-à-
vis embodied others that are also beyond him. What kind
of struggle with respect to his own self/other positioning
is Silentio engaged in here, and why is it only in the context of a God relationship that he can articulate the successful connection of a self (Abraham) with an other
(God)?

Silentio, in his insistence on the lack of analogy between these sketches and the story of Abraham, wants to
put the God relationship in a class by itself: It is only in
the context of a God relationship that a suspension of the
ethical is justified. But the puzzle remains why Silentio
chose these particular sketches to help us understand
Abraham. I argue that Silentio's reading of gender categories makes it problematic for him to conceive of taking
up the feminine position with respect to anyone except
God. On the one hand, he wants to move away from the
masculine position of appealing to fixed categories as the
ultimate justification for meaning and action. On the other
hand, he cannot allow the chaos that would result if those

categories were permitted to crumble. He is thus caught in the dilemma of wanting to maintain both positions at once. He does this by maintaining a masculine position with respect to other human beings and positing the possibility of a feminine position with respect to God. If his gender categories had not prevented him from doing so, the kind of connectedness he posits in a God relationship could have been posited in a relationship with other human beings as well. This kind of connectedness, in turn, could allow new meaning to be translated into the universal that could result in social change.

In the rest of this section I will present five sketches from the "Preliminary Expectoration" and "Problema III" with the following questions in mind: When does Silentio feel that the impulse to assert singularity against the universal is justified? How do the male/female relationships he looks at relate to Abraham's relationship to God?

The situation of the sketch in the "Preliminary Expectoration" is as follows: "A young lad falls in love with a princess, and this love is the entire substance of his life, and yet the relation is such that it cannot possibly be realized, cannot possibly be translated from ideality into reality" (p. 41). Silentio does not say why the relation cannot be realized. He says only that the thoughts the lad summons and rejects, upon examining the conditions of his life, come back and "explain that it is an impossibility" (p. 42). The lad is thus presented with the dilemma of desiring something his rational understanding tells him he cannot have.[13] Not being a "frog of the swamp," he does not merely give up his love but also undertakes the movement of infinite resignation.

In this movement he concentrates "the whole substance of his life and meaning of actuality into one single desire" (p. 42). This focuses him so that his soul is not dissipated into multiplicity.[14] He will recollect his love in pain, but his infinite resignation will reconcile him to existence: "His love for that princess would become for him the expression of an eternal love, would assume a religious character, would be transfigured into a love of the eternal being" (p. 43). Although his desire is denied fulfillment in actuality, the knight of infinite resignation makes consummation possible by expressing it spiritually. Thus, the "desire that would lead him out into actuality but has been stranded on impossibility is now turned inward" (p. 44). From this point it no longer matters what the princess actually does, although if she too chooses to become a knight of infinite resignation these "two will in all eternity be compatible" despite the failure actually to consummate their relationship.[15]

If the lad were to make the double movement of the knight of faith, he would make the additional movement of affirming that he would get the princess by virtue of the absurd. The absurd lies beyond the proper domain of the understanding. It defies human comprehension: "So I can perceive that it takes strength and energy and spiritual freedom to make the infinite movement of resignation; I can also perceive that it can be done. The next amazes me, my brain reels, for, after having made the movement of resignation, then by virtue of the absurd to get every-thing, to get one's desire totally and completely—that is over and beyond human powers, that is a marvel" (pp. 47-48).

Silentio presents this sketch as a concrete example of the difference between the knight of infinite resignation and the knight of faith. The movement of the former he can follow; it is the movements of the latter that bring us to the border of the unknown. The lad of the sketch loves a princess that he cannot have. He feels the impulse to defy the universal because it thwarts his desire. Having the spiritual strength of a knight of infinite resignation, how-ever, he submits his singularity to the universal and re-nounces his love, only to give it expression in spiritual inwardness. Thus, he converts action that would defy the universal into spiritual expression that leaves the univer-sal untouched.

Once this movement involving submission of the indi-vidual to the universal is made, then the further move-ment of faith can justify the suspension of the ethical that would allow actual consummation of the relationship. But because the further movement defies rational understand-ing or any attempt to be justified in words, Silentio can only marvel at the possibility. The knight of infinite res-ignation demonstrates his spiritual power by refusing to give up his love at the same time that he adheres to his ethical task of remaining within the universal. In exercising this power, he has, however, gone beyond the ethical by developing a spiritual inwardness that allows him to maintain the love denied him by the universal. Thus, his love for another has led him to assert his singularity by taking a first step in achieving a relationship with the absolute, which is higher than the ethical. It is not until he can make the movement of faith that the lad is able to translate his impulse into the universal by marrying the princess, despite the fact that according to his rational understanding such a union is forbidden.

This relationship of the knight of faith to the princess parallels Abraham's relationship to God. Just as the lad manages to translate his love for the princess into actuality by virtue of the absurd, so does Abraham translate his love for God by believing God will keep his promise. Both put the relationship with another above the universal, believing that the connection with the other will be consummated despite all rational evidence to the contrary. In the context of this relationship they assert the singularity of their experience against the universal that mediates individual existence in society. Silentio grants that if the lad were a knight of faith, he could have the princess in actuality, but that he himself cannot conceive such a happy ending. We will see in the four sketches of "Problema III" that Silentio continues to explore the assertion of singularity against the universal within the context of male/female relationships. He will increasingly emphasize the difficulty of determining when one is justified in consummating a relationship that brings one in conflict with the universal. In the first ideal case of the "Preliminary Expectoration," Silentio assumes for the purposes of illustration that the knights described actually make the movements of infinite resignation and faith that justify asserting singularity to varying degrees. In the sketches I will now explore, the individual's justification will be more problematic.

In the first sketch of "Problema III," "the bridegroom, to whom the augurs prophesied a calamity that would have its origin in his marriage, suddenly changes his plans at the crucial moment when he comes to get his bride" (p. 89).

The bridegroom must decide what to do.   To remain silent
and get married would be an offense to the girl, as she
would never assent to an alliance that would cause him
harm.   To remain silent and not get married would also be
an offense against the girl.   Ethics demands disclosure of
the individual; it therefore demands that he speak.[16]   If the
pronouncement of the augurs was public property, he
could speak because the suspension of his commitment to
the girl would be superseded by a higher ethics.   Everyone
would be able to understand that the consummation of
their relationship had to be viewed in light of the higher
ethical consideration of a divine sign.   To be silent in such
a case would be to place himself as a single individual
higher than the universal and to forsake the individual's
ethical task to "work himself out of his hiddenness and to
become disclosed in the universal" (p. 82).

If, however, the will of heaven had come to his knowledge privately, then he could not speak.   In being put into
a purely private relation to the will of heaven he would
have been placed as the single individual in an absolute
relation to the absolute (p. 93).   Here again we approach
the unknown territory of the paradox in the context of a
male/female relationship.   The groom wants to consummate his love for the bride.   The will of heaven would seem
to frown on the union.   The groom's impulse is to gratify
his desire.   This could mean defying the universal (if the
information came through an augur) or it could mean
complying with the universal at the expense of his relation to the absolute (if the information was private knowledge).

In the sketch of the lad and the princess the question
was how to make the ethical relative to the absolute.   It was
assumed that both knights had some sort of relationship to
the absolute.   But this relationship could not obviate the
need for a relationship to the ethical.   Justification of
asserting oneself against the universal could come only
after submitting to the universal and making the movement of faith that put one in an absolute relationship to
God.   In the bridegroom sketch we have the additional
problem of one's ethical commitments to others.   The
groom has already pledged he would marry the bride.   It is
thus a matter not merely of consummating his love but of a

promise made to his beloved. It would put him outside the universal to break such a promise unless there was a higher ethical consideration that supersedes that promise.[17] If, however, the information was private knowledge, then doing his duty to the absolute places him outside of the universal. He cannot hope to make the singularity of his experience understandable, and the bride will feel wronged. This gets us closer to the dilemma of Abraham, whose faith put him outside the universal when God requested what was, in ethical terms, murder. A relationship with the absolute puts the groom in conflict with a relationship that is in the ethical realm.

In the second sketch, a merman sees Agnes standing on the shore and wants her as booty; that is, he wants to seduce her and make her one of his conquests—"he cannot give himself faithfully to any girl, because he is indeed only a merman" (p. 95). He calls to her and elicits what is hidden in her. She, "trusting with all her soul . . . gives herself to the stronger one" (p. 94). Because of the power of her innocence—the absolute confidence with which she entrusts her whole destiny to him—he is crushed. He cannot seduce her; he can never seduce again. Instead he struggles with repentance and his desire for Agnes. Because of his guilt about having wanted to seduce Agnes, a love relationship with her is outside of the universal. Agnes fell in love with him in all innocence, thinking that he loved her. The merman agonizes over what to do. Silentio lists some alternatives opened to him.[18] (1) He could destroy Agnes's love by belittling her and making her love ludicrous. He would remain silent with the assistance of the demonic about his anguish at treating her thus, putting himself as the single individual higher than the universal: "The demonic has the same quality as the divine, namely, that the single individual is able to enter into an absolute relation to it. This is the analogy, the counterpart to that paradox of which we speak" (p. 97). (2) He could return to the universal, becoming a tragic hero by speaking and crushing Agnes with the knowledge that he could never make her happy. (3) He could remain in hiding (e.g., by going into a monastery) and hope that Agnes would be saved by taking an absolute relation to the divine. (4) He could be saved by Agnes, become disclosed by revealing the truth, and marry her. For the last option he would have to have the spiritual power to make the movement by virtue of the absurd after having made the infinite movement of repentance (p. 99).

Silentio assumes that the lad and the groom share the desire to carry out the ethical task of translating themselves into the universal.[19] Their dilemmas are how to go about that task and when that task should be suspended in the interests of an absolute relation to the absolute.[20] Here Silentio adds the dimension of guilt. The merman is guilty of wanting to seduce an innocent girl and take her outside the universal—for he had no intention of making the ethical commitment of marriage to her. Her loving trust that he is good and that he will keep them within the bounds of the universal disarms him.[21] He feels guilt and tries to find a way to right his wrong.[22] She fell in love with him in all innocence. The ethical way to translate that love is marriage. But marriage means disclosure of his guilt, which could crush her if he does not have the spiritual power to make the movements of repentance and faith first.

The merman comes to realize that his original impulse to seduce Agnes was wrong. He repents having wanted to take Agnes outside of the universal. He wants to save her, even though he is not sure he can save himself. Saving both of them, in addition to consummating their relationship, seems to him (and Silentio) a miraculous act. Thus, just as God moves Abraham to assert his singularity against the universal in a relation to the absolute, Agnes moves the merman to assert his singularity by consummating a love within the universal when he is outside of it.[23] Both Abraham and the merman would defy rational understanding by asserting their experience of connectedness with another against the universal that denies comprehensible translation of that connectedness. If Abraham were to disclose his singular experience in the universal, he could only say "I'm murdering my son." If the merman were to disclose his experience, he could only say "I'm seducing her." The difference between the two is that Abraham was originally in the universal and the merman outside of it. But both are faced with the dilemma of when it is justifiable to consummate a relationship that requires asserting oneself against the universal.

In the third sketch, "the young Tobias wishes to marry Sarah, the daughter of Raguel and Edna. But the girl has a tragic background. She has been given to seven men, all of whom perished in the bridal chamber" (p. 102). The evil demon who loves Sarah has killed all seven of her previous bridegrooms on their wedding night. From no fault of her own, Sarah has been "defrauded of the highest bliss . . . unlimited, unbounded, uninhibited devotedness" (p. 103). She has been unable to give herself to a lover and unable to express herself in connectedness with another in the universal by getting married (p. 106).

Silentio says that although many would say Tobias was the hero of this story for having the courage to brave the danger of the evil demon, he thinks Sarah is the hero: "What love for God it takes to be willing to let oneself be healed when from the very beginning one in all innocence has been botched. . . . What ethical maturity to take upon oneself the responsibility of permitting the beloved to do something so hazardous! What humility before another person! What faith in God that she would not in the very next moment hate the man to whom she owed everything!" (p. 104). Despite the fact that a situation beyond her control has placed her outside the universal, making it impossible for her to consummate a relationship, she is still willing to let herself be "saved"—to receive the love of another, trusting in all humility that another's love would bring her back within the bounds of the universal.

Whereas Silentio grants this to be a heroic act in a woman, he seems to feel that it would be even more problematic for a man: "Imagine Sarah to be a man, and the demonic is immediately present. The proud, noble nature can bear everything, but one thing it cannot bear—it cannot bear sympathy. In it there is a humiliation that can be inflicted on a person only by a higher power, for he can never become the object of it by himself" (p. 104). The man who chooses the demonic closes himself up within himself. Instead of translating himself into the universal, mediating himself into the idea of society (p. 106), he remains silent, hidden, undisclosed. He is lost in the demonic paradox in which he takes an absolute relation to the demonic.

People such as Sarah are in the paradox by virtue of being set outside the universal by nature or a historical situation: "They are by no means more imperfect than other people, except that they are either lost in the demonic paradox or saved in the divine paradox" (p. 106). Because they are outside the universal and because of the difficulties for translation that poses, they feel the impulse to assert their singularity by taking a relation to the absolute. They could refuse translation, remaining undisclosed to any other including God, thus losing themselves in the demonic. They could also make an infinite movement that maintains their singularity in spiritual inwardness at the same time that it submits them to the demands of the universal, and then through the movement of faith be saved in an absolute relation to the divine. In the latter case, they would be brought back within the universal because of a belief in connectedness with another, a connectedness that defies rational understanding. In Sarah's case, her humble willingness to receive love from a man despite the knowledge that she is outside of the universal allows her to believe she can be saved. Although Silentio, in imagining Sarah as a man, seems to be saying that this kind of receptivity to a human other is possible also for a man, he qualifies this with the notion of the demonic. If Sarah were a man, it would be much more likely for him to become demonic and refuse to disclose himself.

Abraham, in his case, shows to God the same kind of humble willingness to receive love that Sarah shows to a man. This willingness allows Abraham to believe God will keep his promise despite Abraham's violation of the universal in murdering his son. Both Abraham and Sarah defy rational understanding by putting connectedness above the universal. The difference between the two is that Abraham was originally in, whereas Sarah was outside, the universal. Unlike the case of the merman, it is due not to sin but to circumstances beyond her control that Sarah is outside the universal. Thus, for Abraham and Sarah there is an even closer parallel in the dilemma of asserting connectedness above the universal.

In the fourth sketch, Silentio introduces his version of Faust, "the doubter (par excellence), but he has a sympathetic nature" (p. 108). The security and joy men live in are grounded in unreflective bliss rather than the power of the spirit. Thus, Faust, as a doubter, is able "to rouse men up horrified, to make the world totter under their feet, to split men apart, to make the shriek of alarm sound everywhere" (p. 109). But because of his sympathetic nature, "he remains silent . . . he tries as much as possible to walk in step with other men, but what goes on inside himself he consumes and thus brings himself as a sacrifice to the universal" (p. 109).

Because doubt has destroyed Faust's actuality for him and because he would rather remain silent, sacrificing himself to the universal, than throw everything into disorder, he does not tell Margaret of the love he feels for her. Margaret is innocent. To express his love in the universal he would have to disclose himself. Because of his doubt, he cannot do this without wreaking havoc with the universal. If he remains silent about his doubt, ethics condemns him for evading the task of translating his hiddenness into the universal. He can get authorization for his silence only by becoming the single individual who stands in an absolute relation to the absolute. To do this he must make his doubt into guilt.

Here we have a man who, not because of sin or circumstances, is tempted to defy the universal. Faust is in the throes of an infinite passion that pushes him beyond the universal. The question here is whether he can justify expressing his doubt and thus pushing others beyond the universal as well. As the ethical demands disclosure, it would seem he must speak. But if he can make his doubt into guilt and make the infinite movement that would both maintain his singularity in spiritual inwardness and submit him to the universal, he could get authorization for his silence.

Faust's relationship with Margaret is less at issue in this sketch than the other relationships we have looked at. But here again, the question is of connectedness versus the maintenance of the universal. Consummation of a relationship with another would mean disclosure of his doubt, a disclosure that would put not only him but also the other

outside of the universal.   Making an infinite movement
would authorize his silence by putting him into an absolute relation with the absolute; but it would, however, make
consummation of a relationship with another human being impossible.   Here again we approach Abraham's
dilemma.   Abraham maintained connectedness with God
but did so at the expense of his ability to communicate what
he was doing with the human beings closest to him.
Abraham's God relationship justified the suspension of the
ethical, and by virtue of the absurd, by his faith in God,
Abraham believed he would be brought back within the
universal.   God, by commanding the substitution of the ram
for Isaac, did bring Abraham back.   Without such assur-
ance that only the divine can give, Silentio seems to imply,
it is better to be silent.

In all the sketches presented here, the lovers agonized
over justifying action that puts oneself or another outside
of the universal, the ethical standards that one can ra-
tionally understand as being applicable to all.   Silentio
grants the possibility of such justification in only one
case—the case of a God relationship where one will be
brought back within the universal by virtue of the absurd.
That is, in humbly receiving love from an often incomprehensible God, one opens oneself up to possibilities for
being brought back within the universal beyond rational
understanding.

In the following section I will briefly comment on the
category of "woman" that emerges in these sketches.
These comments are preliminary to a discussion of the
masculine and feminine positions of the text.

Woman

Silentio makes no general comments about "woman as
such." By looking at the position of the five women of the
sketches we will be able to establish the parameters for the
conception of "woman" in *Fear and Trembling*.

In the sketch of the young lad and the princess, woman
is depicted as a focusing point.   The lad's love for the
princess becomes the "substance of his life" (p. 42).   If the
lad is a knight of infinite resignation or a knight of faith

(as opposed to a slave of the finite), he will "have the power to concentrate the whole substance of his life and the meaning of actuality into one single desire" (p. 42). Thus, desire for a woman gives the lad the focus necessary for making a movement of the infinite that will promote his spiritual growth.   In the next sketch, the bride awaits her groom in maidenly modesty and humility as he agonizes over whether to tell her about the calamity prophesied by the augurs.   The merman elicits what is hidden in Agnes, thus enticing her to entrust her whole destiny to him in absolute confidence (p. 94).   Sarah has the humble love for God that allows her to love the man willing to let her give herself to him despite the danger presented by the evil demon.   Faust views Margaret in "all her adorable innocence" (p. 109).

In these sketches the woman is the focal point for the man's agony in deciding whether the relationship should be consummated.   The woman, in her love for the man, surrenders herself to his decision.   She is innocent or at least more innocent than the man.   He evokes feelings in her, and she responds without reflection.   She is prepared to receive the man's love without agonizing over whether consummation of the relationship is outside the bounds of the universal, and she will accept the man's judgment about such matters without question—despite the pain it may cause her.   The man has full responsibility for making an ethical judgment about the appropriateness of consummation.   He will weigh her pain in making his decision, but finally it is up to him to decide.   Thus, the "woman" that emerges from these five sketches is a woman prepared to give herself absolutely to the man she loves. Incapable of judging ethical boundaries, she depends on the man to guide her behavior in accordance with the universal.   This may not be Silentio's final position on "woman as such," but we will see that the degree of responsibility assumed by the men in coming to a decision about the relationship, and each one's unwillingness to share any of that burden with the woman involved, indicates Silentio's inability to take up a feminine position with any but a divine other.

The Positions

For Silentio, the duty that marriage presents is a weighty one. If one is married, one is bound to disclose oneself to one's wife and one is also bound to honor the institution of marriage and the social relations that go with it as those relations are laid out in the universal. "Woman" presumably has an easier time honoring the commitments of marriage, as she is willing to sacrifice everything in love for her husband—she lets him determine the parameters of her commitment, and she trusts that he will set those parameters according to the universal. It is the man's duty to uphold the universal so that his wife can unfold and expand within an appropriate space, one in keeping with the universal. Thus, if he is going to go beyond the universal, he has to do it on his own. It would not be fair of him to subvert her when she was trusting him to evoke responses from her that were in keeping with social parameters.

Although Silentio recognizes a calling "higher" than the universal, each subversion of the social categories that make the universal up must find its agonizing justification in the deep soul searching of a God relationship. In such a God relationship, all one's actions are scrutinized to determine whether one is willfully trying to put the single individual before the universal. Only if after submitting oneself to the universal, one discovers oneself to be faced with an incommunicable ordeal (where the ethical poses the temptation to subvert one's absolute duty to God) rather than a spiritual trial (where singularity poses the temptation to subvert the ethical), is such a subversion justified.

To maintain connectedness with God, Abraham needed to suspend the ethical. Just as the men in the five sketches faced the dilemma of confronting women they loved with suspension of the ethical, so did God confront Abraham with suspension of the ethical. The women would have subverted the universal in their love of the men—just as Abraham did in his trusting acceptance of God. The problems for the men were whether they could ask such a thing of their women and whether they could receive new parameters themselves by playing the feminine position with respect to God. In the sketches of Agnes and Sarah,

Silentio intimates the possibility that a woman could save a man, just as God saved Abraham. If man could receive woman the way that Abraham received God, man could, perhaps, have overcome the dilemma presented to him by the universal. This intimation is subordinated to the discussion of a relation to the divine, however. And these stories are not meant as complete analogies: They only hint at the difficulty that Abraham faced in accepting new parameters from God that involved suspension of the ethical. Thus, what Abraham could do with respect to God, the merman or Sarah (imagined as a man)[24] perhaps would have liked to have done with respect to their women, but could not. That is, they wanted to be able to take up a feminine position with respect to their women. They wanted to put aside their role as maintainer of the ethical and subvert the latter by allowing the women to play the role of subject to their other. Through trusting acceptance of the other, they could believe that even though the relationship did not make sense according to the universal, their desire for connectedness would be granted by virtue of the absurd. And the woman, not being bound by the universal in the same way as he, would, because of her love for him, grant him his desire in connectedness despite the restrictions of the universal encoded in rational understanding.

Silentio's dilemma is that his conception of masculine identity dictates that "man" can play only the role of other to God. Man cannot play woman's other because as a man his role is to play subject, to make others his other according to the Law of the Father, which he has inherited. The only one who can subvert that Law is God—a greater father who can reteach him the Law according to his dictates. Only to one "higher" than he can "man" subject himself as a "man," and the only one higher than he is God. Silentio cannot support the idea that another human being could provide him with parameters that would subvert his current conceptual and ethical categories and provide him with new, more fitting categories for the specificity of his experience, because as a man his role is keeper of the Law.

Silentio expresses his masculine allegiance to the Symbolic and his sense of duty toward it in his characterization of the ethical. One does not subvert the Symbolic without cause, and the only cause that can sanction the subversion of the Symbolic is God the Father above, the creator of the Law.   Thus, Silentio allows for a way of subverting the Symbolic, a way of finding categories more in keeping with the specificity of life, without incurring "disrespect" for the Symbolic, disrespect that we will see exemplified in Nietzsche.   Silentio grants an irrational element to life in the form of the commands of a divine father.   But, in his allegiance to the subjectivity of God, he is not willfully creating new values; rather, he is playing the other to God's subjectivity.   He is playing the dutiful son.   He is obeying God even though in all humility he does not comprehend God's wishes, and he does not expect to be able to understand according to his rational and limited human understanding.   Instead he responds with the same faith a woman shows her man when she takes on the form he gives her, conforming to his desire rather than insisting that he take on the form of her desire.   In that way she is stretched beyond her own understanding and creates new meaning in her attempts to understand his desire.

On this reading, the paradox Silentio discusses is the receptivity of man to another, the taking on of the role of other by man.   The dilemma of all five sketches is that the universal in the normal sense of the word cannot be maintained; new meaning has to be found.   The relationship can be consummated only if a new context for it can be formulated.   In all these sketches there is something that makes the relationship unacceptable according to the standards of the Symbolic, but Silentio has nothing but contempt for the suggestion that such an anomaly should render the beloved unlovable.   Instead one is presented with the paradox of the unsuitability of the lover according to the parameters of the Symbolic and with the problem of finding a solution that will allow the concrete specificity of the love expression despite the constraints of the Symbolic that forbid it.   For the relationship to occur, the Symbolic must be subverted.   But when is such a subversion justified and how must it be carried out?

In all cases—including Abraham's—one is tempted to subversion by love of another whose desire is not in keeping with that of the Symbolic.   Only Abraham is really justified in subverting the Symbolic.   The others are trying to play God to a woman; they want to subvert an other to leave the parameters of the Symbolic behind, which is not justifiable. In a human-to-human relationship one or the other must play the subject, and whoever does must do it in keeping with the Symbolic. Just as a man would have to forsake his role as maintainer of the Symbolic to let a woman save him, so would a man have to forsake that role to let himself conform to God's desire in faith. I suggest that it is here that Silentio believes the analogy between the sketches and Abraham's faith ends.

In playing the feminine role with respect to a human beloved, Silentio believes, "man" would be undermining himself as a male. This is the only way, however, that he can subvert the Symbolic. Silentio offers the intriguing suggestion that the only justifiable way to create new values is in the context of a relationship where one takes on another's desire. But in delineating this way out of complete conformity to the Symbolic, he has to posit this feminine position with respect to another as a relationship with one higher than he, a Father higher than the Law, one who creates that Law—God himself—before he will allow the possibility of man taking on such a role.

Owing to his conception of gender categories and his need to maintain a masculine identity, Silentio has to make the dissimilarities between the situations of the sketches and Abraham's situation more striking than they actually are. Silentio delineates a way of subverting the Symbolic within the context of a love relationship that would keep the chaos of complete disruption of all universal categories at bay, but, in keeping with his need to maintain masculine identity, he limits the possibilities of such subversion to a God relationship. This constraint makes impossible such subversion within the context of human relationships that respect the concrete specificity of connectedness over the categories laid out by the Symbolic. It also precludes the possibility of translating into the Symbolic new aspects of human experience disclosed in connectedness with human others. As long as one believes one can have one's desire by virtue of the absurd only with respect to a divine other, the status quo of the Symbolic is safe. What is incomprehensible will remain untranslatable and hence nonsubversive. It is when such faith is taken with respect to human others that the possibility emerges for generating new meaning in connectedness.[25]

Nietzsche: *Beyond Good and Evil*

Introduction

For Nietzsche, the concepts we use to communicate our experience and the values by which we live are human creations imposed upon a chaotic flux in order to give ourselves ballast.[26] We can correlate Nietzsche's values and concepts with Lacan's Symbolic order. Life in all its concrete fecundity is a Dionysian chaos that is completely beyond the generalizing scope of language.[27] Nothing is like anything else and there is no way of distinguishing one "thing" from another.[28] Only via a system of values and concepts encoded in language can some stability be imposed upon this chaos and can one take on both an identity and a position vis-à-vis other things and other human beings. Unlike Lacan, Nietzsche emphasizes a creative moment in which the will to power subverts old moralities in order to create new ones.[29] Rather than being structured by language in the way a Lacanian subject is, Nietzsche's "free spirit," in keeping with his will to power, subverts conventional language.

Thus, we can correlate Nietzsche's notion of the will to power that would defy the Symbolic order with a feminine self-strategy that does not give priority to the Symbolic. Whereas the feminine self-strategy characterized in Chapter 3, however, sought fusion experiences—contact with an other through the fusion of desire—Nietzsche's notion of the will to power makes no reference to desire for contact with an other. This notion does make reference to desire for contact with the subtleties of experience that would defy conventional categories. In listening with the "third ear," the "free spirit" attends to aspects of experience that a less noble soul ignores in his reduction of experience to that which can be communicated to others.[30] The free spirit attempts to capture the subtleties of experience in language despite the risk of being misunderstood by, or incomprehensible to, others. He thus puts language at the service of subtle nuances of bodily sensations and feelings rather than ignoring aspects of his experience that do not fit into a preconceived worldview: "Our eye finds it more comfortable to respond to a given stimulus by reproducing once more an image that it has produced many times before, instead of registering what is different and new in an impression. The latter would require more strength, more 'morality'" (*Beyond Good and Evil*, #192).[31]

Nietzsche, who emphasizes a creative aspect of human existence that Lacan tends to overlook, cannot finally account for the creation of new meaning he claims is possible. The will to power, an irrational force, cannot of itself impose order.[32] If the concepts and values encoded in language stabilize our identities and our world, then the destruction of the old moralities can lead only to nihilism.[33] And yet, the old moralities were, according to Nietzsche, human creations. How could we now go about creating a new, more life-affirming morality? I will suggest that Nietzsche took up a feminine position in *Beyond Good and Evil* in that he refused to give the Symbolic order the reverence granted it by a more masculine self-strategy. But also it was his inability to assert the alternative strategy of seeking fusion experience with others that led to his nihilistic conclusions. Nietzsche, like Silentio, feels the need to respond to something in experience that pushes one beyond conventional language. Part of what characterizes a feminine self-strategy is the need to respond to nuances in concrete experience that defy generalization. Significance is given to these nuances in the shared pleasure that comes from satisfying another's desire. Nietzsche had as much difficulty as Silentio in adopting a feminine position with respect to an embodied other. Unlike Silentio, however, he had no recourse to a divine Other. His attentiveness to aspects of his experience that eluded categorization thus lacks the parameters set by an other's desire.[34]

Nietzsche, although he could talk of attending to nuances of experience not accounted for in the categories of language, could not determine how such nuances could be given meaning, bringing new aspects of experience into the self one posits as well as into one's view of the world. I suggest that such new meaning can come about only through the responsiveness of an other: One needs the mirroring response of an other that brings that meaning into the relational structure of the self. That is, a self can exist and have meaning only in relationship to others, in a position with respect to other selves. Thus only those aspects of experience that have some relationship to others can be incorporated into the subject's sense of self. Those aspects of experience that remain unrecognized and unattended to by others will not be brought into the subject's sense of self because they will not relate to the positioning of that subject with respect to others. Once such aspects have taken on meaning for others, however, they also take on meaning for the subject. Thus, meaning cannot be generated in a vacuum: It is the by-product of a positioning process that determines the subject's place with respect to the world.

The Puzzle

In *Beyond Good and Evil* Nietzsche wants to push us past the old morality that opposes good to evil. In Nietzsche's revaluation what is normally considered "evil" is the "good" of the "free spirit." The Christian ethic of "all equal before God" and democratic egalitarianism are both aspects of a slave morality that reduce everyone to the level of the common man and prevent the evolution of the human race. To counter this disease, Nietzsche wants us to go beyond the old dichotomy that labels anyone who inspires fear as "evil" (#260). We need to encourage a new type to appear, a higher, nobler man who will create a new, more life-enhancing morality: "The noble type of man experiences *itself* as determining values; . . . it is *value-creating.* . . . In the foreground there is the feeling of fullness, of power that seeks to overflow, . . . the consciousness of wealth that would give and bestow" (#260). To prepare the way for this higher man, Nietzsche ("ourselves who are their heralds and precursors, we free spirits" [#44]) wants to reveal all moralities as human creations at the service of the will to power. Far from being a code of unchanging ideals that hold "true" for all time, moralities are sets of concepts and values created by human beings to promote life.[35]

To understand human beings we need to "descend into the depths" (#23) and understand psychology as the doctrine of the development of the will to power. The body is "but a social structure composed of many souls"; willing is a question of the rank of commanding and obeying within this structure; and morals is "the doctrine of the relations of supremacy under which the phenomenon of 'life' comes to be" (#19). One's morality bears witness to who one is by determining "what order of rank the innermost drives of his nature stand in relation to one another" (#6). The strong spirit will be the one who, owing to his morality, is more able than others to discharge his strength (#13) and not splinter it in a conflict of competing drives. His values will discipline those drives to come together in an upsurge of strength.

Thus, instead of the old dichotomy of good and evil, Nietzsche introduces the new dichotomy of "strong" and "weak." Along with that go the dichotomies of noble/contemptible, higher/inferior, and healthy/sick. Nietzsche hopes to prepare the way for a new kind of human being, one who can break the constraints of a morality that has grown too restricting and therefore life-denying. Such a higher man would create the new morality necessary for developing as yet undreamed of aspects of human potential.[36] In the place of the old concepts of good and evil Nietzsche hopes to create, if not *the* new morality, at least transitional concepts and values that will facilitate the evolution of man he envisions.

The puzzle here is why Nietzsche introduces these new dichotomies as if they work better than the old dichotomy of good and evil. I will argue that the dichotomy of strong and weak is undermined by the text. We could say that this is no surprise: Nietzsche is trying to get us beyond all dichotomies. Instead of explaining away discrepancies in the text by positing an author who "intentionally" undermined himself, however, I will return to the text itself. In light of my project, an "I" that confidently proclaims a clear-cut distinction between the strong and the weak is also attempting to position itself as a subject with respect to those categories. That those categories shift in conflicting

ways reveals a conflict in positioning of the speaking "I"
of the text. If we explore this conflict in light of the theory of self thus far developed, we could gain insight into
the difficulties of moving beyond such dichotomies.

By distinguishing between the strong and the weak, the
noble man and the herd animal, Nietzsche attempts to distinguish those who represent the higher hope of humanity from those who should be sacrificed to that higher
hope. We must ask whether the dichotomies introduced by
Nietzsche do the work he wants them to do. I will argue
that they do not. In making these distinctions Nietzsche
seems to shade his concept of the will to power in different
ways. At times the strong manifest a will to power that is a
procreative life force, one that affirms and reveres all life:
"the ideal of the most high-spirited, alive, and world-af-
firming human being who has not only come to terms with
whatever was and is, but who wants to have *what was and
is* repeated into all eternity, shouting insatiably *da capo*"
(#56). At other times the strong manifest a will to power
that is an appropriating life force, one that is intrinsically
and   inevitably   domineering   and   exploitative:
"'Exploitation' does not belong to a corrupt or imperfect
and primitive society: it belongs to the *essence* of what
lives, as a basic organic function; it is a consequence of the
will to power, which is after all the will to life" (#259).
Which interpretation of the "strong" and the will to power
we take will have repercussions for our interpretation of
Nietzsche's higher man. Can there be but one such higher
man—the one who manages to overpower everyone else
and is therefore doomed to solitude? Or can we envision a
community of higher spirits who can live in peaceful
coexistence?[37]

Nietzsche would seem to want the latter: He talks of the
reverence in which a noble soul will hold his equals—"it
honors *itself* in them and in the rights it cedes them"
(#265)—and ends *Beyond Good and Evil* with an "Aftersong"
that appeals for new friends that he, as a precursor of the
higher man, can so revere. But the search for others
equally as "high," "free," or "noble" as he is fraught with
peril. The distinctions he so boldly makes in some places
are undermined in others. In contrast to a clear-cut distinction between the strong spirits that will naturally

come to command and the inferior human beings whose place is to obey, Nietzsche distinguishes a noble soul that needs cleanliness and solitude from the herd that would corrupt him. In an odd reversal it becomes the herd that is strong. Members of the herd use the same words as one another to describe their inner experiences and so are easily understood: "Those more select, subtle, strange, and difficult to understand, easily remain alone, succumb to accidents, being isolated, and rarely propagate" (#268). This points to a conflict in Nietzsche's thought. The noble soul is playing a dangerous game. He is a lover of the great hunt who would probe the human soul and its limits, its unexhausted possibilities (#45), and yet, "it might be a basic characteristic of existence that those who would know it completely would perish" (#39). Thus, strength teeters on a fine line between the spirit who can command because of the self-discipline of drives, resulting in an upsurge of will to power, and the spirit who dares to break down his internal ranking of drives to probe the "truth" that he is, "in which case the strength of a spirit should be measured according to how much of the 'truth' one could still barely endure—or to put it more clearly, to what degree one would *require* it to be thinned down, shrouded, sweetened, blunted, falsified" (#39).

If one were to probe all the "heights, depths and distances" of the range of inner human experiences (#45), one would risk perishing—losing one's ability to act, one's meaning, one's identity in an overwhelming multiplicity of experience no longer controllable with one's fictions. Although we need a new morality more in keeping with the demands of the will to power, in leaving the old moralities behind we are in danger of oblivion. Thus, at the same time as the noble soul is strong—strong in his attentiveness to the pulse of life, which pushes him to discard old values—he is also weak—weak in his inability to leap up in new strength before destroying his old foundations for action. This weakness makes it impossible for him to command and turns his health into a sickness that dooms him to solitude. The noble soul who loves the great hunt and would pass through the "whole range of human values and value feelings" (#211), who would look down from this perspective and create new values, is forced into silence. To speak in the words suited for common experiences, the experiences shared by the many, would destroy what was rare, strange, and subtle in him. The very pulse of life that moves him beyond those words also proves to be his weakness. In isolation to avoid corruption of his delicate rareness, the noble soul shrinks from contact and awaits the new friends who will strengthen his new and higher perspective in the community of shared experiences.

The question is, how is this community to be formed? Again, we come back to Nietzsche's notions of "strong" and "weak." If the strong spirit is the spirit who creates new values, the spirit who commands, who imposes his values on others, then won't the "true" higher man be the higher man who manges to impose the values he creates upon the rest? If this is the case, then each noble soul must sit in solitude, struggling to create his new values alone, and finally, in the attempt to impose his creations on the world, brave the corrupting influences of the common man.

I do not think Nietzsche had this vision and I think he was aware of the conflict at work here. Toward the end of Part 9, the subsections strike a more personal mode. In #278 the wanderer calls out for "Another mask! A second mask!" and in #280 he says, "He is going back like anybody who wants to attempt a big jump." In the following sections I explore Nietzsche's concept of "woman" in *Beyond Good and Evil* and analyze the feminine and masculine positions of Nietzsche's text on the basis of my earlier discussion of those terms. It is my contention that Nietzsche goes a long way toward breaking down old subject/object dichotomies but that his introduction of new dichotomies is an attempt to save his version of masculine identity. An examination of his concept of "woman" demonstrates how his reading of gender categories relates to this attempt. I then explore alternatives he might have taken if he could have freed himself from his version of gender categories.

Woman

Toward the end of Part 7, Nietzsche devotes eight subsections to "a few truths about 'woman as such,'" with the stipulation that one keep in mind "how very much these are after all only—*my* truths" (#231). Throughout his works, Nietzsche goes further in deconstructing the category of "woman" than either Kierkegaard or Sartre does.[38] In the Preface of *Beyond Good and Evil* he asks, "Supposing truth is a woman—what then?" with the implication that the attack he proceeds to make on those who assume there is an absolute Truth waiting to be unveiled and possessed goes for those who would win "woman" as well.[39] He is thus far from unaware that the role that man would have woman play is based on illusion. If there is an absolute Truth behind the confusing array of appearances waiting to be revealed, then man has a focal point, a goal by which to orient his search for knowledge. If there is the essential "woman," the not-man, behind the veils she hides herself in, waiting to be possessed, then man has the ultimate answer to all that he feels himself to lack. Truth will heal his ignorance, woman will make him whole—the problem is to find them both. Once found they can be possessed and man will finally want no more. On this view, at least man knows what he is looking for and can even measure his progress on the way to his goals. But what if both Truth and "woman" were illusions, illusions that he himself invented? Then he is set adrift upon the sea of appearances with nothing to guide him—no goal, no direction, no meaning.[40]

To compensate for the loss of the illusion of Truth as a realm of eternal ideals that men could strive to reflect ever more perfectly, Nietzsche introduces the will to power and emphasizes man's ability to play the creator himself.[41] The old ideals always were illusions anyway. We need fictions to orient ourselves and our actions, to organize our drives into a unified upsurge of life.[42] The trick is to compensate for the loss of an anchor in Truth with a new awareness of our will to power and our ability to create the fictions that would best enhance that will to power. What then of "woman"? Is she free to abdicate from her role as Holy Grail, free as well to play the creator, to create the illusions that will best serve her own will to power? Yes and no. On the one hand, Nietzsche gives woman credit for having always seen through the illusion of "woman" and put it to her advantage: "What is truth to a woman? . . . her great art is the lie, her highest concern is mere appearance and beauty" (#232). On the other hand, to take the next step and discard the illusions given her by man for illusions more to her liking will lead to her degeneration: "As she . . . takes possession of new rights, aspires to become 'master' and writes the 'progress' of woman upon her standards and banners, the opposite development is taking place with terrible clarity: *woman is retrogressing*" (#239).

Because Nietzsche has equal disdain for the scientific man who remains bound by conventional "truths" rather than letting himself go and flowing with the great currents of a free spirit (#206), one could argue that Nietzsche only wants to make sure woman does not do herself the same disservice. But a careful reading of *Beyond Good and Evil* points to more than that. Not only does Nietzsche not want woman to make the same mockery of herself man already has, he wants woman to continue to play her role of being man's illusion: "Let us men confess it: we honor and love precisely *this* art and *this* instinct in woman—we who have a hard time and for our relief like to associate with beings under whose hands, eyes, and tender follies our seriousness, our gravity and profundity almost appear to us like folly" (#232). And he exhorts man to make sure she continues to play this role: "A man . . . who has depth, in his spirit as well as in his desires . . . must conceive of woman as a possession, as property that can be locked, as something predestined for service and achieving her perfection in that" (#238).

In #194 he distinguishes three types of men according to what they consider to be really possessing a woman. The third type combines the criteria of the first two for "having": (1) the use of the woman's body; and (2) the knowledge that "the woman does not only give herself to him but also gives up for his sake what she has or would like to have"; with (3) the knowledge that "when she gives up everything for him, [she] does not possibly do this for a phantom of him," because "he wants to be known deep down, abysmally deep down, before he is capable of being loved at all; he dares to let himself be fathomed." Thus, a woman's desire for self-reliance is one of the worst developments of the general uglification of Europe (#232) because it is in the best interests of man's will to power that she renounce her own will and desire. It may be an illusion that there *is* a "something Eternally-and-Necessarily-Feminine" (#239), a "something more refined and vulnerable, wilder, stranger, sweeter, and more soulful . . . something one has to lock up lest it fly away" (#237), but if this illusion is necessary for the development of the higher man, then it is an illusion we should keep.

Again we are brought back to Nietzsche's notions of "strong" and "weak." If the higher man is to be a creator of values, then to distinguish himself from those inferior to him he must not only create those values but also impose them on those he has subjected to his will. On this reading of the will to power as domination, only the one who imposes his morality has the opportunity to manifest an upsurge of strength. Those around him—such as women and slaves—must be sacrificed to his superior ability to create and impose on others the values that will expedite his own will to power: "To a being such as 'we are' other beings must be subordinate by nature and have to sacrifice themselves" (#265). It is only when such a being has determined whether another being is of equal rank that "it moves among these equals with their equal privileges, showing the same sureness of modesty and delicate reverence that characterize its relations with itself" (#265).

The same problem arises of determining one's rank with respect to woman as arose earlier with respect to the "weak." If woman is to be possessed, her desire subsumed by man's, her illusions put in man's service, then presumably she is "weak." She is not part of Nietzsche's "we free spirits." Her reasons for shame (such as superficiality and petty presumptuousness) should continue to be kept "repressed and kept under control by *fear* of man" (#232). Clearly it is not to her that we turn in our watch for the higher man. Thus, to allow her to attempt the creation of values could only lead to retrogression. Woman can and should chase away worries, fathom man's depths, and play into his faith that within her lies concealed a "basically different ideal" that must be maintained and protected (#239). All these roles are based on illusions that will give him some relief from his struggles and even help him on his way. But only he is capable of the great hunt that will lead the human race to its higher glory.[43]

From this discussion of "woman," one can obtain some additional clues to the problem of distinguishing the "strong" from the "weak." According to Nietzsche's doctrine of will to power, all who can should, and must, struggle to manifest as much of their will to power as possible—such is life. The only constraints on that struggle are the need to maintain orienting fictions and the need for the mastery of others stronger than oneself. Thus, far from surrendering her desire for the sake of man, woman should be struggling for as much self-reliance and self-mastery as it is in her power to achieve. If man can keep her in his service, then so be it—but to ask her to sacrifice her own will to power voluntarily is not in keeping with Nietzsche's conception of will to power. That is, it is one thing to suggest that the noble souls will come to command because of a superabundance of energy, but it is another to suggest that a group of human beings (i.e., women) should prefer to help man find the fictions best suited to his will to power rather than attend to the pulse beat of her own. Presumably, it is the desire to render such service that Nietzsche is thinking of when he worries about her unlearning her fear of man. "She unlearns her *fear* of man: but the woman who 'unlearns fear' surrenders her most womanly instincts" (#238); "what is the meaning of all this if not a crumbling of feminine instincts, a defeminization?" (#239).

This brings us to another point: If Nietzsche's "strong" spirit turns out to be not so strong, and if sacrifices need to be made by the "weak" for the "strong" to become stronger, just what is the relationship between the strong and the weak? Why does Nietzsche want woman to continue to play her womanly role? Would it not be better for the whole human race to struggle for self-reliance and self-mastery, letting the best man win—the higher man, the one who is the culminating achievement of the struggle of a multitude of wills, to dominate? Or is something else needed for the "strong" to become strong, something already hinted at in the previous section, something that would undermine the distinction between strong and weak entirely?

In "Positions," I relate Nietzsche's text to the two positions I laid out in Chapter 3. I argue that Nietzsche's notion of the will to power represents an attempt to speak from the feminine position. In his attention to the pulse of life that defies categories, to the continual becoming that cannot be contained, he attempts to take into account aspects of experience denied by the extreme of the masculine position.[44] This attempt brings him up against the limits of masculine identity. If woman is to exercise her feminine instincts in his service, then he must be man enough to subject her to his service, to command. And yet how can he command when faced with the danger of the great hunt—his own dissolution?

My contention is that Nietzsche, despite his breakdown of the category of "woman," still cannot allow himself to exercise what he refers to as "feminine instincts." What for him falls under the category of "feminine instincts" indicates his version of gender categories. That what he puts in that category is what he is not—what is forbidden to him as a man—indicates an oppositional self-strategy at work. By laying out the elements of the text that speak from the two positions and by examining the conflict alluded to in "The Puzzle" and "Woman" within the framework of those elements, I hope to go beyond Nietzsche's new dichotomy of strong and weak. The questions my analysis addresses are, what constitutes for Nietzsche "feminine" or "weak" instincts, instincts he will not allow himself; and how would these instincts enable him to surrender his solitude for a *community* of free spirits?

The Positions

In Part 1, Nietzsche undermines the notion of a fixed human essence by looking at human beings as a process that makes use of concepts and values to enhance the development of will to power. Out of the vast range of possibilities open to a human being, who that human being is, her identity, is an effect of her morality—that which ranks her instincts so that the order of command is clear, conflict between instincts is reduced, and action is facilitated. By undermining Truth, dogmatism, and Platonism, he intends to challenge the belief that there are eternal, transcendent, road maps in the sky by which to guide our identities and our actions. For Nietzsche, not only are

there no such road maps, but also our real guide is the
surging process of life itself, the will to power in whose
service we create our concepts and moralities, rather than
vice versa.[45]

Nietzsche's concept of will to power can be considered a
way of representing the source of individual life in
chaotic flux. As such, it is his version of the origin—not a
gift from God the Father above who beckons us onward, but
the underground turbulence of life in all its bewildering
multiplicity. Phenomena, rather than being the pale reflection of an eternally unchanging realm, are the result
of a chaotic, irrational upsurge of life always struggling to
surge ever higher and more forcefully, taking the most
expedient, rather than most "rational," forms for getting
there. Thus, there is no such thing as a "soul," a "motive,"
a "law," a "right" or a "wrong"—there is only the will to
power that creates the concepts and values that will feed
its continual need to grow and expand.

The recognition that all rankings, all boundaries, all
categories are created undermines and subverts the authority of the Symbolic order of social meaning in favor of
the concrete specificity of life. The recognition of the
guiding force of the will to power is the "feminine"
recognition that life is growth and becoming and that the
Symbolic order should be subordinate to becoming—life-
enhancing rather than life-denying. Nietzsche speaks
from the feminine position in his attentiveness to the
pulse of life that defies all categorizations and that says no
more than "I want to live." It is that pulse of concrete living things that the feminine responds to—the
"indiscriminate" response she makes to enhance the
chances of any living thing simply because it makes that
appeal.[46] In valuing the will to power over morality itself,
in saying that the latter should serve the former, Nietzsche
is taking the feminine position of putting the concrete
specificity of actual living things before the preservation
of eternal ideals. He is advocating the destruction of an
outmoded Symbolic order that impedes rather than fosters
the growth of the human beings subject to it. In doing so,
he is listening with a "third" ear, an ear that can tune in to
the subtleties of experience that elude the Symbolic—
experiences that would take humanity higher if given the

nourishment they deserve. This is the kind of sensitivity a woman gives to her loved ones, attending to the inarticulate longing of each, giving her loved ones a hearing, and through her mirroring, providing new aspects of experience, of life, the response the loved one needs to give him- or herself form.

But this attempt to incorporate aspects of the feminine position into his work put Nietzsche into a quandary. The oppositional strategy of masculine identity relies on the repetition of fixed relationships for continuity. The Symbolic order is a static order of fixed positions by which one can place one's self and others. Thus, in defying the Symbolic Nietzsche is defying the very order that sustains his identity. Nietzsche refers to just this dilemma in speaking of the dangers of the hunt. How can he defy the mechanical repetition of fixed patterns and sterile con-cepts for the subtle richness of experiences that elude it, without perishing in the attempt? His response is to brave the danger of chaotic flux "like a man." Single-handedly and boldly he must go forth, leaving the charted realm of the Symbolic order behind, and create a new order on his own. He will be "strong," he will be "noble," he will play the "creator" on his own, making a map of positions as he goes.

Thus, Nietzsche's new dichotomies and his order of rank can be seen as aspects of the masculine position. They are attempts to maintain identity through the imposition of one's own creations, the imposition of a new self/other pattern that one can repeat in the same way one could re-peat the old one. That this strategy cannot work is attested to by the contradictory nature of these dichotomies. In a world of flux and becoming how can any fixed self/other pattern hold? If one is to navigate a new realm of life ex-perience that follows no rules and adheres to no order, one needs a new strategy. We all know of such a strategy—we have all experienced a time where every moment was new and there were no patterns to repeat—and yet we managed to create an identity from a realm of chaotic flux that served to order the whole of our existence. I am referring to infancy. To create a new identity, one more responsive to the subtler aspects of life that elude the Symbolic order as we know it, one might take some hints from that earlier experience. I think Nietzsche has done that in his fresh responsiveness to elusive aspects of experience. But in his need to maintain the masculine illusion of self-sufficiency, he has overlooked another self-strategy and the vital role played by connectedness in it. To brave chaotic flux "like a man" one must overlook the other self-strategy because it requires exercising those "feminine instincts" Nietzsche is so loath for women to give up.

The extreme of the masculine position would have us ignore chaotic flux in order to crank out mechanical patterns based on the repetition of pre-fixed categories. The extreme of the feminine position involves surrendering to that flux to the point of losing all sense of self, of things, of continuity or order at all. Nietzsche, by trying to incorporate some of the feminine position into the masculine one, is struggling to bring order to flux—to maintain an identity and meaning while being faithful to every last nuance of concrete life—an impossible task, and he knows it. But at the very least he wants us to do a better job of it than we are doing. He wants us to leave behind some of our old guideposts and to find a morality in keeping with a new range of subtleties, aspects of human experience that once attended to could allow new forms of life to flourish. The "man" with the masterful and domineering will to power imposes order upon flux. He is the great hunter who leaves the Symbolic behind to play creator in an uncharted realm. The woman, with her "feminine instincts," has no wish to impose her will. Instead, she surrenders the desire for order and mastery and gives herself up to the life around her; she does not surrender her will to power, but she surrenders to the responses life evokes from her, responses that defy all order and all categorization. A woman who finds her perfection in service to a man is one who has forsaken the repetition of a self/other pattern and instead lets a man evoke whatever response comes forth. It is thus that a man can feel himself fathomed to his depths, his every move, his every thought reflected in her responsiveness to him as if she were his mirror.

This same responsiveness is a crucial feature of the mother/infant dyad from which the infant's original self is precipitated. Here, the reciprocal responsiveness of the two form a whole in which meaning is generated in the interest of life. The infant, rather than repeating a self/other pattern of its own, conforms to the other of the mother's self/other pattern. If the mother is reasonably nurturing, the self/other pattern she imposes will not be that of the extreme male position but one that is responsive to the infant's cues and bodily needs. Thus, although she structures her experiences via the Symbolic order, she will ignore or subvert that order in the interest of enhancing the life of the infant. A man who finds a woman to possess will obtain some of the benefits of the infant/mother relationship. Her responsiveness will mirror him the way his mother did, allowing him a similar feeling of connectedness, of being known ("fathomed"). But if he cannot lay aside the need for repetition of a fixed self/other pattern, if he cannot brave the terrors of flux within the safety of another's embrace, he will never be able to leave the restrictions of the Symbolic order behind.

What Nietzsche has overlooked in his call for the higher man is that the only way the human race can evolve is together. No one man can do it alone—no matter how "strong" or "noble." There is a simple reason for this. Human beings form and maintain their identity in connectedness; the only way for them to change that identity is in connectedness. Thus far men have been able to veil that fact by denying both their dependency as infants and their continuing dependency on the others in their lives willing to give them the attentive responsiveness they need. If we all desired only to make others conform to our fixed self/other patterns, we would starve for human contact and lose the richness of life. If we all desired only to conform to another's self/other pattern, we would lose all stability. In trying to find a meeting ground for flux and order, Nietzsche, I believe, was struggling to create a new identity, a new subjectivity for himself—one that could respond to the nuances of life as well as make sense of it. On the way to that new subjectivity, his need to maintain a masculine identity steered him into an impasse. Narrowing the distance between the poles of masculine and feminine threatens not only neat categorizations of gender but also our habitual strategies for maintaining self-identity. In braving that task Nietzsche has shown us

some of the pitfalls involved—as well as given us suggestions for where to go from here.

Sartre: *Being   and   Nothingness*

Introduction

In *Being and Nothingness* (Sartre 1956) Sartre also emphasizes a creative moment that determines a Symbolic
order rather than saying we are structured by the
Symbolic. He thus moves away from a masculine position
that would revere the Symbolic as is. Instead he emphasizes the free acts that give rise to Symbolic orders—categories that order experience in light of an individual project.[47]   Sartre also talks about the way one's free acts are
given social meaning by the other who externalizes one's
acts.   Here he is also approaching a feminine position by
recognizing that others play a role in the creation of
meaning (in contrast to a masculine position, which would
deny the part played by the other). He sees the part played
by the other as a completely negative moment, however.

I suggest that although Sartre takes a feminine position
in his refusal to defer to a socially sanctioned Symbolic
order, he does not substitute a desire for fusion experiences for the masculine self-strategy of revering the
Symbolic order. Instead he tries to substitute individual
Symbolic orders. Like Nietzsche, he expects each individual to create a law unto himself—a Symbolic order of his
own that may or may not conflict with the socially sanctioned Symbolic order. Unlike Nietzsche, however, Sartre
does not advocate receptivity to new feelings and bodily
sensations that may subvert one's categories. Sartre assumes that subversion of socially sanctioned categories
must be done through the assertion of categories structured by one's fundamental choice of being.[48]   Thus Sartre
proposes that the law of categories represented by the
Symbolic order should come from each individual.

The Puzzle

Sartre ends Part 4 of *Being and Nothingness* with the following passage: "Each human reality is at the same time a direct project to metamorphose its own For-itself into an In-itself-For-itself and a project of the appropriation of the world as a totality of being-in-itself, in the form of a fundamental quality. . . . Thus the passion of man is the reverse of that of Christ, for man loses himself as man in order that God may be born. But the idea of God is contradictory and we lose ourselves in vain. Man is a useless passion" (p. 784). Sartre's pessimistic conclusion that humanity's fundamental project is contradictory and therefore unachievable stems from his view that consciousness cannot be its own foundation. Humans want to transform the negating activity of the for-itself (consciousness) that distinguishes them from inert matter into a self-causing substance. Mere for-itself is nothingness—it gives the in-itself (brute existence) meaning by revealing it in the light of an end that has not yet been achieved.[49] Thus, for-itself introduces possibility into the fullness of being that is sufficient unto itself. But in so doing, human reality also posits itself as a lack—as a being that is not yet what it is.[50] Its fundamental project is to retain the freedom of making choices among its possibilities and yet to attain the self-sufficiency of a complete being that no longer lacks, hence, Sartre's alternate description of this project as the project of being God.[51]

The question I will investigate here is, why is the Sartre of *Being and Nothingness* so drawn to a project that he claims to be doomed to failure? A careful reading of Part 4 of *Being and Nothingness* reveals that Sartre overlooks a fairly obvious way in which human consciousness can be its own foundation. I will sketch out his views on for-itself, being-for-others, and the project of becoming in-itself-for-itself in order to highlight the dilemma as Sartre sees it.

Sartre posits a split between for-itself and in-itself. Human consciousness is consciousness *of* something. This something is transphenomenal being.[52] That is, consciousness reveals phenomena in the light of the possibilities it projects before it. Thus, phenomena are revealed only with reference to a concrete, individual project. But the being of such phenomena is beyond all individual projects. This in-itself "is an immanence which cannot realize itself, an affirmation which cannot affirm itself, an activity which cannot act, because it is glued to itself" (p. 27). It is beyond all negation or affirmation, passivity or activity, transition or becoming: "It is full positivity. It knows no otherness; it never posits itself as *other-than-another-being*. It can support no connection with the other. It is itself indefinitely and it exhausts itself in being" (p. 29).

For-itself, in contrast, is an escape from the in-itself that gives the latter meaning: "It is only because I escape the in-itself by nihilating myself toward my possibilities that this in-itself can take on value as cause or motive. Causes and motives have meaning only inside a projected ensemble which is precisely an ensemble of non-existents. And this ensemble is ultimately myself as transcendence" (p. 564).

Human reality perpetually puts its being into question. It thereby opens a hole in the heart of being by considering itself vis-à-vis nonbeing. That is, human reality, nihilating what it is by projecting itself toward possibilities that it is not, gives meaning to itself and its situation. My place, my past, the things around me, are all interpreted in view of the end toward which I project my possibilities. Each human project has its own empirical shape, but all share the fundamental project of becoming in-itself-for-itself. This project can take different forms according to the type of relation to being a for-itself adopts. That is, the for-itself projects an ensemble of nonexistents in light of its initial choice of a particular kind of relation to being. Choices of concrete objects of desire are integrated as secondary structures into this totality. Although the initial choice can be changed, such a change cannot be achieved through mere reflection. In fact, merely willing a change would be in bad faith.[53] It is action taken in the spontaneous upsurge of the for-itself that most accurately reflects one's project in its totality.

Each for-itself finds itself in a world that includes others. These others also have the freedom to nihilate what is, in light of their possibilities.[54] When I see an

Other in the distance, "suddenly an object has appeared which has stolen the world from me. Everything is in place; everything still exists for me; but everything is traversed by an invisible flight and fixed in the direction of a new object" (p. 343). When there is no Other in my vicinity, the world stretches out around me according to *my* project, and things are understood as obstacles or as helpful in light of the possibilities *I* am reaching for. I am the center of my world. But when I see an Other on the horizon I become aware that my perspective is not the only one. The Other has his own perspective, one that, for example, places the bench that is thirty feet from *me* two feet from *him*. Furthermore, the for-itself is responsible for revealing the Other's conduct in the world as techniques (p. 668).[55] As I watch the Other sit on the bench, I turn what he lives as a free project into a technique that exists outside of him. The world "is revealed to me . . . by collective and already constituted techniques which aim at making me apprehend the world in a form whose meaning has been defined outside of me" (p. 657). By manifesting certain techniques, I manifest my membership in various collectivities such as the human race, a nation, a professional or family group. But in choosing my acts I always go beyond the internal technical organization that expresses my memberships, toward myself—the transcendent me of my individual project. Thus, although the for-itself gives the Other an exterior that makes objective rules of human conduct, this conduct is always grounded in the free acts of individuals with individual projects.

As a for-itself living with other for-itselves, I am aware of other freedoms that create perspectives different from my own and that can exteriorize my behavior in the light of their own projects. Exteriorizing another's behavior gives that behavior meaning that can form techniques I can choose to take on or reject in living my own project. Thus, a new dimension of being arises, being-for-others: "By means of the upsurge of the Other there appear certain determinations which I *am* without having chosen them. . . . All this I am *for the Other* with no hope of apprehending this meaning which I have *outside*, and, still more important, with no hope of changing it. Speech alone will inform me of what I am" (p. 671).

The situation that I reveal in the free choice of my project is alienated from me and comes "to exist as a form in itself for the Other" (p. 673). Because I exist as a for-itself for other for-itselves, I can be freely apprehended by them in light of ends that are not my own. Because the Other apprehends me as an Other-as-object, reducing my free conduct into an objective form, he limits my freedom. The Other tells me who I am, and although there is an infinity of attitudes I can assume with respect to what I am told, I cannot not assume some attitude. The things others say I am (e.g., ugly, brilliant, a coward, a Jew) cannot actually refer to me because I am a free nothingness that projects itself toward its possibilities. But I can choose to interiorize such "unrealizables" by incorporating them in the structure of my free projects (p. 678). These unrealizables cannot be realized because as a being that lacks and is always projecting itself toward what it is not, I am never a completed being that can see myself from the outside. Instead, I am always waiting for a "repose which would be *being* and no longer a waiting for being . . . that is, evidently, a plenitude of the type 'in-itself-for-itself'" (p. 688).

Death, far from enabling me to attain this repose, is the triumph of the Other's point of view over my own: "Death reapprehends all this subjective which while it 'lived' defended itself against exteriorization, and death deprives it of all subjective meaning in order to hand it over to any *objective* meaning which the Other is pleased to give to it" (p. 696). As long as I am alive I can escape what I *am* for the Other. I can demonstrate that whatever the Other discovers about me can be surpassed by projecting myself toward other ends. Thus, I can prove that "my dimension of being-for-myself is incommensurable with my dimension of being-for-others" (p. 695). But once death has canceled my possibilities, I exist only through the Other. I can no longer nihilate my outside with the absolute, subjective positing of a freedom that interprets itself and its world in the light of its own, freely chosen project.

The ultimate goal of the for-itself is not death but *being-as-for-itself* (p. 723). It wants to be a being that is what it is (rather than always be projecting itself toward what it lacks), but it also wants to be this being as consciousness.

The fundamental value guiding this project is "the ideal of a consciousness which would be the foundation of its own being-in-itself by the pure consciousness it would have of itself" (p. 724). Thus, the for-itself wants to be an in-itself that founds its existence by constituting that existence in the free choice of itself. Like the in-itself, such a for-itself would be complete, lacking nothing, a full positivity. But unlike the in-itself, such a for-itself would choose to be exactly what it is and constitute its very existence in the making of that choice. Like God, such an in-itself-for-itself would be a self-causing being, completely free and always choosing, yet already realized and always complete.

For Sartre, the project of becoming in-itself-for-itself is doomed from the start. Because "choice and consciousness are one and the same thing" (p. 595) and in-itself is an immanence that cannot realize itself, the two realms of being are radically opposed. Consciousness cannot found itself because it must choose itself by projecting itself toward nonexistents. Once it failed to pose such transcendent ideals, it would lapse into the inert immanence of an in-itself that cannot choose. The only way for consciousness to escape the in-itself is to negate it. The only way for consciousness to escape the Others that would give it an objective form not of its choosing is to negate that form by continuing to engage in a project of its own choice. And yet, if for-itself can give others an outside meaning, revealing an Other in the same way it reveals an in-itself, then a natural solution to the project of in-itself-for-itself emerges. Although an individual for-itself may not be able to found its own consciousness, perhaps an interlocking network of human consciousnesses could. Obviously Sartre did not see this as a possibility.[56] In "Woman," I relate his discussion of appropriation and the quality of "slimy" to the category of "woman" that emerges from his text. In "The Positions," I argue that his rigid adherence to his version of gender categories blocks him from resolving the dilemma he depicts, despite the suggestions implicit in his text for just such a resolution.

Woman

Like Kierkegaard, Sartre does not discuss "woman as such," but he mentions women and the feminine in enough places for us to reconstruct what "woman" means to him, at least within the confines of *Being and Nothingness*. The sections most pertinent to my present topic are found in Part 4, Chapter 2. There Sartre introduces his conception of "existential psychoanalysis." Sartre does not propose that human behavior can be understood by tracing its origins to sexuality or the will to power, as traditional psychoanalysis does. Instead, he proposes understanding human behavior in view of the original way in which each individual has chosen his being. Because the fundamental human project is to become in-itself-for-itself, desire of what one lacks can be understood in view of this project of being that which no longer lacks. An empirical study of concrete desires will indicate various approaches to this project. A "thousand empirical examples" (p. 736) show that desire comes in three categories—to do, to have, to be. "To do" reduces to "to have" (p. 742) which reduces to "the desire to be related to a certain object in a certain *relation of being*" (p. 751).[57] Thus, a discussion of appropriation reveals various ways of approaching the ideal of in-itself-for-itself.

Sartre discusses various kinds of appropriation. In all forms of appropriation, for-itself attempts to become its own foundation by appropriating an object that is indifferent to consciousness (thus an in-itself) at the same time that the object represents for-itself by belonging to for-itself (thus an in-itself-for-itself). A thing that is mine is *me*, because possession of a particular object means "*to have for myself*; that is, to be the unique end of the existence of the object" (p. 752). Because possession means I have exclusive rights to utilize the objects I possess in light of my own project, I found my possessions in their being by creating their meaning. As this creation is an emanation of the transcendent me of my chosen possibilities, the object is me. Thus "in possession, I am my own foundation in so far as I exist in an in-itself" (p. 755).

In the appropriation of objects of knowledge, "what is seen is possessed; to see is to *deflower*. . . . The unknown object is given as immaculate, as virgin, comparable to a *whiteness*. It has not yet 'delivered up' its secret; man has not yet 'snatched' its secret away from it." I transform the known into me by appropriating it in the form of a thought that receives its existence from me. And yet because it is also an objective fact that will never lose its form, at the same time that it is "assimilated, transformed into myself, and . . . entirely *me*," it is also "impenetrable, untransformable, entirely smooth, with the indifferent nudity of a body which is beloved and caressed in vain" (p. 740).

In the appropriating activity of the scientist, the artist, and the sportsman, the object of appropriation (knowledge, artistic medium, or physical environment) appears "simultaneously to be a kind of subjective emanation of ourselves and yet to remain in an indifferently external relation with us." In such activity we attempt to found the existence of an in-itself that is me because it is mine: "The 'mine' appeared to us then as a relation of being intermediate between the absolute interiority of the me and the absolute exteriority of the not-me. There is within the same syncretism a self becoming not-self and a not-self becoming self" (p. 751).

Furthermore, "each possessed object which raises itself on the foundation of the world manifests the entire world, just as a beloved woman manifests the sky, the shore, the sea, which surrounded her when she appeared. To appropriate this object is then to appropriate the world symbolically" (p. 760). In the drive to become that which does not lack, for-itself wants to appropriate not only a particular object but also the world. As long as I am choosing myself by negating what I am in order to project myself toward what I am not, I cannot be in-itself. But if I can appropriate the whole world, I can found my own existence in the in-itself. That is, I can reveal all that is as the result of the free choice of a transcendent me that turns out to be exactly what the in-itself is.

But appropriation is merely symbolic: The objects I make mine are only symbolic representations of me. No matter how many objects I appropriate, I am still nothingness—a free for-itself that must be what it is not. Appropriation of others in sexual relationships is as

doomed to failure as the appropriation of knowledge of
things: "The lover's dream is to identify the beloved object
with himself and still preserve for it its own individuality;
let the Other become me without ceasing to be the Other"
(p. 740). This "impossible synthesis of assimilation and an
assimilated which maintains its integrity" (p. 739) can
never come to pass. As long as for-itself can choose itself
only by negating itself in light of what it is not, for the
Other to become me, (s)he would have to become the nothingness of a for-itself.

The attempt to attain in-itself-for-itself through appropriation takes an interesting twist in Sartre's discussion of
the "slimy."[58]   In the third and final section of Chapter 2,
Sartre proposes a psychoanalysis of things (p. 765).
Things have qualities that reveal being in certain ways. If
we bring out the ontological meaning of qualities, we can
understand how particular qualities symbolize being. We
can then better understand an individual's original choice
of being by noting the particular attitudes he takes with
respect to particular qualities. To give us an idea of how
such an ontology might work, Sartre explores the meaning
of the slimy. Here, appropriation fails, and the "mine" that
related absolute interiority with absolute exteriority turns
into "a possibility that the In-itself might absorb the For-
itself" (p. 776). That is, the project to attain in-itself-for-itself is reversed into the attack of an in-itself on the for-itself that would "draw the For-itself into its contingency,
into its indifferent exteriority, into its foundationless existence" (p. 776).

Just as Sartre's discussion of appropriation was laced
with references to women as objects to be possessed, his
discussion of the slimy is laced with references to the
feminine that would engulf one. Both discussions refer to
a realm of being between the absolute freedom of the for-
itself and the absolute immanence of the in-itself. Making
something "mine" was a symbolic attempt to bridge the two
realms that led to failure. The slimy symbolizes a being "in
which the for-itself is swallowed up by the in-itself" (p.
783). This ambiguous substance is "between two states" (p.
774). Ironically, although attempts to bridge the two
realms in an appropriation that would lead to in-itself-for-
itself are doomed to failure, attempts made by the in-itself

to swallow up the for-itself seem more likely to succeed. References to women and the feminine in the discussion of appropriation refer us to the ideal, if doomed, project of becoming in-itself-for-itself; however, references to women and the feminine in the discussion of the slimy refer us to dangerous aspects of an ambiguous being between two states. In the former "woman" was in the appropriate relationship to for-itself; in the latter "woman" threatens to derail the for-itself's project entirely. In possession the for-itself remains the assimilating and creative power. "It is the For-itself which absorbs the In-itself. In other words, possession asserts the primacy of the For-itself in the synthetic being In-itself-For-itself. Yet here is the slimy reversing the terms; the For-itself is suddenly *compromised*. . . . It is a soft, yielding action, a moist and feminine sucking. . . . I am no longer the Master in *arresting* the process of appropriation" (p. 776). Thus, "slime is the revenge of the In-itself. A sickly-sweet, feminine revenge" (p. 777).

The horrible image of a consciousness become slimy haunts us. Such a consciousness would be held back from the freedom of a for-itself projecting itself toward its possibilities. It would "be slyly held back by the invisible suction of the past and . . . would have to assist in its own slow dissolution in this past which it was fleeing, would have to aid in the invasion of its project by a thousand parasites until finally it completely lost itself" (p. 778). This type of being does not exist any more than the in-itself-for-itself, but just as the latter is an ideal toward which I project myself, the former is an "antivalue" from which I flee. This antivalue represents the kind of being one does not want to become, "a threatening mode of being which must be avoided" (p. 779).

Through these discussions we can begin to make sense of Sartre's refusal to explore the possibility that human consciousnesses could found one another. It is one thing for a for-itself to attempt to appropriate the in-itself. It is entirely another for it to allow itself to be appropriated. The moment a for-itself allows itself to be held back by a "moist and feminine sucking," allows its free project to be invaded by a "thousand parasites," it is compromised. The only acceptable way for a for-itself to approach the project

of becoming in-itself-for-itself is by retaining mastery
throughout.   Such a reading of the project naturally dooms
it from the start.   A for-itself that is forever fleeing in-itself by insisting on its freedom to negate everything that
is will never be able to repose in the objective form
granted it by another.   And yet, in his description of the
antivalue, Sartre himself suggests the form that such repose could take.   In the next section I will set the ultimate
value of the in-itself-for-itself against the antivalue of the
slimy by relating the two to the masculine and feminine
positions of my interpretive framework.   I argue that incorporation of the antivalue of the slimy with the value of
the in-itself-for-itself could resolve the dilemma presented
by man's "useless passion."

The Positions

Sartre's concept of the transphenomenality of being
moves him away from the extreme of the masculine position and brings him closer to a feminine one.   The in-itself
exceeds all categories because there are as many ways of
illuminating it as there are for-itselves to illuminate it.
Reality exceeds the social categories used to define it.   The
specificity of one's life goes beyond those categories.   The
human conduct of particular for-itselves is given objective
forms by others who perceive that behavior from the outside.   Such exteriorization of what were free acts gives rise
to a Symbolic structure of techniques and characteristics
with social significance.   But all that can be said about another's conduct is an exteriorization of that conduct, which
distorts by giving it an outside meaning that cancels out
the free upsurge of an individual project.   In taking various attitudes to the Symbolic, the various techniques and
meaning structures available to one, each person surpasses the Symbolic in choosing his or her own particular
relation to being.   The original choice of one's relation to
being sets the parameters for all one's other choices.   It is
not a rational choice in the normal sense of the word.
There are no possible grounds for making such a choice, as
it is the choice itself that constitutes one's end and thus

one's situation in light of that end. That is, it is this choice that reveals the in-itself and gives it meaning.

Sartre's emphasis on one's absolute freedom of choice challenges the Symbolic's authority to tell me who I am. I do not create a self by taking up a position granted me by the Law of the Father—I create a self by projecting myself toward my own possibilities. I reveal and interpret the positions laid out in the Symbolic in light of an end of my own choosing. Because I am making the choice I make, the positions of the Symbolic appear to me as they do. Sartre rejects any transcendental source of values. My values do not come from God, the Law of the Father, Platonic ideals, or others. Even though meaning structures may exist outside of me, I surpass them in living out my own choice of being. The transcendent me I project in light of the fundamental relation to being I have chosen informs my attitudes to these meaning structures. Thus, in choosing or rejecting the positions offered by the structures that embody social relations, I pass beyond those meaning structures.

My freedom can be experienced only from the inside. Any attempt to characterize it from the outside cancels it out by freezing my choice of being into a technique with an objective form. Such a technique cannot capture the moment of choice in which I hurl myself toward a future of my own making or the possibility that my relation to being could be transformed at any moment, given my next act, my next choice. Thus, my interior life defies all description in the Symbolic. The moment that one's life is exteriorized from the viewpoint of the other, one's possibilities are extinguished. The only thing one cannot choose is whether or not one is free. I am condemned to freedom. When I try to evade my freedom I am in bad faith. To avoid bad faith, I must accept that the choices I make are finally beyond rationality and beyond the comprehension of others. I must accept a freedom so absolute that it has no foundation, no final court of appeal for the fundamental choice of being it makes.[59]

Sartre moves away from the masculine position of someone enthralled by transcendental ideals coming from above to a feminine position with respect to one's own freedom. In both Nietzsche and Kierkegaard there is the feminine element of letting go and allowing themselves to be formed—Nietzsche in his receptivity to the subtlety of experience, to new feelings and sensations that would subvert categories, and Kierkegaard in his receptivity to an incomprehensible God. Sartre emphasizes nothingness, the nothingness that distinguishes the for-itself from the in-itself and thereby saves the for-itself from being meaningless matter.[60] Sartre thus narrowly confines his move toward the feminine position. All three grant a lack of rational foundation for ultimate values, but Nietzsche confronts a seething array of conflicting forces and Kierkegaard confronts the incomprehensible will of God, whereas Sartre confronts nothingness. We do not simply take up a position in the Symbolic; we choose one. And in choosing such a position we authorize it in light of our fundamental project. We have nothing to guide us in choosing our project. We reject the security of being inheritors of the Law of the Father, only to assert that it is our freedom that creates that Law. Thus, Sartre rejects the authority of the Symbolic in order to assert the authority of each individual to create a Law unto himself.

There is a price to be paid for making this move. In fact, far from feeling supremely confident with this new position of power, Sartre is terribly burdened with the responsibility that goes along with it.[61] Now, being a person not only means upholding the Law of the Father, it means creating it. A person must continue to stake out an identity, but with the understanding that the Symbolic given him as aid and support is a fraud. It cannot tell him who he is or how to be because no matter what position he takes up in it, his choice surpasses it. Sartre has reoriented the project of subjectivity by saying that each one of us must posit our own ideals, our own transcendence—and take complete responsibility for it. But it is still nonexistent ideals that pull us away from the in-itself, that allow us to escape the in-itself by negating it. On Sartre's view, each one of us must become the Father of the Law on our own. Having granted to being a transphenomenality that ever threatens to overflow the categories of thought, and having done away with the possibility of a transcendental grounding from above (God) or an instinctual upsurge for grounding from within (such as the will to power), Sartre is left staring straight in the face of a world that threatens to absorb him entirely, with only the negating power of nothingness to protect him.[62]

The slimy is ambiguous, soft, between two realms. It threatens to appropriate the for-itself, to turn the for-itself into the in-itself. It is a feminine sucking that lures the for-itself into forgetting its freedom and its responsibility for creating a Law unto itself. If the for-itself allows the slimy to trap it, it will fail to attain its ideal of in-itself-for-itself, and instead it will be drawn to the anti-ideal of a being in which the foundationless in-itself has priority over the for-itself (p. 778). Both ideals involve an intermediate being between two realms of being. And yet Sartre sets them at opposite poles—one is an ideal to be attained, the other an ideal to flee. But how different are the two ideals? Feminine slime is soft and leechlike. It wants to be an individual and yet allows itself to be dissolved into its past. It invites the for-itself to appropriate it but then compromises the for-itself's appropriating activity. The antivalue of the slimy draws the for-itself into a realm of being where the for-itself's freedom is put into doubt. It is no longer creatively appropriating an object in light of its own project; it is being appropriated. Its freedom is contaminated and the radical split between in-itself and for-itself is compromised. The value of the in-itself-for-itself draws the for-itself into a realm of being where the for-itself's freedom remains intact and the radical split between in-itself and for-itself is maintained.[63]

Sartre undermines the authority of the Symbolic and moves toward a feminine position. "Woman"—soft and leechlike, tending toward dissolution—beckons him to receive her, but he must refuse the invitation. She may accept the ambiguous status of being between two realms, of being both appropriator and appropriated, but he cannot. He can take up a position of receptivity that goes beyond all rational categories only with respect to his own freedom. The pull to forsake his masculine role is apparent, but he resists the temptation by setting up the slimy as an antivalue. He heads resolutely toward an ideal that will allow him to keep his masculine self-strategy intact. Leechlike sucking is feminine. Letting one's project be invaded by a thousand parasites is feminine. In rejecting such feminine strategies Sartre closes out the possibility of a new approach to the ideal of in-itself-for-itself.

If I could accept such feminine strategies, I might not be able to achieve the status of the in-itself in my continual projection of myself toward a transcendent me. But I could freely choose to be founded by other consciousnesses. In receptive attentiveness to another's desire, I could allow myself to be appropriated, to be the in-itself that fulfilled that other's current lack. I could appropriate an other by giving him or her meaning in light of my own project. At the same time I could allow myself to be appropriated by him or her by taking on the meaning (s)he gives me in light of his or her project. If both for-itselves involved remained true to their original choice of being but allowed the concrete form taken by secondary choices to be shaped by the other, they could form a reciprocal relationship. Both would be in-itselves for the other, but both would also exercise their free choice as for-itselves. Two individuals could find the meeting point between two free projects that could grant both repose, if both were receptive to conforming to the desire of the other within the parameters set by their own projects. Each would then be an "emanation" of the other at the same time that each remained in an "indifferently external relation" with the other because each had a project of his/her own that was unaffected by the other's project. Together they would be in-itself-for-itself—all consciousness, yet complete and self-causing. Obviously, such a state of repose could not last for long. But if one took Sartre's project of becoming in-itself-for-itself as a project for humanity as a community rather than for humanity as individuals, one could resolve Sartre's dilemma. A community of consciousnesses each with a unique perspective, each revealing various aspects of other for-itselves and fulfilling various lacks, could conceivably achieve a state of self-causing repose. It may not be a "realistic" project, but it is not the hopeless dead end of a "useless passion."

Conclusion

In this section, I will draw some tentative conclusions from the readings of Kierkegaard, Nietzsche, and Sartre discussed in this chapter, which will be of use in Chapter 5 when I delineate two poles that represent the extremes of masculine and feminine positioning and the self-strategies correlated with these two poles.

Kierkegaard. For Silentio, subverting Symbolic categories involves deferring to the desire of an other, which means using a feminine self-strategy that values satisfying the desire of an other over maintaining Symbolic categories. A masculine self-strategy would sacrifice connectedness in order to maintain a self positioned in the Symbolic.

Once we relate the universal to the Symbolic and the position of Abraham to a feminine position that values deferring to the desire of the other—being what that other desires—over maintaining the Symbolic, we can say that such a priority can lead one to be "taken out of the universal" and fill out what that means. Thus, we can see how the feminine position can jeopardize one's standing in the Symbolic order and therefore jeopardize one's identity. Letting another's desire inform one can take one beyond the universal without destroying one's identity if one receives the desire of the other with faith that one will be returned to the universal.

Nietzsche. Whereas Kierkegaard does not address the question of how one goes about changing Symbolic categories, Nietzsche does. Correlating Nietzsche's values and concepts with the Symbolic, we can take the feminine position as one that chooses to give first place to something other than those values and concepts. Symbolic categories are created not through attentiveness to the desire of an other but through receptiveness to subtle messages of the body. This relates to the desire for body connectedness and responsiveness (Chapter 2) as well as to Irigaray's "sensation-ideas" (Chapter 3).

Sartre. My reading of Sartre revealed a masculine self-strategy that is afraid of losing its legitimacy. If man cannot maintain a masculine self-strategy with respect to woman, he will become what she wants and so lose the ability to position himself. Unlike Kierkegaard and Nietzsche, Sartre does not take up a feminine position with respect to either God or body sensations. Sartre needs to impose categories upon the world. His not being able to see the feminine self-strategy as a viable alternative means that any breakdown in the masculine self-strategy will lead to a failure of identity.

Notes

1. A "deconstructive" reading is a reading that is in the post-structuralist tradition, especially as exemplified by Derrida. I use this term here because it seems appropriate for the kind of interpretive strategy developed here, a strategy in keeping with the Lacanian view of the self as radically contingent and "decentered." For more on deconstruction and its influence on the interpretation of texts, see Derrida (1978), Dews (1987), Felman (1982), Harari (1979), Leitch (1983), Moi (1985), Silverman and Inde (1985), Sturrock (1979), and Taylor (1987).

2. Mark Taylor, in commenting on a paper I gave based on the Kierkegaard section of this chapter, said that the Lacanian notion of "woman" is inseparably bound to the Real and that which eludes binary oppositions. To understand the Lacanian notion of "woman" we would thus need to think through the Lacanian notion of the Real. Woman as the Real is the Goddess, the figure for what cannot be figured, that which is the condition of the possibility of sexual difference as such, an other of a more radical sort than the other of a male/female opposition—an other that is always already excluded from the Symbolic order and yet always speaking through that order. Taylor's comments on "woman" led him to posit Kierkegaard's God as a Goddess; Kierkegaard's divine Other is the maternal Other rather than the transcendent father.

I have not had the space in this work to do justice to Lacan's notion of the Real. Although Taylor's comments are suggestive—especially in light of the ambiguity of positioning with respect to female and divine others in *Fear and Trembling* that I explore—I feel that they enhance rather than challenge my interpretation of *Fear and Trembling*. To suggest, as Taylor has, that Lacan and

Kierkegaard are more interested in the moment of the Real that is irreducibly other, a moment that cannot be domesticated in self/other relations, and to assert that the Real is *irreducibly* other in an oppositional sense, speaks to the male positioning of all three. Woman as the Real, as Goddess, as irreducibly other—the maternal Other that is not oneself—this is precisely the kind of opposition I am challenging in positing both the possibility of connectedness between embodied others and the possibility of generating new meaning in the play space of such connectedness.

3. It is misleading to say decisions in Kierkegaard's sense are made in the aesthetic sphere, as the aesthete prefers to reflect on possibilities, but Kierkegaard also thinks that at this stage there is no actual self to take up a position. See Taylor (1975, 128-130).

4. For writing this section, I found useful the discussions of the differences among the three spheres, their interrelationships, and the positions taken up by various Kierkegaardian pseudonyms in Dunning (1985), Mackey (1972), Malantschuk (1971), and Taylor (1975).

5. Thompson (1967) suggests that Kierkegaard, in writing his pseudonymous works, was engaged in a form of self-therapy designed to provide him relief from the misery of his life. Others (e.g., Croxal 1956 and Taylor 1975) have emphasized Kierkegaard's characterization of these works as a form of "indirect communication" designed to enable the reader to come to a subjective understanding of possibilities for existence. Although Thompson's reading strikes me as a bit crass (reducing Kierkegaard to a patient on the couch), the idea that Kierkegaard was engaged in his own process of self-transformation in the act of writing, at the same time as he was encouraging his readers to engage in that process, is in keeping with my claim that the production of meaning is also a self-constituting process.

6. Dunning claims Silentio's point of view is an ethical interpretation of how the religious stage differs from the ethical (1985, 124).

7. For discussions and/or characterizations of the two Kierkegaardian concepts that I found useful, the "universal" and the "ethical," see Robert Perkins's "For Sanity's Sake: Kant, Kierkegaard, and Father Abraham," Merold Westphal's "Abraham and Hegel," Paul Holmer's "About Being and Person: Kierkegaard's *Fear and Trembling*," and C. Stephen Evans's "Is the Concept of an Absolute Duty Toward God Morally Unintelligible?" all in Perkins (1981).

8. This reading of the ethical realm as involving duty as well as communication is borne out in *Fear and Trembling* by Silentio's emphasis on revealing oneself: "His [the single individual's] ethical task is to work himself out of his hiddenness and to become disclosed in the universal" (Kierkegaard 1983, 82). See also David Wren's "Abraham's Silence and the Logic of Faith" and Mark Taylor's "Sounds of Silence," both in Perkins (1981).

9. See Lemaire (1977) for a discussion of Lacan's "Symbolic" as a term referring to a hierarchy of both social positions and symbolic/linguistic codes. Some have argued against any such "facile" correlation. Since I am arguing here that a social position is the function of taking up a position as a grammatical subject within symbolic/linguistic codes, however, I feel the correlation is warranted.

10. The story of Abraham and Isaac is given in Genesis 22:1-18. Biblical comments on it include Hebrews 11:17-19 and James 2:21-23.

11. For a historical discussion of some interpretations of the Abraham/Isaac story preceding Kierkegaard's, see Louis Jacobs's "The Problem of the *Akedah* in Jewish Thought" and David Pailin's "Abraham and Isaac: A Hermeneutical Problem Before Kierkegaard," both in Perkins (1981).

12. The positioning of the beloved as the other in my discussion is not entirely unproblematic. I am primarily interested in the analogy/disanalogy of lover/beloved relationships with the Abraham/God relationship. It is because of loving someone the lover cannot have according to the strictures of the universal that he feels the impulse to defy the universal, just as it is Abraham's love for and desire to maintain connectedness with God that lead Abraham to defy the universal. As we will see, however, in the discussion of the sketch about the lad/princess relationship, the lad as the knight of faith can get the princess "by virtue of the absurd," just as Abraham can get his son back "by virtue of the absurd." Here the lover/beloved relationship is more in keeping with the Abraham/Isaac relationship than with the Abraham/God relation. The possibility for consummation of a male/female relationship is undermined by the only sketch that suggests it because that sketch situates the beloved in the Isaac position rather than the God position. Just as Abraham cannot communicate his connectedness with God to Isaac, the lad cannot communicate his connectedness with God to the princess. This leaves full translation of their union into the universal an impossibility.

13. On the terms of the theory of self I developed here, we could put this situation as follows: Given who he is and who the princess is, connection between the two is forbidden. The self/other patterning the lad uses to maintain self-continuity does not allow him to have the princess as an object that can satisfy his desire. For the connectedness of satisfied desire, either the lad or the princess would have to shift positions. Such a shift of position would involve a rupture in identity that would defy rational self-understanding. And yet, the lad loves the princess as an embodied other in a way that defies all such positioning.

14. Again, on my terms, we might put this thus: He constitutes himself as a self that desires this other, the princess. Instead of canceling out his felt response to the princess by denying his love, he chooses to remember her, despite the disruption this causes his self/other patterning.

15. On my terms: His self/other patterning vis-à-vis embodied others remains the same, but he retains the self created in contact with the princess by maintaining a spiritual inner self distinct from the outer self that navigates the universal of social positionality.

16. Mark Taylor argues in "Sounds of Silence" (in Perkins 1981) that although silence is a necessity in the immediate moment of the aesthetic sphere and in the religious sphere, the ethical person must speak: "The absence of individual selfhood and the inability to use language necessitate the silence of aesthetic immediacy. . . . The direct, unmediated radically privatized individualized relation of the believer to God cannot be conveyed in the universal categories of thought and language" (p. 186); "the ethicist argues that a person is duty bound to speak, to come out of concealment and to reveal publicly the ground of his deeds. Silence is a moral transgression in which one refuses to express himself in terms of universality and clings to particularity" (p. 180).

17. This point is made by Silentio's sketch of the story of Agamemnon (Kierkegaard 1983, 87). Agamemnon is a "tragic hero" rather than a knight of faith because his actions are readily intelligible to us. His having to sacrifice his daughter, Iphigenia, was tragic. Killing her was not in keeping with the ethical commitment to love one's daughter. But since he did it because of the "higher" ethical consideration of saving a whole city, we can accept his act as an act of sacrifice.

18. For a discussion of the merman's four alternatives in terms of silence see Taylor's "Sounds of Silence," in Perkins (1981).

19. In my terms, such translation comes down to adopting a position as a subject that is intelligible to oneself and others.

20. Again, in my terms, the interests of an absolute relation to the absolute would be the desire for the pleasure of connectedness with an other that defies the possibilities for positioning available to one in the Symbolic.

21. As an aesthete, the merman is engaged in poeticizing the woman to be the other that will satisfy his lust. Her innocence disarms him into wanting to make a commitment to her. This takes him into the ethical sphere.

22. C. Stephen Evans (1983) argues that the ethical person determined to maintain commitments and live up to an ethical ideal is doomed to failure and thus to feel guilt for being unable to become what she has taken responsibility to become. Such guilt pushes the ethical person into the religious sphere because of the realization that the only way toward salvation from sin (one's inevitable failure to be all one could be) is through the grace of God—i.e., through recognition of one's dependence on an Other.

23. As an aesthete, the merman has no self. He is at the mercy of fleeting desires. His positioning is that of one who attempts to avoid all positioning entirely. For discussions of this kind of positioning of the aesthete in terms of a failure to achieve selfhood, see Taylor (1975).

24. "Imagine Sarah to be a man, and the demonic is immediately present. The proud, noble nature can bear everything, but one thing it cannot bear—it cannot bear sympathy. In it there is a humiliation that can be inflicted on a person only by a higher power" (Kierkegaard 1983, 104).

25. Dunning (1985) demonstrates that self-development from one sphere of existence to the next can be traced in the pseudonymous works as a complicated dialectical development of inner and outer natures and of self and other that (ideally) ends up in the sphere of existence Kierkegaard calls religiousness B. On his view, one's inner and outer natures are furthest apart in the aesthetic and religious spheres of life and are closest together in the ethical sphere. Commentators on Kierkegaard have criticized him for stressing the inwardness of religiousness B (the ultimate goal of selfhood) in a way that renders any prospect for community problematic. For example, Mackey comments: "The existence of other men presents him [the religious man] not with a public in which he is firmly set as a part sustained by an organic whole, but only with further possibilities—beckoning, tempting, or threatening—that he must take into

the gamut of his inner life. . . . His own inwardness is the only reality . . . with which he is properly occupied" (1972, 190).

26. This comes out most clearly in the *Birth of Tragedy*
(Nietzsche 1968b) where Nietzsche draws a distinction between the
Dionysian and the Apollonian. In this work he seems to suggest
that the Dionysian is the primal state of existence—a state of pure
undifferentiated flux ("the objectification of a Dionysian state . . .
represents . . . the shattering of the individual and his fusion with
primal being" [65]; "the primordial contradiction and primordial
pain in the heart of the primal unity . . . beyond and prior to all
phenomena" [55]). It is therefore real in a way that the Apollonian
attempts to organize that flux are not: "For Apollo wants to grant
repose to individual beings precisely by drawing boundaries between them and by again and again calling these to mind as the most
sacred laws of the world, with his demands for self-knowledge and
measure" (72); "the Apollonian tears man from his orgiastic self-
annihilation and blinds him to the universality of the Dionysian
process, deluding him to the belief that he is seeing a single image
of the world" (128).

27. With the renewed interest in Nietzsche there have been up-
dated readings that argue that Nietzsche went beyond an
Apollonian/Dionysian dichotomy. That is, although in his earliest
work, *The Birth of Tragedy*, Nietzsche seems to argue that "reality"
is ultimately chaotic and anything we say about it no more than a
dream or illusion, his later works go beyond even this appear-
ance/reality split to assert that there is nothing beyond appearances. Thus, people like Nehemas (1985) and Megill (1985) argue
that Nietzsche's perspectivism comes down to an aesthetic theory of
truth.

Nietzsche associates Dionysian chaos with the "feminine": "By
the mystical triumphant cry of Dionysus the spell of individuation
is broken, and the way lies open to the Mothers of Being, to the innermost heart of things" (*The Birth of Tragedy* [1968b, 99-100]).
Also see Kelly Oliver's discussions of the "feminine" in Nietzsche
(Oliver 1984, 1988). In keeping with my reading of the female
position as one that attends to bodily sensations of the other in
order to satisfy the other's desire, I take Nietzsche's concept of
Dionysian chaos as life experience beyond the generalizing scope of
language. Thus, my notion of Dionysian chaos is not something beyond appearances, a reality out of our reach; rather, it is intrinsic
to human experience. Also see Jean Granier's "Nietzsche's

Conception of Chaos" and "Perspectivism and Interpretation," both in Allison (1985).

28. See the section of "On Truth and Lie in an Extra-Moral Sense" published in Nietzsche (1968a) and Hinman's article on Nietzsche's view of metaphor (1982). Hinman argues that Nietzsche felt all concepts are metaphorical since no two experiences are the same. Thus, Nietzsche breaks down the distinction between literal and metaphorical language: "The categories and concepts in terms of which we order experience have no more epistemic justification than other metaphors, except for the fact that we have forgotten their metaphorical origins and let them harden into normative measures of reality itself" (p. 189). Also see Kofman (1972).

29. "With a creative hand they reach for the future, and all that is and has been becomes a means for them, an instrument, a hammer. Their 'knowing' is *creating*, their creating is a legislation, their will to truth is—*will to power*" (*Beyond Good and Evil*, #211 [Nietzsche 1968b, 326]). Also see *Beyond Good and Evil*, #260, and "On the Thousand and One Goals" in *Thus Spoke Zarathustra* (Nietzsche 1966).

30. See *Beyond Good and Evil*, #246. Schutte comments: "One might say that the self engaged in authentic understanding of itself needs to have a fine ear for the tunes that the body and the unconscious are playing in it and for it" (1984, 46). Kofman, in a talk she gave at a Nietzsche conference (University of Massachusetts, Amherst, spring 1986), referred to Nietzsche's "third ear" as the intuitive ear of woman that situates itself beyond metaphysical oppositions of truth and error, good and bad, clarity and obscurity. See Lorraine et al. (1986). Also see Derrida's discussion of Nietzsche's "ear" in *Otobiographies* (1984).

31. All quotes from Nietzsche in the text are from *Beyond Good and Evil* (Nietzsche 1968b). I cite section numbers from this work.

32. For a discussion of the irrationality of the will to power, see Alphonso Lingis's "The Will to Power" in Allison (1985).

33. For discussion of Nietzsche's nihilism see Deleuze (1983) and Maurice Blanchot's "The Limits of Experience: Nihilism" and Eric Blondel's "Nietzsche: Life as Metaphor," both in Allison (1985).

34. We could say that although Nietzsche does not explicitly address the desire of an other in the text, the speaking "I" of his text subverts conventional language in order to respond attentively to the desire of his own Other. That is, repetition of the same self/other pattern is thwarted in order to attend to and attempt to

reflect the barely audible, barely intelligible signals of an Other not yet incorporated into such patterning. This Other, made up of all aspects of his experience not yet incorporated into his self-system, is a bit more amorphous than Kierkegaard's God, who at least desires specific things of his creations.

35. "Whatever makes them rule and triumph and shine, to the awe and envy of their neighbors, that is to them the high, the first, the measure, the meaning of all things" ("On the Thousand and One Goals," *Thus Spoke Zarathustra* [Nietzsche 1966, 58]).

36. "Your love of life shall be love of your highest hope; and your highest hope shall be the highest thought of life. Your highest thought, however, you should receive as a command from me—and it is: man is something that shall be overcome" ("On War and Warriors," *Thus Spoke Zarathustra* [Nietzsche 1966, 48]).

37. Schutte argues that there are two uses of the will-to-power notion in Nietzsche: "In one case, power is used in the sense of domination, whereas in the other it is used in the sense of recurring energy" (1984, 76). She relates the former to Nietzsche's notion of the higher man of *Beyond Good and Evil* who overcomes morality and the latter to the overman of *Thus Spoke Zarathustra* who engages in the self-overcoming of morality: "Self-overcoming involves the overcoming of the Apollonian principle of individuation and drive to permanence in favor of the greater reality of the Dionysian flow of existence in which the boundaries between subject and object, time and eternity disappear" (1984, 86). Schutte feels that Nietzsche's analysis of nihilism was not radical enough to get him beyond the dualisms of strong versus weak, master versus slave (p. 190). She further claims that this failure manifests itself in his depiction of love between the sexes (the sex drive seen as an instinct of domination [p. 177]) and in his tendency to distrust the human need for community (p. 180).

38. For interesting discussions of Nietzsche's "deconstruction" of "woman" see Derrida (1979), Krell (1986), and Oliver (1984, 1988).

39. See Derrida's *Spurs* (1979) and Oliver's rendition of Derrida's position (1984).

40. Of course, man, in his attempts to assume self-sufficiency, must evade this feeling of lack through mastery. It is woman, or Truth, that is dependent on him and his mastery and not vice versa, and it is he who possesses them. By mastering both of them, he will finally be the whole man that he is supposed to be. Despite Nietzsche's "deconstruction" here of the notions of "truth" and

"woman," we will see that he is still drawn to the notions of mastery and possession.

41. "The 'world,' 'essence' are themselves texts written by a particular type of will. The idea of an original music of the world is replaced by an original text of which human texts function only as metaphors: all text becomes correlated with an interpretation that constitutes a determined sense, provisional, symptomatic of the domination of the world and other types of life by a certain type of life" (Kofman 1972, 121—my translation). Also see Kaufmann (1968) and Nehemas (1985).

42. "In effect all construction is the expression of an internal architecture, that is, a certain hierarchization of instincts, the subordination of a multiplicity of instincts to the strongest instinct that thus serves as a provisional center of perspective" (Kofman 1972, 90—my translation).

43. In *Spurs* (1979), Derrida refers to three kinds of women in Nietzsche: "Woman, inasmuch as truth, is scepticism and veiling dissimulation" (p. 57); "Feminism is nothing but the operation of a woman who aspires to be like a man. . . . Feminism too seeks to castrate. . . . Gone the style" (p. 65); and "In the instance of the third proposition . . . woman is recognized and affirmed as an affirmative power, a dissimulatress, an artist, a dionysiac. . . . She affirms herself, in and of herself, in man" (p. 97), and comments: "He [Nietzsche] was, he dreaded this castrated woman. He was, he dreaded this castrating woman. He was, he loved this affirming woman" (p. 101). Krell (1986) picked up on this Derridean view of Nietzsche as the deconstructor of "woman" who moved beyond gender categories by taking up feminine positions in his text. On this reading, Nietzsche's misogynist comments refer to social constructions of "woman" rather than to women themselves. This view is more sophisticated than Kaufmann's view that we can simply bracket Nietzsche's misogynist comments as aberrations of Nietzsche's time (Kaufmann 1968). I am in agreement with Oliver, however, when she says: "Nietzsche does not, as both Derrida and Krell suggest, want to become woman" (1988, 28); "rather, he desires to *possess* woman. Nietzsche's desire, then, is not a feminine desire. It is not the desire of a woman. Rather, it is a masculine desire (the desire to possess through impregnation)" (1988, 25).

44. The true, undissembled voice of Dionysian art cries: "Be as I am! Amid the ceaseless flux of phenomena I am the eternally creative primordial mother, eternally impelling to existence, eternally finding satisfaction in this change of phenomena!" (*Birth of*

Tragedy, section 16 [Nietzsche 1968b, 104]). Oliver comments: "Nietzsche repeatedly uses metaphors of biological reproduction— 'womb of being,' 'mother eternally pregnant,' 'procreative life'—to describe the Dionysian force. Nietzsche's Dionysian type is the 'eternally pregnant mother.' She affirms herself continually by reproducing. The biological metaphors which Nietzsche uses to describe the will to power are metaphors of reproduction, procreation, motherhood" (1988, 26). Also see Eric Blondel's "Nietzsche: Life as Metaphor" (in Allison 1985) for a discussion of Nietzsche's "central" image of the "*vita feminia.*"

45. See Kaufmann (1968).

46. Deleuze refers to life-enhancing and life-denying forces of life as becoming-active and becoming-reactive forces: "Becoming-active is affirming and affirmative, just as becoming-reactive is negating and nihilistic" (1983, 68). Schutte, however, feels that Deleuze's distinction "remains conceptually tied to the old notion of the struggle for power between the forces of good and evil" (1984, 90). She distinguishes two versions of Nietzsche's will to power: "The Übermensch stands for will to power as creativity. The higher man stands for will to power as power" (p. 127). It is the Übermensch who symbolizes "the ability of human beings to be at one with the process of life and death without building up walls and mental barriers against it. It is a Dionysian symbol reminding one of the dynamic continuity of life" (p. 124).

47. "There is a *situation* for consciousness to the extent it views existent things in their totality and in their relation . . . to itself, arranging them as a world around itself" (Jeanson 1980, 123). Also see Warnock (1965, chap. 5).

48. For discussions of how one's fundamental choice of being affects one's relationship to the world and others, see Catalano (1980, 196-202), Hayim (1980, 50-58), and Jeanson (1980, 180-187).

49. "The For-itself is not a person, nor a substance, nor a thing; it is merely revelation of the In-itself" (Desan 1954, 10). I have been influenced by Catalano (1980, part 2), Desan (1954, 10-56), and Jeanson (1980, chap. 1-4) in my rendering of the "For-itself."

50. "Consciousness, in general, is a desire for 'things'; it is at all times aware of an object, with the realization that it can never coincide with that thing which it desires or with that which it is conscious of. . . . It is a mere desire or lack" (Hayim 1980, 12-15). Also see Catalano (1980, 103-106), Grene (1983, 126-136), and Warnock (1965, 42-43).

51. "What it [the For-itself] lacks is being, which would make it a totality, a self, i.e., itself an In-itself. . . . The For-itself is a failure. A Being-for-itself can never be a Being-in-itself without losing, ipso facto, its most characteristic feature of consciousness [i.e., freedom or nothingness]. If such a being could be hypostatized, realizing this utopian identification of For-itself and In-itself, it would be God" (Desan 1954, 32-33). Also see Jeanson (1980, 140).

52. "The phenomenon of being is being as revealed to consciousness, *encountered* by it, while the being of phenomenon [transphenomenal being] is *apprehended* by it as the objectivity that inevitably overflows and grounds any knowledge that consciousness has of it" (Jeanson 1980, 112). Also see Catalano (1980, Introduction) and Grene (1980, 114-119).

53. For discussions of Sartre's notion of bad faith, see Catalano (1980, 78-91), Hayim (1980, 24-26), Jeanson (1980, 127-135), and Warnock (1965, 50-62).

54. "Ontologically, the Other appears as an alien freedom, as the upsurge of another subjectivity with its own consciousness as well as with its own desire for a human world" (Hayim 1980, 32). Other commentators that have also influenced my reading of Sartre's "other" are Catalano (1980, part 3), Desan (1954, 65-95), Grene (1980, chap. 5), Jeanson (1980, chap. 5), and Warnock (1965, chap. 3).

55. Also see Desan (1954, 116).

56. It is important to remember that I am restricting my discussion to the Sartre of *Being and Nothingness*. Although it would be interesting to compare this Sartre to the later Sartre of, say, the *Critique of Dialectical Reason*, especially on this point, I will not do that here.

57. For discussions of this trio (to do, to have, to be), see Catalano (1980, part 4), Desan (1954, 121-131), and Hayim (1980, 61-63).

58. See Margery Collins and Christine Pierce's article on the sexist nature of this discussion (Collins and Pierce 1979). Also see Warnock's comments on the "viscous" (her translation of slimy) (1965, 99-107).

59. As Desan puts it: "His extreme notion of freedom needs a For-itself which is void, completely void. He thinks that the slightest granule of being would provide something for deterministic influence to take hold of and that the freedom of his pure and translucid consciousness would thereby be destroyed" (1954, 158).

60. "Because it is not a fixed attribute with a certain nature, consciousness as the for-itself is also characterized by Sartre as *nothingness.* . . . In contrast to the for-itself, . . . the in-itself possesses no lack or desire. . . . Every act of consciousness is an instance of negation, that is, of breaking away from the in-itself" (Hayim 1980, 14-15).

61. "The Sartrean individual is utterly alone, wholly responsible, making himself as the negation of a barren field of being, in itself wholly devoid of meaning" (Grene 1983, 92). Also see Hayim (1980, 17).

62. "It is . . . inevitable that the nihilating power of consciousness, unable to indefinitely sustain everything and remain present to everything, will allow phenomena to be reabsorbed one by one into the in-itself from which consciousness had made them emerge *for itself*" (Jeanson 1980, 151).

63. Many commentators have criticized Sartre's conception of human freedom and his insistence on the radical split between the for-itself and the in-itself (see, for example, Desan 1954 and Grene 1983). Judith Butler comments on the repercussions of this dualist thinking in the context of Beauvoir's reading of "woman" as "other": "Women are 'Other' according to Beauvoir in so far as they are defined by a masculine perspective which seeks to safeguard its own disembodied status through identifying women generally with the bodily sphere. . . . From this belief that the body is Other, it is not a far leap to the conclusion that others *are* their bodies, while the masculine 'I' is a non-corporeal soul. . . . Beauvoir's dialectic of self and Other argues the limits of a Cartesian version of disembodied freedom, and implicitly criticizes the model of autonomy upheld by these masculine gender norms" (1987a, 133).

5

Conclusion

The interpretive framework developed here is a restricted one. I have generated it using the idealist tradition of Western continental nineteenth- and twentieth-
century philosophers, Lacanian psychoanalysis, and
feminist critiques of psychoanalysis. This framework reorients a theory of self to a theory about a self in process,
presents the formation and continuing reconstitution of a
self in and through social practices and meaning structures as a problem that human beings need to solve if they
are to survive as social agents, and posits fear of the threat
of self-dissolution as a motivation in human behavior.
This framework also delineates two kinds of strategies for
maintaining selves, correlates these strategies with gender, and points to a range of possible strategies that fall
between the two. It posits the production of meaning as a
self-constituting activity and provides some suggestions
for reading out strategies in self-construction from a text.
Reading out the contents of a particular text's gender categories enables us to target a conceptual barrier in the use
of self-strategies presented by the conception of gender
categories peculiar to that text. This, in turn, lets us explore the different ways of filling out the content of gender categories as well as the effects gender categories have
for the production of meaning.

I have offered this interpretive framework for rendering gender-sensitive analyses of texts in the hope of encouraging further exploration of gender categories and
their effects. It is important that we take the threat of
self-dissolution seriously in developing theories that pro-

mote social change. Psychoanalysis and its conception of the unconscious—a range of human significance not immediately accessible to us and yet still exerting its effects—provides us with a theoretical tool for explaining how we form and maintain (relatively) coherent selves in the face of the chaotic range of our embodied experience. The Oedipus complex need not be a universal phenomenon—either within our own culture or cross-culturally. The gendered self-strategies characterized on its basis are highly problematic if taken as a definitive answer to the question of sexual difference. But they do constitute two kinds of strategies for maintaining some sense of stability and continuity. Relating strategies to gender allows us to interpret a subject's gender identity as an effect of positioning rather than as an attribute related to bodily anatomy. Contrasting two strategies and offering a range of intermediary strategies between them show the large number of solutions human subjects can propose to the problem of human identity. But correlating the two strategies with gender in the way that I do vastly oversimplifies the ways that people play out their answers. In fact, what I have done is to abstract one form the binary opposition of masculine/feminine has taken in certain discourses and tried to amplify it—by filling out in a more positive way the "feminine" side of the story, the shadowy counterpart of the "masculine" one.

The gendered self-strategies here help illuminate a particular phenomenon of my experience that I believe to be gender-informed. I have often experienced the strange and disconcerting feeling in particular relationships that I was not really there for the other person. Although not peculiar to women it is an experience more prevalent among women—being spoken to, related to, even obsessed about, and yet somehow not seen—as if I were a projection screen or a placeholder for a drama that had very little to do with me or my thoughts, perceptions, desires, and goals. It is the experience of objectification—not merely sexual, but a kind of objectification that extends into relationships where one has supposedly gone beyond superficial appearances. In such relationships, in addition to denial of myself, I felt concern about the connection between me and the other person. My stepping out of the role of other often precipitated paranoia on the part of the "self/subject" involved. Sometimes it was easier to maintain the role of other than to risk breaking the connection, which there are often reasons to keep (e.g., financial dependence or fear of being on one's own), but I was curious about the pleasure this role gave me—an inherent satisfaction in satisfying another that did not seem to me to be necessarily self-destructive.

It is this facet of masculine/feminine relationships I have chosen to explore here. I am very sympathetic to feminist discussions about the differences among women and the feminist concern about women oppressing one another with definitions of women as exclusionary as any ever created by men. Women come from different races, ethnic groups, and economic backgrounds, differences that often seem more striking than the shared identity of one's gender.[1] The kind of relationship discussed above could occur between two women, two men, or a woman (as the subject) and a man (as the other), so why bother trying to distinguish the two positions according to gender at all? Am I simply reifying gender categories rather than deconstructing them in keeping with this concern for differences among human individuals?

I believe that it is only by amplifying gender stories, filling in the content of both sides of the dichotomy, that we can work through the categories that bind us. We are not self-transparent. My conscious self-understanding has to be set in the context of the broader background of meaning systems out of which it emerges. If we elaborate stories that resonate for us, we may see more clearly some of the conceptual barriers that constrain us and be able to remove them. Just as nightmares lose their power to terrify once we confront them, so may half-submerged notions of what it means to be masculine or feminine lose their power to control us once we recognize them. Although my analysis of gender categories will not resonate for everyone, I believe it will for some—and in such a way that it will free them to explore alternatives in self-strategies rather than prompt them to adhere more rigorously to the one "appropriate" to their sex.

I argued that the philosophers discussed here could not make the move to incorporate the two strategies past a certain point owing to the conceptual barrier of their gender categories. Moreover, there is a critical point for each individual—a point of no return—when he/she is faced with the not trivial dilemma of the collapse of gender categories. Because my particular interest here is the limitations of masculine positioning, I chose three male writers. I believe, however, that female writers can also exemplify male positioning. In addition, the impact of gender categories on the self-constituting activity of women and the range of feminine positions (or a textual position beyond gender categories?) are both interesting issues that bear further study.

The repercussions of our self-strategies occur not only in the writing of theory but in our relationships in the world as well. Truly reciprocal relationships require the abandonment of a rigid, mutually exclusive, two-gender system. Although such reciprocal relationships may require something approaching "androgyny," I do not use that term here for two reasons. First, despite my belief that we need to move toward a "new" kind of subjectivity, one that incorporates the two self-strategies without the conceptual barrier of rigid gender categories, I want to avoid the connotation that there should be a uniform self-strategy for human subjects. It is not differences between human individuals that should be eradicated—but restrictions on differences in self-strategies arising from gender categories. Self-strategies should evolve out of the context of a particular individual's life experience in response to that individual's particular problems in creating and maintaining subjectivity. As we have seen, Kierkegaard, Nietzsche, and Sartre, because of their own reading of gender categories, could not resolve certain problems. I am interested in solutions we might find for such problems if we could get past the gender categories that restrict us.

Second, "androgyny" is too easily read as effeminate masculinity: Because the masculine self-strategy is the accepted "norm" for personhood in dominant Western culture, attempts to envision a new kind of human subject tend to be based on this norm with a few "feminine" aspects mixed in. Before we can articulate what the incorporation of two self-strategies—in a way that breaks the conceptual barrier of gender categories—might entail, we need to be able to articulate and valorize the "repressed" self-strategy—the feminine.[2] I will therefore suggest a way of incorporating two gendered self-strategies into one in order to conceptualize what it might mean to go beyond gender. But because I have pursued one characterization of the binary opposition between masculine and feminine, my attempt is doomed to failure; it can do no more than speak to one moment in the continuous struggle of an entire network of interdependent selves to reconstitute identities that are not only sexed and gendered in complicated and conflicting ways but that are also refracted according to other aspects of identity only hinted at here.

With this caveat, I will now amplify the two stories I tell about gendered self-strategies even further. I will also provide some suggestions for incorporating the two self-strategies into one.

Interpretive Framework

My interpretive framework stands as follows: We can characterize two poles that represent "pure" femininity and "pure" masculinity. That is, we can characterize two modes of being that are so radically distinct from each other that they are opposed and mutually exclusive in the strictest sense of those words. No one could actually personify either one of these poles.

The Feminine Pole

The purely and eternally feminine is chaotic flux. It is life in its concrete specificity—so concrete that it escapes all attempts to characterize it via general categories. The eternally feminine mode of being takes each aspect of life as completely unique and unrepeatable—so much so that the attempt to characterize this mode of being in words immediately falsifies it. It is beyond language, beyond all attempts to label, describe, or even point it out. Even to say that "each aspect of life is unique" is false, since without names or any kind of generalizations to help us distinguish one aspect of life from another, all aspects flow into one another and there is an overwhelming chaos within which no distinctions can be made and in which no selves or perspectives can distinguish themselves. This pole can only be a limit because a self at this position is a contradiction in terms. There can be no purely feminine self: Such a self would be completely unable to distinguish itself from the life around it. It would be dissolved into a chaotic flux of life that pulsated along with no beginning, middle, or end.

The Masculine Pole

The purely and eternally masculine is changeless, eternal, harmonic order. It is a complete, self-sufficient, completely rational map of the universe in which everything and everyone has its unique place plotted out for all time. It contains all categories necessary for capturing every nuance of life. It is the real rendered orderly, the real with everything in its proper place, the proper order toward which the universe is striving. This is the only order where absolutely everything and everyone has the place that is in harmony with all other places, and this is the harmony of the whole where all of life is finally harmonized, where all things follow their appropriate course and nothing is in conflict. It is life made perfect, rendered completely intelligible and rational, where all connections are clear and intelligible and everything is connected to everything else. It is completely characterizable via the perfect language that reflects all the categories it has. Everything has its boundaries and definable ways of relating to everything else; nothing is muddled, confused, or blurred. All is complete clarity and distinctness. This pole can only be a limit because a self at this position is also a contradiction in terms. There can be no purely masculine self: Such a self would be motionless; being perfect, it would not need to change. It would remain in a state of suspension in the only place in which it truly belongs. All would be known, desire would be sated, and all would remain fixed in their positions with no need or desire to move, no lack to push them to reach for what they do not have. Thus, no change, no movement, no life. Having set up these two poles, we can relate the extreme of each of the two self-strategies already characterized to the pole which is its guiding ideal.

The Feminine Self-Strategy

The feminine self-strategy is based in connectedness. The self who makes predominant use of the feminine self-strategy maintains self-continuity through connectedness with others. She must always be connected to an other who informs her, giving her her meaning and her function by demanding that she play the role of other. That is, she takes on the shape that will satisfy the desire of a self. She reflects back to that self the image it desires to see. She conforms to the self/other pattern set by another by responding to that self's desire, with no self parameters of her own holding her back. She becomes whatever self will fit the form provided by the "other" of the other's self/other pattern. She gives first priority to connectedness, to the fusion experienced by fitting so closely to the desire of an other that she feels that other's desire as her own, thus desiring what the other desires: that she be the "other" that will affirm the other's self. She cares very little about the pattern of social positions laid out by the Symbolic. Instead, her attention is completely on the specificity of those others in her life whose "other" she plays. She cares very little about the "rational" code for translating and transposing a particular self-identity through the positions of the Symbolic. She attends instead to the concrete specificity of the particular individuals in front of her taking on whatever shape they give her. It is fine with her if this is within the socially acceptable parameters of the Symbolic. If not, she is perfectly content to subvert those parameters. Her priority is satisfying the concrete desire of a particular other for an "other" that will satisfy that other's self/other pattern.

The Masculine Self-Strategy

The masculine self-strategy is based on opposition. The self who maintains himself with a masculine self-strategy must always oppose himself to those around him. He assumes the self of a self/other pattern created in early childhood, and he attempts to translate and transpose this self through the social positions of the Symbolic by finding others to play the "other" of his self/other pattern, others who will repeatedly confirm and so maintain a recognizable form of his original self. Unless the other is willing to conform to *his* self/other pattern, he must establish a connection with the other by using his self/other pattern as a guide to staking out the Symbolic positions between them. Thus, with the help of the Symbolic categories available to him, he can build up the layers of his identity to fit various situations and social contexts by using the logic of the same—rules of analogy and similarity—to translate his identity. To find the self/other pattern suitable for a situation that he encounters for the first time, he orders that situation via socially accepted categories and finds his appropriate position vis-à-vis those categories. By finding others in the situation that take the positions toward him that his self/other pattern specifies, he can maintain self-identity, even though specific people and events have changed. His priority is the laying out of a clear self/other pattern by means of categories that càn be related to one another in an orderly and "rational" fashion. Everything has a category, a place within the Symbolic. This place can be found by using rules of similarity and analogy to deduce what categories currently pertain to one's self from a history of self/other patterning that extends back to one's original self/other relationship. Any messiness must be cleared up and properly categorized so that the transposition of self/other patterning through the network of already established categories can occur. Ordering of experience through such categories makes transposition and translation easier by clearly labeling and defining the boundaries of things. Then all one has to do is maneuver through those positions via the transposition of one's self/other pattern.

Summary

I have delineated these two self-strategies as extremes approaching the limits set by the two poles. A self that used only the feminine self-strategy would be so pliable, so dependent on others to determine her form for her, that she would take on absolutely any form some other in her vicinity desired of her, with no questions asked. A self that used only the masculine self-strategy would so rigidly adhere to his own fixed conception of himself that he could never change but had to repeat continually, with no variation, the same self/other pattern. He would thus need an other who was very pliant, changing to fit his need in whatever new situation presented itself, or he would need a very stable external situation with rigid Symbolic categories.

As we have seen, it is likely for the particular position between the poles taken up by an individual to combine the two self-strategies in some form or other. There would be a critical point for each individual, representing his/her own conception of gender categories, the point of "no return" for these individuals for incorporating any more of the opposite-sex self-strategy than they already had. By testing particular texts for this critical point we have gained insight into the conceptual barriers preventing authors from making use of their own suggestions for solving dilemmas they confront. The analysis of a text's category of "woman" suggested new ways of getting beyond certain impasses of the text from which the author, because of his conception of gender categories, could not escape. Such an analysis suggests an internal critique of the gender categories of the text; reworking them can resolve problems presented by the text. The "deconstruction" of gender categories a gender-sensitive reading of philosophical texts provides could, in turn, have ramifications in the broader realm of social relations between men and women.

Variations   in   a   Masculine   Position

Each individual divides humanity into the groups of
"masculine" and "feminine" a bit differently. Indeed,
many individuals may divide the two groups with a greater
or lesser overlap of the masculine and feminine
characteristics that both sexes can share without putting
their gender into question. But as long as there are gender
categories, there will always be a point where a person of
one sex cannot manifest characteristics of the other sex.
That is, there is a point of no return where if I, as a man,
were to go any further toward the feminine pole, I would
be so in danger of losing my masculine identity that I
would be threatened with a complete loss of identity. The
same is true for a woman, coming from the feminine pole
and going toward the masculine one. I have chosen a
binary opposition involving deferring desire through
signifying chains versus fusion experiences as a way of
representing the two poles of gender between which this
point of no return could fall.

On the reading of gendered self-strategies developed
here, a certain interdependency between the two self-
strategies emerges. A purely "feminine" self would get lost
in the broader realm of social positions. Because her priority is connectedness with an embodied other, she acts in
responsiveness to another rather than on the basis of social acceptability. To the extent that she takes on a masculine self-strategy, she can position herself in a socially acceptable way. To be guaranteed a position in the broader
social realm, she is to a greater or lesser extent dependent
upon a masculine self to position her. In her responsiveness to this self she takes on the role of other that will
guarantee her a position in the social realm.

A purely "masculine" self would lose the richness of his
embodied experience. Because his priority is positioning
himself vis-à-vis Symbolic categories, he orders his experience via categories in accordance with the self/other
pattern that maintains his identity. Like any theory that
refuses to respond to data it has not yet been able to explain, such a self-strategy would soon lead to falsification
of one's experiences by reducing them to inadequate categories. To incorporate new aspects of experience into

one's self/other pattern, however, one needs a responsive other. It is only through the responsive mirroring of an other who anticipates one's desire that heretofore meaningless bodily sensations can be incorporated into one's self/other pattern.

Each individual has his/her own sense of when a strategy would no longer be supported by an opposite-sex strategy, threatening the individual's own self with extinction. Depending on one's upbringing and cultural background, this threat would come at various places between the two poles. Thus, there is a place between the two poles at which each person can no longer conceive of the kind of response necessary for maintaining self-identity, the place where his/her own strategies would fail because there would be no strategy out there to complement it. This threat of self-extinction renders any attempt to incorporate the two self-strategies a tenuous one. As we have seen, such attempts can take different forms. Kierkegaard, Nietzsche, and Sartre all have different conceptions of gender categories—that is, the "critical point," or conceptual barrier, past which they cannot push incorporation of two self-strategies further, differs for the three of them. I will now characterize the critical point for each of them, relating that critical point to what we learned about their particular category of "woman."

Kierkegaard

Kierkegaard could conceive of a woman taking a feminine self-strategy with respect to a man. That is, he could conceive of a woman's being receptive enough to a man to allow an experience beyond her conceptual categories to occur. The princess waited for the knight of infinite resignation or the knight of faith (depending on the way it turned out) to make up his mind about how to deal with the unsuitability of their match. The bride waited in all modesty for the groom who never came. Agnes was ready to entrust her destiny to the merman. Sarah was ready to let herself be saved by Tobias. All the women characterized by Silentio in *Fear and Trembling* were either innocently receptive—waiting for someone to take them by the hand—

or actively entrusting themselves to the judgment of another. Thus, all these women were willing to receive another, to entrust themselves to the judgment of another,
even though that other's reasoning may have seemed irrational according to their own sense of the Symbolic.
Because they were women, willing to take the feminine
position with respect to another, they put connectedness
with another first. That is, they were willing to override
their own sense of the Symbolic in order to satisfy the desire of the other.

The man who won this woman's trust, in contrast, had
the weighty responsibility of respecting that trust by
keeping the woman within the bounds of the Symbolic.
Silentio's conception of "woman" was of someone who utilized a feminine self-strategy of surrendering herself to
the form given her by the "other" of another's self/other
pattern, and who took no responsibility for maintaining
Symbolic order. This passivity, in turn, made it necessary
that the man take all responsibility for maintaining
Symbolic order. It was next to impossible, and inconceiv-
able as far as Silentio was concerned, for a man to let go of
his self/other pattern enough to allow himself to be informed by the woman's "other." As the responsibility of
maintaining the Symbolic order was his and his alone, and
as overflowing his own self/other pattern to receive another could subvert Symbolic categories, he could not
"indulge" in a feminine self-strategy. And yet, Silentio felt
the restriction of Symbolic categories. He granted a kind
of experience beyond all categories, beyond the universal,
within the context of a God relationship.

Silentio could more easily justify taking up the feminine
position with respect to God, of conforming to God's desire
by playing the role of "other" in God's self/other pattern.
He could not, however, conceive of taking up this role with
respect to women. For someone in a God relationship,
someone who attended to the will of God, who had a faith in
God that went beyond all Symbolic categories, there were
feelings and acts that went beyond the Symbolic, beyond
what could be communicated in language, beyond the rational. Thus, without forsaking his role as upkeeper of the

Symbolic order, man could take up a position of innocent receptivity with respect to God.

Social relations were protected from an exploration of inwardness that included opening oneself up to the desire of the other and letting it inform one. Silentio allowed the possibility of individual transformation but stopped short of social transformation. The external demeanor of a knight of faith remained the same, social categories remained the same, traditional notions of masculine and feminine remained the same. It was only in inwardness that one could explore the possibility of breaking down traditional ways of dividing the task of self and other that maintain subjectivity. But the new kind of subjectivity Silentio posited in the inwardness of the knight of faith could not be translated into the outwardness of social relations. The receptivity with respect to God that defied all categories was a realm of inward experience that man would not introduce into the Symbolic. He would keep it to himself, knowing that his actions could not be expressed via any available categories. Man could take up a feminine position with respect to God, just as woman could, but Silentio could not conceive of man's taking this position with respect to woman or other men.

Silentio's critical point, then, did not come in positing a man in the feminine position. It came in determining the "other" with respect to whom this position could be posited. Silentio could not conceive of a man who would risk subversion of Symbolic categories, because it was the masculine sex that must preserve those categories. If men gave up the responsibility for maintaining the Symbolic order, then the Symbolic would be threatened with dissolution and chaos would ensue. To counter this possibility, man had to make sure that he did not forsake his role. For Silentio, getting beyond restrictive Symbolic categories involved a different kind of self-strategy carried out in an inwardness that would not affect one's external relations with the world. Thus, he could conceive of further incorporating the two self-strategies only as long as the Symbolic order itself could be kept safe from tampering.

Nietzsche

Nietzsche went further than either of the others in questioning the boundary between the two self-strategies. His free spirit could make use of both. But Nietzsche still felt that different self-strategies had to be divided between different groups of people. He recognized the importance those with "feminine instincts" had for the "strong," but he failed to see that if the "strong" were to incorporate two self-strategies into one, other individuals of the human community would have to make corresponding changes. Nietzsche's critical point comes in his failure to recognize the interdependency of self-strategies. The free spirit should be able to impose his self/other patterning on others and yet challenge Symbolic categories by overflowing any and all categories that do not respect the specificity of his own experience. Thus, Nietzsche's free spirit should impose a patterning that requires the support of the Symbolic at the same time as he should respect life's specificity in a way that would subvert Symbolic categories. He should create the categories that speak to his own experience, but he should be able to create them with no help from another. Thus, in his attempt to incorporate the "masculine" and "feminine" self-strategies, Nietzsche overlooks their interdependent nature. Silentio suggests that an attempt to subvert categories needs to be contained within the context of a relationship. Nietzsche does not provide this context, which leaves him vulnerable to being overwhelmed by chaotic flux.

Nietzsche's conception of "woman" is that she should stick to her feminine role so that man can perform his task of incorporating the two self-strategies. But he fails to recognize that an incorporation of the two self-strategies would require a change in the other that played another's "other." Since human identity is created and maintained in interdependent relationships, and since self-strategies are mutually affecting, a change in one self-strategy necessitates a change in the other. For Nietzsche's vision of subjectivity, of the free spirit, to work, all must change to support this new kind of subjectivity in the interdependent network of human relations. Nietzsche fails to recognize that the change he envisions cannot be of one individual or an elite group of individuals: It must be of a whole community of individuals. Thus, whereas Silentio's conception of a new kind of subjectivity takes into account its relational nature, Nietzsche's critical point leads him to believe that a new kind of subjectivity can be imposed on others in the same way that the old, masculine identity was.

Sartre

Sartre recognized that there is no particular reason that any particular group of people should take on one or the other of the two self-strategies. But he could not conceive of incorporating the two strategies. If there were not a group of people to play the other, if the distinction between self and other were not complete, then identity, and human agency, would fail completely. He could not tolerate any overlapping of the two strategies, although the possibility of such an overlap comes out in his work. His critical point comes in not being able to conceive that a man could make use of a feminine self-strategy. He concedes that others may refuse to don the feminine self-strategy, but this refusal only makes it harder and more unlikely that one will find an "other" to fit one's own self/other pattern. The task of being a man is thus harder than ever, but it is still the same task. One cannot count on the Symbolic because it turns out not to be sanctioned the way that one thought. One cannot count on the Law of the Father to preserve one's identity. If one is to preserve an identity, one must continually impose one's self/other pattern. With the legitimacy of the Symbolic in doubt, this task is harder than ever, but at the very least one must make sure that one does not become an "other" for another's self/other pattern.

Thus, Sartre's critical point comes in taking on the feminine position with respect to any other—be (s)he God or human. He shares Nietzsche's feeling that the Symbolic is arbitrary, but rather than challenge or subvert it in light of one's own specificity or in light of a God relationship, he focuses on the need to legitimate Symbolic categories on one's own. One must take responsibility—there is nothing else to appeal to, neither God nor subtler nuances of life. One must admit that all is arbitrary and take responsibility for the categories one chooses to affirm as being arbitrary. Unlike Silentio, Sartre does not feel that man has a responsibility to maintain the Symbolic as it is. He does not specify the conditions under which one is justified to subvert the Symbolic because he believes that one is always recreating the Symbolic. Like Nietzsche, he thinks the Symbolic is an arbitrary creation that has no claim to legitimacy or authority. Unlike Nietzsche, he does not think that there is anything beyond the Symbolic to inform one. If the Symbolic has no legitimacy, no authority, then nothing does. There is nothing with respect to which one can take up a feminine position of receptivity, nothing one can entrust oneself to, in order to let oneself be informed by a new shape that will give rise to new categories.

If the Symbolic has no legitimacy, then there is nothing to inform one and one is entirely on one's own, to make sense of an inert in-itself as best one can. Unlike Silentio, Sartre does not think there is any other with respect to which one can take on a feminine self-strategy. Unlike Nietzsche, Sartre does not think there is any pulse of life waiting to inform one. For any meaning at all to exist, one must create one's own categories out of the nothingness of one's own freedom. Thus, unlike Silentio, Sartre throws the Symbolic into doubt but refuses to take up a feminine position with respect to anything else. He thus can conceive of the failure of a masculine self-strategy, but he cannot conceive of an alternative self-strategy with any efficacy.

Critical Points

All three have varying critical points that constitute varying conceptual boundaries in their ability to incorporate into a new self-strategy the two self-strategies characterized here as masculine and feminine. Whereas Silentio will allow the possibility of his being informed by God's desire, and Nietzsche allows the possibility of his being informed by a will to power beyond rational categories, Sartre will not allow himself to be informed by anything at all. All three share the refusal to be informed by a human other. The mark of the masculine position that they all share is the refusal to take on the "other" of a human other's self/other pattern. At the same time, all three consider taking on the "other" as a mark of the feminine position, of "woman" as she appears in their texts. Tracing out these three masculine positions has thus allowed us to find a critical point that they have in common. I next will explore the possibilities that going beyond this critical point lead us to.

Suggestions for a New Subjectivity

We are now ready to move to an incorporation of the two positions into one. Until this point, the two strategies have been approached as needing to be performed by one or the other of the self/other dyad; there has been a critical point—a point where the individual could not envision any more overlap of the two strategies without endangering the possibility of subjectivity entirely. There may have been a greater or lesser overlap of the masculine and feminine, but finally each according to his/her gender had to bear responsibility for one or the other of two kinds of functions designed to maintain the identities of both interdependently. If either the one or the other failed to carry out the function he/she was responsible for, then identity, subjectivity, would fail. This would entail obliteration of the worst sort for both parties.

In a relatively static society with rigid Symbolic categories, an individual would assume an identity at birth, which he would keep the rest of his life. For example, a man living in a small, isolated community would not have much opportunity for any change in his identity. It would be staked out in terms of his relationships to the people around him. These relationships, being relatively static, would ensure a relatively static self. For the breakdown of static social relations to occur without a loss of stable subjectivity, there must be a group of people willing to mirror back the desire of those who would create new identities. For example, a daughter who habitually thought of herself as subservient and lacking in decision-making abilities would need someone to reflect back to her her dawning desire to fight back rather than submit to family demands. A mother reacts to the infant's initial attempts to reach out for something by putting an object in his hand. She notes what he is reaching for and anticipates a desire the infant may not have yet recognized in himself. The woman, or man, who notices the daughter's impatience with her position and reflects back to her an angry person with the power to act will be able to affect the daughter's subjectivity by allowing her to incorporate new aspects of her experience (e.g., shortness of breath, which now signifies her anger to her) into her self/other pattern. Thus a social position takes on new meaning in the context of concrete relationships with others.

In our complex society there has been a proliferation of symbolic structures. Mass media and cable television, along with accelerated methods of transportation, have created a clash of all the symbolic structures various cultures have created. With this complicated Symbolic, the positions one may take up with respect to others have become more diverse. A new option exists—the possibility that we can all learn to perform the role of other without losing the role of self. We can all play the self because the variety of symbolic structures available to us is great enough to fit a wide range of experience. This makes it more likely that two people with conflicting experiences can find common ground in the Symbolic. We can also play the other, without sacrificing our own self/other pattern, because there are parameters that can open up between two selves that allow such mingling. That is, there is room in the overlap between the two selves for both to play "other" to the other's self at the same time that the other continues to confirm his/her own self/other pattern. This creates a kind of play space similar to that discussed with respect to Winnicott (Chapter 2). Both selves need confirmation of their social position and yet can release new aspects of their experience in keeping with their other's "other."

For example, I may be a masculine professor with an authoritative approach to teaching. My self/other pattern with a student requires that he give me a certain amount of deference and so forth. If I could allow myself to play the other's "other" in a way that gave priority to concrete connectedness rather than to Symbolic categories, I might find myself playfully engaging with the student. Instead of disqualifying any aspect of our interaction that did not fit my self/other pattern, I would allow my body to respond to his body. I would then give these responses meaning by attending to them and articulating them in one form or another, such as picking up on his body stiffening when I gave an order in a certain way and modifying my order. The same would hold true for the student's engagement with me. This kind of interaction occurs all the time, of course. The point here is that two modes of interacting can be going on at the same time, with either one mode (the masculine self-strategy) or the other (the feminine self-strategy) predominating. It is interesting to contemplate how quickly the form of the professor/student relationship would change if both parties made the use of a feminine self-strategy predominate. (How acceptable this change would be to the rest of the academy is, of course, another matter.)

Gender-sensitive readings of philosophical texts can help us explore and articulate how gender affects our worldview and our ways of relating to human others. Articulating two strategies, valorizing both of them, and demonstrating how they can come together into one strategy could help pave the way toward a new kind of subjectivity in which both strategies could be used by all individuals in our day-to-day living as well as in our theorizing.

I have tried to suggest how such an incorporation of the two strategies might work. For reciprocal relations to be successful, individuals must be able to use both strategies equally well. They must be both responsive to the desire of the other and clear on their own parameters. They cannot let themselves be taken over by the desire of the other, and they cannot let themselves turn into dictators of the form the other will take.[3] Instead, both must utilize both strategies in an equal give and take, which is within the confines of the Symbolic in the sense that it makes use of the positions the Symbolic makes available. It also defies the Symbolic in the sense that it readily subverts Symbolic categories, for example, those of status (as we saw in the example of the professor) or gender, in order to create new categories in keeping with the concrete specificity of the concrete relationship.   But this new kind of relationship is not merely the imposition, transposition, of the self-same identity of one onto an other; it is the creation of two new identities in reciprocal responsiveness to the desire of the other.

Kierkegaard, Nietzsche, and Sartre

I have explored the possibilities for a new subjectivity presented by each of the three philosophers discussed here.   In his relationship to God, Silentio talks of a receptivity to the incomprehensible desire of an other.   If Silentio could take this position with respect to a human other without losing his own identity, he could stretch his identity beyond "rational" standards.   Thus, what he says about a relationship to God is instructive for a relationship with another that does not take one outside of one's own parameters.   The new self-maintaining human being will allow a receptivity to an other, defying all "rational" meaning given to life and one's own experiences, like the receptivity Silentio suggests Abraham felt with respect to God's command, despite its apparent irrationality.   If all individuals—whether male or female—involved with an other could allow this "irrational" moment to creep into their own project of maintaining self-identity, they could allow faith in the other to carry them to a new moment where things made sense in an entirely new perspective. That is, they could take a "leap of faith" by trusting that in taking on the role of "other" to another's self/other pattern, they would not entirely forfeit their own position.
Nietzsche suggests that we are not tied to any one position in the Symbolic, but his taking on of the feminine position does not have the parameters of Kierkegaard's. Nietzsche attempts to take on the feminine position with respect to life, which is admirable, but it also makes the danger of losing identity much more immediate.   Nietzsche has no answer to the question of how to protect one's identity when one has abdicated from the masculine strat-

egy in order to take on the feminine one. If one were to attend to every nuance of one's embodied experience, one's self and perspective would unravel. Without parameters to guide one's attentiveness, the world would quickly lose its coherence. Attending to the nuances of one's embodied experience in responsiveness to an other in order to respond to the other's desire is the feminine self-strategy for providing such parameters.

Kierkegaard protects himself from the loss of all identity by speaking of dropping the masculine strategy only within the context of a God relationship. Nietzsche tries to adopt feminine relationships with respect to all life experience and yet insists that it is one's personal responsibility to maintain identity. He tries to say that one individual can take on both strategies and not have his identity fail; Nietzsche should have suggested that if his vision is to work, both parties must take on both strategies so that both can continue as identities working in a reciprocal relationship. Instead he insists that woman continue to play her role—even if it is an arbitrary one—and he insists that even though man should push toward the feminine position, he should be able to protect himself from a loss of identity, not by insisting on a reciprocal change in any other, but through sheer strength of will.

Sartre's suggestion that the Symbolic order is not sacrosanct breaks down the legitimacy of a masculine self-strategy. Although he does not offer a feminine self-strategy as an alternative, we can trace the struggle toward a new kind of subjectivity in his discussion of the project of becoming God. Sartre says that such a project is impossible, but he is operating on the assumption that each individual has the project of becoming God. No single individual can be both in-itself (an object subject to the gaze of another) and for-itself (the consciousness that gazes) at once. A community of individuals could conceivably attain a state of in-itself-for-itself if they could achieve reciprocal relationships. If the self-strategies of the individuals of the community perfectly "match" one another, then it is possible for the community to form a harmonious, self-sufficient, self-causing whole.

The   New   Self-Strategy

The   new   self,   incorporating   feminine   and   masculine
self-strategies,   would   be   based   in   both   opposition   and   connectedness   as   two   moments   in   a   dynamic   process   of   self-
maintenance.   A   self   that   made   equal   use   of   both   strategies
would   be   one   that   would   treat   the   positions   laid   out   by   the
Symbolic   as   vehicles   for   translating   and   transposing   its
own   self/other   pattern   to   new   situations   and   contexts.
Such   a   self   would   be   open   to   being   informed   by   the   desire
of   an   other   within   the   parameters   set   by   the   overlap   of   its
and   the   other's   self/other   patterns.   That   is,   it   would   adhere   to   the   form   of   its   self/other   pattern,   but   it   would   also
be   flexible   enough   to   "overflow"   the   boundaries   of   its   own
pattern   in   order   to   conform   to   the   "other"   of   a   self/other
pattern   of   someone   of   his   or   her   choosing.

In   the   reciprocal   relationship   of   a   fusion   experience   in
which   both   selves   are   able   to   take   on   a   feminine   self-strategy   with   respect   to   each   other,   each   will   anticipate   the
desire   of   the   other   in   a   mutual   attempt   to   pleasure   one   another.   Thus,   neither   will   dictate   the   exact   shape   the   other
should   conform   to.   Instead,   the   two   selves   will   create   a
new   self/other   pattern   for   both,   by   mutually   conforming
to   the   as   yet   unarticulated   desire   of   the   other.   Through
attentive   receptivity   to   the   other's   concrete   specificity
that   defies   all   categorization,   each   self   will   anticipate   the
other's   desire   and   attempt   to   satisfy   it   before   it   is   voiced.
In   this   mutual   attentiveness   where   each   attempts   to   conform   to   the   other's   "other,"   the   parameters   of   both   selves'
self/other   patterns   will   change.   The   desire   to   satisfy   the
other   will   lead   each   to   overflow   the   self-boundaries   set   by
their   self/other   patterns   in   the   Symbolic.   But   this   overflow   of   self-identity   will   remain   within   the   parameters   of
taking   on   an   "other"   that   will   satisfy   another.   Each   one's
transformed   self/other   pattern   will   also   derive   from   each
one's   original   self/other   pattern   since   that   pattern   was   the
context   within   which   the   other   attended   to   the   self's   desire.

For   example,   two   colleagues   may   have   very   decided
views   on   their   relationship   vis-à-vis   the   other   and   the
book   they   want   to   write   together.   If   both   take   on   a   feminine   self-strategy   with   respect   to   the   other,   those   views

will swiftly change. The individual, rather than attempting to fit the other and the project into his/her self/other pattern, will attend to the pleasure of the other. Again, a play space is created in which both try to tune in to and anticipate the desire of the other. In this state of reciprocal attentiveness the project and the individual's relationship to each other take on a form that is different from either individual's preconception of it. Thus, the self/other pattern of both is transformed in the process of creation.

Philosophy and Feminism

Most people who have investigated human self-understanding in the Western idealist tradition have not directly addressed the question of gender. They have written analyses that are "gender-blind": They have excluded or ignored the feminine perspective by either marginalizing it or putting it completely offstage. Feminist theory has, of course, tried to correct this limitation. In this work I have suggested an interpretive framework that would allow us to utilize the insights of these gender-blind analyses of human nature and self by reading the same texts in such a way that gender is brought to the fore.

Even a gender-blind text is informed by gender. As long as gender is a crucial component of our identity, every theorist will speak from a position that is gender-informed, a perspective that makes use of either a "masculine" or a "feminine" self-strategy, however those self-strategies may be construed. I have here sketched one way of construing the contrast between such gendered self-strategies. My reading was developed in line with a certain thread of continental philosophy, psychoanalytic theory, and feminist literature that attempts to target what might be universally true of "women's" experience. Since, as I pointed out in Chapter 1, the latter project is dubious, and since the philosophical and psychoanalytic traditions I have looked at are by no means the only or even the most adequate sources for human self-understanding, there are certainly other stories we could tell about self-strategies. But if it is granted that the self-strategies I describe operate in some times and places and that one's conception of gender categories may in some times and places affect the use of these self-strategies, the interpretive framework developed here may illuminate gender-related conflicts in the construction of self as well as in the production of meaning. When these texts are read with such an interpretive framework in mind the gender categories at play in a particular text become obvious. This, in turn, demonstrates the importance of these categories as conceptual barriers to envisioning a new mode of being for humanity—one that goes beyond gender categories, reaches beyond relations to others built upon opposition and domination, and instead strives for relations built upon connectedness and cooperation.

Human identity is a product of a social and communal enterprise—no single individual can form and maintain an identity without the help and support of the others around her. We need to recognize and affirm the interdependence of us all and our need for self-strategies, whatever form they take, in order to maintain human identity. A gender-sensitive reading of philosophical texts can help us further articulate the interdependent nature of human identity. Once we have put the self into context, positing it as one moment in the whole of a self/world relation rather than isolating it from the world, we can further elaborate that context by investigating the other kinds of selves a self needs in order to continue in a particular form. Once we start seeing how various kinds of selves constitute one another in a community of interlocking human relations, we can better understand what kind of contextual transformation would be needed to effect certain changes. In particular, we could better understand the way current gender categories work in preserving both masculine and feminine selves; then we could envision a transformation of gender categories that would respect the way in which gender categories play off one another.

Given my account of human identity as the product of an interlocking network of self-strategies, and given the role human identity has to play in the constitution of a particular worldview, a better understanding of gender, along with other components of identity such as class, race, and ethnicity, is important to human self-understanding and an understanding of how we shape the reality we attempt to describe. Philosophers who have any interest in a deeper self-understanding or in the way our self-understanding enters into knowledge of the world we live in can therefore not afford to marginalize identity issues. We can no longer assume that the experience of a particular group of people can give us the whole picture. Not only are the experiences of the rest of humanity crucial for an understanding of the human race as a whole—they are crucial to an understanding of the perspective represented in dominant discourses as well.

In addition to what I have called one version of the "feminine" perspective, we could distinguish alternate perspectives that form the background to dominant discourses. The "marginal" perspectives that are not incorporated into the current hegemony of current dominant discourses take many different forms. As we grow up we learn to marginalize various parts of our identity—we learn which aspects of our experience find expression in the dominant discourse and which ones are marginalized according to various other categories: race, class, geographical region, or other "deviancies" (such as being handicapped). To create a self that is acceptable in all walks of life, we constitute ourselves according to the social categories that apply most universally. This may lead us to attempt to restrict other aspects of our identity to the social contexts where they are accepted—our particular geographical region or a particular group of people. If we try to introduce these particularistic identities into the dominant discourse, we will create tension.

Gender is an entry point for investigating how certain self-identities have been marginalized. Feminine self-strategies in various forms obtain for roughly one half of the population, and yet, according to the dominant discourse, they are still considered "marginal." Feminist theory that attempts to characterize and valorize feminine self-strategies is still considered marginal in academic departments all across the country. Female academics have learned to marginalize their feminine experience, just as male academics have. To have a voice in the dominant discourse as given expression by the academic community, one must marginalize the feminine aspects of one's experience and speak with a masculine voice.

It is only if we articulate the feminine as well as the masculine perspective that we will be able to explore the relationship between the perspectives and ways of changing them. Both perspectives capture aspects of human experience. Do we want to valorize only one of the two perspectives as our standard for the "human" perspective, or do we want an entirely new perspective that can be shared by all? By a "new perspective," I don't mean the perspective of a God's eye view that finally captures all of human experience. If such a view is possible, it is too far in the future for me to envision. I mean a perspective that can see all perspectives as interdependent and mutually affecting—and all the different perspectives that go into the perspective of a human community as equally valid.[4] A philosophy that takes gender and gender issues seriously must provide a theoretical framework in which various perspectives are viewed as mutually supporting and enriching. Thus, instead of valorizing any one perspective as the "correct" view of human experience, we will be able to see how various perspectives not only fill out the picture of reality, but also make other perspectives possible.

I believe that the struggle of each individual or larger group for recognition is crucial to the development of a new worldview based on the collective human experience rather than that of certain elite groups. Just as the individual needs a self-identity that integrates the fullest range of her experience, thus allowing flexibility without sacrificing passionate commitment, responsibility, or effective agency, so do we as a world community need a self-identity that integrates the fullest range of human experience without trivializing or canceling out the experiences of those who live on the "margin." Theory should provide individual and collective struggles for recognition with a framework flexible enough to incorporate new viewpoints without bringing the whole edifice down, a worldview that respects multiplicity and allows new categories to multiply without threatening to destroy any possibility of categories at all. This framework should value and respect all life and experience rather than just the small range manifested by a particular group of people.

It is with respect to their refusal to accept conventional categories at face value that I am very sympathetic to poststructuralists like Michel Foucault and Derrida who carry on a continual practice of deconstruction. I do, however, feel that there is at least the possibility of achieving a new worldview more satisfying than the present one— even if such a worldview would be quickly outmoded. This worldview would emerge from multiple perspectives and be a group identity constructed by myriad individuals. Just as a self is constructed from countless fragments of embodied experience and is continually in transition and transformation in the face of its imminent dissolution, so would such a worldview be continually revised in keeping with the myriad perspectives of the embodied individuals from which it emerges.

On the reading of masculine identity given here, a masculine self-strategy opposes itself to a feminine other. It may oppose itself to other groups of human beings as well, depending on its race, class, and so forth, but its most fundamental opposition is to a feminine other.[5] Thus, gender is one key to exploring how the authorial identity (the self) constructed in a philosophical text relates to the text's construction of human others and the world (the other). Gender-sensitive analyses can thus be important tools in the philosophical enterprise of theorizing the human condition.

Notes

1. For discussions of the problem of difference in a feminist context see, for example, Bulkin, Pratt, and Smith (1984), Hooks (1984), and Spelman (1982). This problem has been of concern in the women's movement because of the difficulty of forming a collective identity as "women." Feminist theory has taken on the challenge of being sensitive to these differences at the same time that it attempts to provide a comprehensive theory. My remarks in this chapter are informed by this discussion.

2. I am influenced here by Janice Raymond's discussion of problems with the concept of "androgyny" for feminism in *The Transsexual Empire: The Making of the She-Male* (1979, chap. 6).

3. For a discussion of problems due to the "ego-permeable-boundaries" of the female gender see Flax (1978).

4. This is a Hegelian view in the sense that I am assuming a sort of "coming together" of perspective along the lines of absolute spirit.   Any self-respecting postmodern poststructuralist would turn over in her grave!   I here admit a yearning for this kind of ultimate closure at the same time that I accept deconstructing practices as more feasible for a day-to-day understanding of human experience.

5. I am thus, for the purposes of this book, emphasizing gender as an identity category.   For a discussion of other identity categories (e.g., race, class, gender) and their relationship to gender, see Elizabeth Spelman (1988).   That the opposition of male and female is the most fundamental opposition is subject to debate both in and outside feminist circles.   Although I am advocating gender as an important category of analysis, it is not crucial to my project that it be accepted as *the* most fundamental identity category.

References

Abel, Elizabeth, ed. 1982. *Writing and Sexual Difference.* Chicago: University of Chicago Press.

Allison, David B., ed. 1985. *The New Nietzsche, Contemporary Styles of Interpretation.* Cambridge, Mass.: MIT Press.

Anderson, Thomas C. 1979. *The Foundation and Structure of Sartrean Ethics.* Lawrence: Regents Press of Kansas.

Andrew, Edward. 1977. "The Science of Marx and Nietzsche." In *Political Theory and Praxis.* See Ball 1977.

Balbus, Isaac D. 1982. *Marxism and Domination: A NeoHegelian, Feminist, Psychoanalytic Theory of Sexual, Political and Technological Liberation.* Princeton: Princeton University Press.

Ball, Terence, ed. 1977. *Political Theory and Praxis.* Minneapolis: University of Minnesota Press.

Bart, Pauline. 1983. "Review of Chodorow's *The Reproduction of Mothering.*" In *Mothering.* See Trebilcot 1983, 147-152.

Bartky, Sandra Lee. 1979. "On Psychological Oppression." In Sharon Bishop and Marjorie Weinzweig, eds. *Philosophy and Women.* Belmont, Calif.: Wadsworth.

Baynes, Kenneth, James Bohman, and Thomas McCarthy. 1987. *After Philosophy: End or Transformation?* Cambridge, Mass.: MIT Press.

Beauvoir, Simone de. 1961. *The Second Sex.* Trans. H. M. Parshley. New York: Bantam.

Benjamin, Jessica. 1980. "The Bonds of Love: Rational Violence and Erotic Domination." In *The Future of Difference.* See Eisenstein and Jardine 1980, 41-70.

Benvenuto, Bice, and Roger Kennedy. 1986. *The Works of Jacques Lacan: An Introduction.* New York: St. Martin's Press.

Bergmann, Peter. 1987. *Nietzsche, "The Last Antipolitical German."* Bloomington: Indiana University Press.

Bordo, Susan. 1986. "The Cartesian Masculinization of Thought." *Signs* 11 (3), 439-456.

Bowie, M. 1979. "Jacques Lacan." In *Structuralism and Since.* See Sturrock 1979.

Bulkin, Elly, Minnie B. Pratt, and Barbara Smith. 1984. *Yours in Struggle.* New York: Long Haul Press.

Burke, Carolyn. 1980. "Introduction to Luce Irigaray's 'When Our Lips Speak Together.'" *Signs* 6 (1), 66-68.

Butler, Judith. 1987a. "Variations on Sex and Gender: Beauvoir, Wittig, and Foucault." In Benhabib, Seyla, and Drucilla Cornell, eds. *Feminism as Critique.* Minneapolis: University of Minnesota Press, 1987, 128-142.

————. 1987b. *Subjects of Desire: Hegelian Reflections in Twentieth-Century France.* New York: Columbia University Press.

Catalano, Joseph S. 1980. *A Commentary on Jean-Paul Sartre's Being and Nothingness.* Chicago: University of Chicago Press.

Caws, Peter. 1979. *Sartre.* Boston: Routledge and Kegan Paul.

Chodorow, Nancy. 1974. "Family Structure and Feminine Personality." In *Women, Culture and Society.* See Rosaldo and Lamphere 1974, 43-66.

————. 1978. *The Reproduction of Mothering: Psychoanalysis and the Sociology of Gender.* Berkeley: University of California Press.

————. 1980. "Gender, Relation and Difference in Psychoanalytic Perspective." In *The Future of Difference.* See Eisenstein and Jardine 1980, 3-19.

Collins, Margery L. and Christine Pierce. 1979. "Holes and Slime: Sexism in Sartre's Psychoanalysis." In *Woman in Western Thought.* See Osborne 1979, 319-322.

Coward, Rosalind, and John Ellis. 1977. *Language and Materialism: Developments in Semiology and the Theory of the Subject.* London: Routledge and Kegan Paul.

Craib, Ian. 1976. *Existentialism and Sociology, A Study of Jean-Paul Sartre.* Cambridge, Mass.: Cambridge University Press.

Cranston, Maurice. 1975. "Jean-Paul Sartre: Solitary Man in a Hostile Universe." In A. de Crespigny and K. Minogne, eds. *Contemporary Political Philosophers.* New York: Dodd, Mead and Co.

Croxal, T. H. 1956. *Kierkegaard Commentary.* London: James Nisbet and Company.

Dannhauser, Werner J. 1974. *Nietzsche's View of Socrates.* Ithaca, N.Y.: Cornell University Press.

Davis, Robert Con, ed. 1981. *The Fictional Father: Lacanian Readings of the Text.* Amherst: University of Massachusetts Press.

Deleuze, Gilles. 1983. *Nietzsche and Philosophy.* Trans. Hugh Tomlinson. New York: Columbia University Press.

Den Ouden, Bernard. 1982. *Essays on Reason, Will, Creativity and Time: Studies in the Philosophy of Friedrich Nietzsche.* Washington, D.C.: University Press of America.

Derrida, Jacques. 1978. *Writing and Difference.* Trans. Alan Bass. Chicago: University of Chicago Press.

———. 1979. *Spurs/Eperons.* Chicago: University of Chicago Press.

———. 1984. *Otobiographies.* Paris: Éditions Galilée.

Desan, Wilfrid. 1954. *The Tragic Finale, An Essay on the Philosophy of Jean-Paul Sartre.* Cambridge, Mass.: Harvard University Press.

Descartes, René. 1977. *The Philosophical Works of Descartes,* vol. 1. Trans. E. S. Haldane and G. R. Ross. Cambridge, Mass.: Cambridge University Press.

Descombes, Vincent. 1982. *Modern French Philosophy.* Trans. L. Scott-Fox and J. M. Harding. Cambridge, Mass.: Cambridge University Press.

Dews, Peter. 1987. *Logics of Disintegration: Post-structuralist Thought and the Claims of Critical Theory.* New York: Verso.

Dinnerstein, Dorothy. 1977. *The Mermaid and the Minotaur: Sexual Arrangements and Human Malaise.* New York: Harper and Row.

DiStefano, Christine. 1983. "Masculinity as Ideology in Political Theory: Hobbesian Man Considered." *Women's Studies International Forum* 6 (6).
——. 1989. "Rereading J. S. Mill: Interpolations from the (M)otherworld." In M. Barr and R. Feldstein, eds. *Discontented Discourses: Feminism/Textual Intervention/Psychoanalysis.* Urbana: University of Illinois Press, 160-172.
Dunning, Stephen N. 1985. *Kierkegaard's Dialectic of Inwardness: A Structural Analysis of the Theory of Stages.* Princeton: Princeton University Press.
Dworkin, Andrea. 1974. *Woman Hating.* New York: E.P. Dutton.
Eichenbaum, Louise, and Susan Orbach. 1983. *Understanding Women: A Feminist Psychoanalytic Approach.* New York: Basic Books.
Eisenstein, Hester. 1984. *Contemporary Feminist Thought.* London: Allen and Unwin.
Eisenstein, Hester, and Alice Jardine, eds. 1980. *The Future of Difference; Vol. 1 of the Scholar and the Feminist: Papers from the Barnard Women's Center Conference.* Boston: G. K. Hall and Company.
Elrod, John W. 1975. *Being and Existence in Kierkegaard's Pseudonymous Works.* Princeton: Princeton University Press.
Epstein, Seymour. 1973. "The Self-Concept Revisited, Or a Theory of a Theory." *American Psychologist* 28 (5), May.
Evans, C. O. 1970. *The Subject of Consciousness.* London: George Allen and Unwin.
Evans, C. Stephen. 1983. *Kierkegaard's "Fragments" and "Postscript": The Religious Philosophy of Johannes Climacus.* Atlanta Highlands, N.J.: Humanities Press.
Felman, Shoshana, ed. 1982. *Literature and Psychoanalysis: The Question of Reading: Otherwise.* Baltimore: Johns Hopkins University Press.
Ferguson, Ann. 1983. "On Conceiving Motherhood and Sexuality: A Feminist Materialist Approach." In *Mothering.* See Trebilcot 1983, 153-182.
——. 1985. "Public Patriarchy and How to Fight It: A Tri-Systems Theory." Unpublished draft.

————. 1987. "A Feminist Aspect Theory of the Self." *Canadian Journal of Philosophy*, supplementary vol. 13, 339-356.

Flax, Jane. 1978. "The Conflict Between Nurturance and Autonomy in Mother/Daughter Relationships and Within Feminism." *Feminist Studies* 4 (1).

————. 1980. "Mother-Daughter Relationships: Psychodynamics, Politics and Philosophy." In *The Future of Difference*. See Eisenstein and Jardine 1980, 20-40.

————. 1983. "Political Philosophy and the Patriarchal Unconscious: A Psychoanalytic Perspective on Epistemology and Metaphysics." In *Discovering Reality*. See Harding and Hintikka 1983, 245-281.

————. 1986. "Gender as a Social Problem: In and For Feminist Theory." *American Studies/Amerika Studien*.

Freeland, Cynthia A. 1986. "Woman: Revealed or Reveiled?" *Hypatia* 1 (2), 49-70.

Freud, Sigmund. 1957. *A General Selection from the Works of Sigmund Freud*. Ed. John Rickman. Garden City, N.Y.: Doubleday.

————. 1963. *Sexuality and the Psychology of Love*. Ed. Philip Rieff. New York: Macmillan.

Frye, Marilyn. 1983. *The Politics of Reality*. Trumansburg, N.Y.: Crossing Press.

Fuss, Peter. 1977. "Theory and Practice in Hegel and Marx." In *Political Theory and Praxis*. See Ball 1977.

Gadamer, Hans-Georg. 1982. *Truth and Method*. New York: Crossroad.

Gallop, Jane. 1982. *Feminism and Psychoanalysis: The Daughter's Seduction*. London: Macmillan.

————. 1985. *Reading Lacan*. Ithaca, N.Y.: Cornell University Press.

Gilligan, Carol. 1979. "Woman's Place in Man's Life Cycle." *Harvard Educational Review* 49 (4), November.

————. 1982. *In a Different Voice: Psychological Theory and Women's Development*. Totowa, N.J.: Littlefield, Adams.

Gould, Carol. 1984. *Beyond Domination: New Perspectives on Women and Philosophy*. Totowa, N.J.: Rowman & Allanheld.

Green, André. 1966. "The Logic of Lacan's *objet* (a) and Freudian Theory: Convergences and Questions." In

Interpreting Lacan. See Smith and Kerrigan 1983, 161-191.

Greenberg, Jay R., and Stephen A. Mitchell. 1983. *Object Relations in Psychoanalytic Theory*. Cambridge, Mass.: Harvard University Press.

Grene, Marjorie. 1983. *Sartre*. Lanham, Md.: University Press of America.

Griffin, Susan. 1978. *Woman and Nature: The Roaring Inside Her*. New York: Harper and Row.

Grimshaw, Jean. 1986. *Philosophy and Feminist Thinking*. Minneapolis: University of Minnesota Press.

Guignon, Charles B. 1983. *Heidegger and the Problem of Knowledge*. Indianapolis, Ind.: Hackett.

Habermas, Jürgen. 1971. *Knowledge and Human Interests*. Trans. Jeremy J. Shapiro. Boston: Beacon Press.

Hamilton, Victoria. 1982. *Narcissus and Oedipus: The Children of Psychoanalysis*. London: Routledge and Kegan Paul.

Harari, Josue V., ed. 1979. *Textual Strategies: Perspectives in Post-structuralist Criticism*. Ithaca, N.Y.: Cornell University Press.

Harasym, Sarah. 1988. "Practical Politics of the Open End: An Interview with Gayatri Chakravorty Spivak." *Canadian Journal of Political and Social Theory* 12 (1-2).

Haraway, Donna. 1985. "A Manifesto for Cyborgs: Science, Technology, and Socialist Feminism in the 1980's." *Socialist Review* 80.

Harding, Sandra. 1982. "Is Gender a Variable in Conceptions of Rationality? A Survey of Issues." Reprinted in *Beyond Domination*. See Gould 1984, 43-63.

———. 1983. "Why Has the Sex/Gender System Become Visible Only Now?" In *Discovering Reality*. See Harding and Hintikka 1983.

———. 1986. *The Science Question in Feminism*. Ithaca, N.Y.: Cornell University Press.

———. 1987. "The Method Question." *Hypatia* 2 (3).

Harding, Sandra, and Merril B. Hintikka, eds. 1983. *Discovering Reality: Feminist Perspectives on Epistemology, Metaphysics, Methodology and the Philosophy of Science*. Dordrecht: Reidel.

Harper, Ralph. 1965. *The Seventh Solitude, Metaphysical Homelessness in Kierkegaard, Dostoevsky and Nietzsche.* Baltimore: Johns Hopkins University Press.

Hartsock, Nancy. 1983. "The Feminist Standpoint: Developing the Ground for a Specifically Feminist Historical Materialism." In *Discovering Reality.* See Harding and Hintikka 1983, 283-310.

————. 1984. *Money, Sex and Power: Towards a Feminist Historical Materialism.* Boston: Northeastern University Press.

Hayim, Gila J. 1980. *The Existential Sociology of Jean-Paul Sartre.* Amherst: University of Massachusetts Press, chap. 1-3.

Hayman, Ronal. 1980. *Nietzsche: A Critical Life.* New York: Penguin.

Heath, Stephen. 1978/79. "Difference." *Screen* 19 (4), Winter.

Hegel, G.W.F. 1977. *Hegel's Phenomenology of Spirit.* Trans. A. V. Miller. Oxford: Oxford University Press.

Heidegger, Martin. 1962. *Being and Time.* Trans. J. Macquarrie and E. Robinson. New York: Harper and Row.

al-Hibri, Azizah. 1983. "Reproduction, Mothering, and the Origins of Patriarchy." In *Mothering.* See Trebilcot 1983, 81-93.

Hinman, Laurence M. 1982. "Nietzsche, Metaphor, and Truth. *Philosophy and Phenomenological Research* 43, 179-200.

Hirschmann, Nancy J. 1987. "Women and Obligation: A Feminist Analysis." Ph.D dissertation, Swarthmore College, Swarthmore, Penn.

Hooks, Bell. 1984. *Feminist Theory from Margin to Center.* Boston: South End Press.

Hume, David. 1978. *A Treatise of Human Nature*, 2d ed. Ed. P. H. Nidditch. Oxford: Oxford University Press.

Irigaray, Luce. 1985a. *Speculum of the Other Woman.* Trans. Gillian C. Gill. Ithaca, N.Y.: Cornell University Press.

————. 1985b. *This Sex Which Is Not One.* Trans. Catherine Porter. Ithaca, N.Y.: Cornell University Press.

Izenberge, Gerald N. 1976. *The Existentialist Critique of Freud: The Crisis of Autonomy.* Princeton: Princeton University Press.

Jaggar, Alison. 1983. *Feminist Politics and Human Nature.* Totowa, N.J.: Rowman and Allanheld.

Jardine, Alice A. 1985. *Gynesis: Configurations of Woman and Modernity.* Ithaca, N.Y.: Cornell University Press.

Jeanson, Francis. 1980. *Sartre and the Problem of Morality.* Trans. Robert V. Stone. Bloomington: Indiana University Press.

Jones, Ann Rosalind. 1981. "Toward an Understanding of *L'Écriture Féminine.*" *Feminist Studies* 7 (2), 247-263.

Juranville, Alain. 1984. *Lacan et la philosophie.* Paris: Presses Universitaires de France.

Kain, Philip J. 1982. *Schiller, Hegel and Marx: State, Society, and the Aesthetic Ideal of Ancient Greece.* Montreal: McGill-Queen's University Press.

Kappeler, Susanne. 1986. *The Pornography of Representation.* Minneapolis: University of Minnesota Press.

Kaufmann, Walter. 1968. *Nietzsche, Philosopher, Psychologist, Antichrist*, 3rd ed. Princeton: Princeton University Press.

Keller, Evelyn Fox. 1978. "Gender and Science." Reprinted in *Discovering Reality.* See Harding and Hintikka 1983, 187-205.

Keohane, N. O., M. Z. Rosaldo, and B. C. Gelp, eds. 1981. *Feminist Theory: A Critique of Ideology.* Chicago: University of Chicago Press.

Kerrigan, William. 1983. "Introduction." In *Interpreting Lacan.* See Smith and Kerrigan 1983, ix-xxvii.

Kierkegaard, Søren. 1983. *Fear and Trembling; Repetition.* Trans. H. V. Hong and E. H. Hong. Princeton: Princeton University Press.

Klein, Melanie. 1937. *The Psychoanalysis of Children.* London: Hogarth Press.

Kofman, Sarah. 1972. *Nietzsche et la Métaphore.* Paris: Payot.

Kramarae, Cheris. 1981. *Women and Men Speaking: Frameworks for Analysis.* Rowley, Mass.: Newbury House, 64-89.

Krell, David Farrell. 1986. *Postponements, Woman, Sensuality, and Death in Nietzsche.* Bloomington: Indiana University Press.

Kuykendall, Eleanor H. 1983. "Toward an Ethic of Nurturance: Luce Irigaray on Mothering and Power." In *Mothering.* See Trebilcot 1983, 263-274.

Lacan, Jacques. 1966. *Écrits.* Paris: Éditions du Seuil.

———. 1975. *Le Séminaire livre XX: Encore.* Paris: Éditions du Seuil.

———. 1977. *Écrits: A Selection.* Trans. Alan Sheridan. New York: Norton.

———. 1981. *The Four Fundamental Concepts of Psycho-Analysis.* Trans. Alan Sheridan. Ed. Jacques-Alain Miller. New York: W. W. Norton and Co.

La Capra, Dominick. 1978. *A Preface to Sartre.* Ithaca, N.Y.: Cornell University Press.

Laplanche, Jean. 1976. *Life and Death in Psychoanalysis.* Trans. Jeffrey Mehlman. Baltimore: Johns Hopkins University Press.

Lauretis, Teresa de, ed. 1986. *Feminist Studies: Critical Studies.* Bloomington: Indiana University Press.

Leitch, Vincent B. 1983. *Deconstructive Criticism.* New York: Columbia University Press.

Lemaire, Anika. 1977. *Jacques Lacan.* Trans. David Macey. Boston: Routledge and Kegan Paul.

Lloyd, Genevieve. 1984. *The Man of Reason: "Male" and "Female" in Western Philosophy.* Minneapolis: University of Minnesota Press.

Lorraine, Tamsin, et al. 1986. "Nietzsche after 1968: A Conference Report." *Telos* 68 (Summer), 129-137.

Lugones, Maria C., and Elizabeth V. Spelman. 1983. "Have We Got a Theory for You! Feminist Theory, Cultural Imperialism and the Demand for the Woman's Voice." *Women's Studies International Forum* 6 (6), 573-581.

MacCannell, Juliet Flower. 1986. *Figuring Lacan: Criticism and the Cultural Unconscious.* Lincoln: University of Nebraska Press.

Mackey, Louis. 1971. *Kierkegaard: A Kind of Poet.* Philadelphia: University of Pennsylvania Press.

Magnus, Bernd. 1985. "The End of 'The End of Philosophy.'" In *Hermeneutics and Deconstruction.* See Silverman and Inde 1985, 2-10.

Mahawald, Mary B., ed. 1978. *Philosophy of Woman: Classical to Current Concepts*. Indianapolis, Ind.: Hackett.

Mahler, Margaret S., F. Pine, and A. Bergman. 1975. *The Psychological Birth of the Human Infant: Symbiosis and Individuation*. New York: Basic Books.

Malantschuk, Gregor. 1971. *Kierkegaard's Thought*. Ed. and Trans. H. V. Hong and E. H. Hong. Princeton, N.J.: Princeton University Press.

———. 1980. *The Controversial Kierkegaard*. Trans. H. V. Hong and E. H. Hong. Waterloo, Ont.: Wilfrid Laurier University Press.

Marks, Elaine. 1978. "Women and Literature in France." *Signs* 3 (4), 832-842.

Marks, Elaine, and Isabelle de Courtivron, eds. 1980. *New French Feminisms*. Amherst: University of Massachusetts Press.

Megill, Allan. 1985. *Prophets of Extremity: Nietzsche, Heidegger, Fourcault, Derrida*. Berkeley: University of California Press.

Millett, Kate. 1971. *Sexual Politics*. New York: Avon Books.

Mitchell, Juliet. 1975. *Psychoanalysis and Feminism*. Harmondsworth, U.K.: Penguin.

Mitchell, Juliet, and Jacqueline Rose, eds. 1985. *Feminine Sexuality, Jacques Lacan and the École Freudienne*. Trans. Jacqueline Rose. New York: W. W. Norton and Co.

Modell, Arnold H. 1968. *Object Love and Reality: An Introduction to a Psychoanalytic Theory of Object Relations*. New York: International Universities Press.

Moi, Toril. 1985. *Sexual/Textual Politics: Feminist Literary Theory*. New York: Methuen.

Muller, John P., and William J. Richardson. 1979. "Toward Reading Lacan: Pages for a Workbook." *Psychoanalysis and Contemporary Thought* 2.

———. 1982. *Lacan and Language, A Reader's Guide to Écrits*. New York: International Universities Press.

Nehemas, Alexander. 1985. *Nietzsche, Life as Literature*. Cambridge, Mass.: Harvard University Press.

Nietzsche, Friedrich. 1966. *Thus Spoke Zarathustra*. Trans. Walter Kaufmann. New York: Penguin.

———. 1968a. *The Portable Nietzsche*. Trans. Walter Kaufmann. New York: Penguin.

————. 1968b. *Basic Writings of Nietzsche.* Trans. Walter Kaufmann. New York: Modern Library.

O'Brien, Mary. 1981. *The Politics of Reproduction.* London: Routledge and Kegan Paul.

O'Hara, Daniel, ed. 1985. *Why Nietzsche Now?* Bloomington: Indiana University Press.

Okin, Susan K. 1979. *Women in Western Political Thought.* Princeton: Princeton University Press.

Oliver, Kelly A. 1984. "Woman as Truth in Nietzsche's Writing." *Social Theory and Practice* 10 (Summer), 185-199.

————. 1988. "Nietzsche's Woman: The Post-structuralist Attempt To Do Away with Women." *Radical Philosophy* 48 (Spring), 25-29.

Ortner, Sherry. 1974. "Is Female to Male as Nature Is to Culture?" In *Women, Culture and Society.* See Rosaldo and Lamphere 1974, 67-87.

Osborne, Martha, ed. 1979. *Woman in Western Thought.* New York: Random House.

Pasley, Malcolm, ed. 1978. *Nietzsche: Imagery and Thought, A Collection of Essays.* Berkeley: University of California Press.

Perkins, Robert L., ed. 1981. *Kierkegaard's Fear and Trembling: Critical Appraisals.* University: University of Alabama Press.

Plant, Raymond. 1983. *Hegel: An Introduction,* 2d ed. Oxford: Basil Blackwell.

Ragland-Sullivan, Ellie. 1986. *Jacques Lacan and the Philosophy of Psychoanalysis.* Urbana and Chicago: University of Illinois Press.

Raymond, Janice G. 1979. *The Transsexual Empire: The Making of the She-Male.* Boston: Beacon Press.

Ree, Jonathan. 1974. *Descartes.* New York: Pica Press.

Reiter, Rayna Rapp, ed. 1975. *Toward an Anthropology of Women.* New York: Monthly Review Press.

Rosaldo, M. Z., and L. Lamphere, eds. 1974. *Women, Culture and Society.* Stanford, Calif.: Stanford University Press.

Rose, Hilary. 1983. "Hand, Brain and Heart: A Feminist Epistemology for the Natural Sciences." *Signs* 9 (1), 73-90.

Rose, Jacqueline. 1985. "Introduction II." In *Feminine Sexuality.* See Mitchell and Rose 1985, 27-57.

Rubin, Gayle. 1975. "The Traffic in Women: Notes on the 'Political Economy' of Sex." In *Toward an Anthropology of Women.* See Reiter 1975, 157-210.

Ruddick, Sara. 1980. "Maternal Thinking." Reprinted in *Mothering.* See Trebilcot 1983, 213-230.

Sargent, Lydia, ed. 1981. *Women and Revoltuion.* Boston: South End Press.

Sartre, Jean-Paul. 1956. *Being and Nothingness.* Trans. Hazel E. Barnes. New York: Washington Square Press.

Scheman, Naomi. 1983. "Individualism and the Objects of Psychology." In *Discovering Reality.* See Harding and Hintikka 1983, 225-244.

Schneiderman, Stuart. 1983. *Jacques Lacan: The Death of an Intellectual Hero.* Cambridge, Mass.: Harvard University Press.

Schrag, Calvin O. 1985. "Subjectivity and Praxis at the End of Philosophy." In *Hermeneutics and Deconstruction.* See Silverman and Inde 1985, 24-32.

Schutte, Ofelia. 1984. *Beyond Nihilism, Nietzsche Without Masks.* Chicago: University of Chicago Press.

Segal, Hanna. 1964. *Introduction to the Work of Melanie Klein.* New York: Basic Books.

Sherman, J., and E. T. Beck, eds. 1979. *The Prism of Sex: Essays in the Sociology of Knowledge.* Madison: University of Wisconsin Press.

Shklar, Judith N. 1976. *Freedom and Independence: A Study of the Political Ideas of Hegel's Phenomenology of Mind.* Cambridge, Mass.: Cambridge University Press.

Silverman, Hugh J., and Don Inde, eds. 1985. *Hermeneutics and Deconstruction.* Albany: State University of New York Press.

Silverman, Lloyd H., and Joel Weinberger. 1985. "Mommy and I Are One: Implications for Psychotherapy." *American Psychologist*, December.

Smith, Dorothy. 1974. "Women's Perspective as a Radical Critique of Sociology." *Sociological Inquiry* 44.

———. 1979. "A Sociology for Women." In *The Prism of Sex.* See Sherman and Beck 1979, 135-187.

Smith, Joseph H., and William Kerrigan, eds. 1983. *Interpreting Lacan: Psychiatry and the Humanities* 6. New Haven: Yale University Press.

Snitow, Ann, Christine Stansell, and Sharon Thompson, eds. 1983. *Powers of Desire: The Politics of Sexuality*. New York: Monthly Review Press.

Spelman, Elizabeth V. 1982. "Theories of Race and Gender: The Erasure of Black Women." *Quest* 5 (4).

———. 1988. *Inessential Woman: Problems of Exclusion in Feminist Thought*. Boston: Beacon Press.

Sturrock, J., ed. 1979. *Structuralism and Since: From Levi-Strauss to Derrida*. Oxford: Oxford University Press.

Swinglewood, Alan. 1975. *Marx and Modern Social Theory*. New York: John Wiley and Sons.

Taylor, Mark C. 1975. *Kierkegaard's Pseudonymous Authorship, A Study of Time and the Self*. Princeton: Princeton University Press.

———. 1980. *Journeys to Selfhood: Hegel and Kierkegaard*. Berkeley: University of California Press.

———. 1987. *Altarity*. Chicago: University of Chicago Press.

Thompson, Josiah. 1967. *The Lonely Labyrinth: Kierkegaard's Pseudonymous Works*. Carbondale: Southern Illinois Press.

Trebilcot, Joyce, ed. 1983. *Mothering, Essays in Feminist Theory*. Totowa, N.J.: Rowman and Allanheld.

Valone, James J. 1983. *The Ethics and Existentialism of Kierkegaard*. Lanham, Md.: University Press of America.

Vance, Carole S., ed. 1984. *Pleasure and Danger: Exploring Female Sexuality*. Boston: Routledge and Kegan Paul.

Veisland, Jørgen S. 1985. *Kierkegaard and the Dialectics of Modernism*. New York: Peter Lang Publishing.

Warnock, Mary. 1965. *The Philosophy of Sartre*. London: Hutchinson and Company.

Wawrytko, Sandra A. 1981. *The Undercurrent of Feminine Philosophy in Eastern and Western Thought*. Washington, D.C.: University Press of America.

Weedon, Chris. 1987. *Feminist Practice and Poststructuralist Theory*. Oxford: Basil Blackwell.

Whitbeck, Caroline. 1982. "The Maternal Instinct" and "Afterword." In *Mothering*. See Trebilcot 1983, 185-198.

———. 1983. "A Different Reality: Feminist Ontology." In *Beyond Domination*. See Gould 1984, 64-88.

Wilden, Anthony. 1968. *The Language of the Self*. Baltimore: Johns Hopkins University Press.

Winant, Terry. 1987. "The Feminist Standpoint: A Matter of Language." *Hypatia* 2 (1), 123-148.

Winnicott, Donald W. 1958. *Through Paediatrics to Psychoanalysis*. London: Hogarth Press.

———. 1965. *The Maturational Process and the Facilitating Environment*. New York: International Universities Press.

———. 1971. *Playing and Reality*. New York: Basic Books.

Wright, Elizabeth. 1984. *Psychoanalytic Criticism: Theory in Practice*. London: Methuen.

Young, Iris Marion. 1983. "Is Male Gender Identity the Cause of Male Domination?" In *Mothering*. See Trebilcot 1983, 129-146.

Index